Contents

Brecht, Turkish Theater, and Turkish-German Literature

Studies in German Literature, Linguistics, and Culture

Brecht, Turkish Theater, and Turkish-German Literature

Reception, Adaptation, and Innovation after 1960

Ela E. Gezen

CAMDEN HOUSE

Rochester, New York

First published 2018
by Camden House

Camden House is an imprint of Boydell & Brewer Inc.
668 Mt. Hope Avenue, Rochester, NY 14620, USA
www.camden-house.com
and of Boydell & Brewer Limited
PO Box 9, Woodbridge, Suffolk IP12 3DF, UK
www.boydell.co.uk

ISBN-13: 978-1-64014-024-0
ISBN-10: 1-64014-024-7

Library of Congress Cataloging-in-Publication Data

Names: Gezen, Ela E., 1977– author.
Title: Brecht, Turkish theater, and Turkish-German literature : reception, adaptation,
    and innovation after 1960 / Ela E. Gezen.
Description: Rochester, New York : Camden House, 2018. | Series: Studies in
    German literature, linguistics, and culture | Includes bibliographical references and
    index.
Identifiers: LCCN 2017053770| ISBN 9781640140240 (hardcover : alk. paper) |
    ISBN 1640140247
Subjects: LCSH: German drama—20th century—History and criticism. | German
    literature—Turkish authors—History and criticism. | Theater—Turkey—
    History—20th century. | Brecht, Bertolt, 1898–1956—Stage history—Turkey. |
    Brecht, Bertolt, 1898–1956—Influence.
Classification: LCC PT668 .G49 2018 | DDC 832/.91409—dc23 LC record
    available at https://lccn.loc.gov/2017053770

This publication is printed on acid-free paper.
Printed and bound in Great Britain by
TJ International Ltd, Padstow, Cornwall

Anneme ve Babama

Illustrations

Acknowledgments

I HAVE BEEN FORTUNATE TO BENEFIT FROM the support of many individuals and institutions. While my doctoral dissertation dealt with a different subject, the seed for the idea for this book was planted during my time as a PhD student at the University of Michigan in Ann Arbor. It was my doctoral adviser Kader Konuk who first noticed in my analysis that Bertolt Brecht seemed to assume a significant "supporting role" as a recurring source of influence for the artists I was discussing. I am indebted to her for getting me to think about the connection between Brecht and Turkish-German studies scholarship, and for her continued support and encouragement. Two colleagues (and close friends) accompanied this project from its initial phases to the very end: Seth Howes and Christian Rogowski. I owe Seth Howes, my *Wegbegleiter* for over a decade, more than I could express in words. His limitless generosity in reading my work, his reassuring words in moments of stasis and his unparalleled enthusiasm for my project have been indispensable. I am grateful to Christian Rogowski, a friend, colleague and mentor, who supported this project not only by generously reading the entire manuscript and providing valuable feedback but also with lively conversations in Amherst and beyond. I would like to thank my colleagues, Gülru Çakmak and Marisol Barbon, for their friendship and for their tireless support of all aspects of my life: you make Amherst home. I have been lucky to work with tremendously supportive colleagues, mentors, and friends in my program: I owe thanks to Andrew Donson, Barton Byg, Jonathan Skolnik, Robert Sullivan, Sherrill Harbison, Kerstin Mueller-Dembling, Frank Hugus, Sky Arndt-Briggs, and Sara Jackson. They ensured that I had time for writing, and they provided crucial feedback (and cheer) at various stages of the manuscript and kept me afloat (and sane) through hallway conversations, dinner gatherings, field trips, and meetings. I also want to thank Annette Damayanti Lienau, Jon Olsen, and Hiltrud Schulz for always having an open door and ear. I owe thanks to my German studies colleagues in the Five College community, especially Anna Schrade, Jocelyn Kolb, Karen Remmler, Jeff Wallen, and Ute Brandes, for their support, encouragement, and feedback during our faculty seminar meetings. I would like to thank my fellow team members of the Mellon Mutual Mentoring Grant at UMass, especially Sara Lennox and Laura Doyle, for their crucial feedback in the early stages of the conceptualization of this project, and the Institute for Teaching Excellence and Faculty Development, especially Brian Baldi and Jung Yun, for generously supporting it.

I would like to thank Nina Berman, whose support and mentorship has been invaluable, Bala Venkat Mani for our many productive exchanges during our wonderfully regular chance encounters, and Sonja Klocke, whose reassuring words gave me the needed push to overcome my own hesitations. Thanks to Berna Güneli, my coconspirator on a variety of projects, a friend and a colleague who stood by my side with her infinite optimism. Additionally I would like to thank Leslie Adelson, David Gramling, Marc Silberman, Martin Kagel, Deniz Göktürk, Kira Thurman, Randall Halle, Yasemin Yildiz, Andrew Zimmerman, Damani Partridge, Daniel Kojo Schrade, Stuart Parker, Olivia Landry, Irene Kacandes, Kristin Dickinson, Vera Stegmann, and Priscilla Layne for stimulating conversations and productive exchanges at conferences, workshops, and professional meetings.

I am grateful for my time in the multidisciplinary research program EUME (Europe in the Middle East—The Middle East in Europe), which provided a tremendously productive forum for engaging in interdisciplinary conversations with colleagues who share many of my concerns, even if they work on different subjects and employ different methodologies. I would like to thank especially its academic coordinator, Georges Khalil, and my fellow participants, Erol Ülker, Banu Karaca, Margaret Litvin, Beth Holt, and Saima Akhtar.

I would like to thank the University of Massachusetts and the Forum Transregionale Studien for financially supporting research for this project. My heartfelt thanks to the colleagues at the Interlibrary Loan (ILL) office at UMass; their resourcefulness to attain seemingly unattainable texts never ceases to amaze me. I will never forget holding a first edition of the first Turkish Brecht translation from Boğaziçi University in Istanbul. I owe thanks to Jim Kelly, our research librarian, who tirelessly figured out ways to bring any kind of materials here (from anywhere). I would like to thank Annie Sollinger for her support, help and expertise with the images.

I want to express my gratitude to Iliane Thiemann and Anett Schubotz at the Bertolt-Brecht-Archiv, and Katja Geisler at the Stadtarchiv Erlangen. I would like to thank Helga Neumann at the Archiv der Akademie der Künste in particular for her helpfulness and patience for all my questions and queries. I am grateful to Aras Ören and Emine Sevgi Özdamar for granting me permission to use their photos and unpublished sources.

By coincidence I met Jim Walker at the Symposium of the International Brecht Society in Oxford in June 2016. That is where our collaboration began, and now that it is nearing its end, I can say that I could not have wished for a better editor. I thank him for his generous guidance and his enthusiasm from beginning to end. I also would like to extend my deepest gratitude to both anonymous reviewers for their careful attention to the manuscript and their helpful critical suggestions for improving it.

I want to thank my parents, who had to leave Turkey during the tumultuous upheavals this book addresses. They taught me everything I know. I dedicate this book to them. I am grateful to my husband Diogenes for knowing what I needed when I did not, for his unconditional love (and patience), and for always being a sounding board to my ideas. I could not have done it without you. And lastly, I would like to thank Cem, my little tortoise, I will never forget our joint writing sessions, your endless cheer and support.

Earlier versions of sections in chapter 2 appeared as "Aras Ören and the (West) German Literary Left," *Literature Compass* 13, no. 5 (2016): 324–31; and "Convergent Realisms: Aras Ören, Nazım Hikmet, and Bertolt Brecht," *Colloquia Germanica* 45, no. 3/4 (October 2015), 377–93. Chapter 3 revises material previously published as "Staging Berlin: Emine Sevgi Özdamar's *Seltsame Sterne starren zur Erde*," *German Studies Review* 38, no. 11 (2015): 83–96. A small excerpt from "Brecht on the Turkish Stage: Adaptation, Experimentation, and Theatre Aesthetics in Genco Erkal's *Dostlar Tiyatrosu*," *German Life and Letters* 69, no. 2 (2016): 269–84, appears in revised form in chapter 1.

Introduction

In 1968 dramaturg Käthe Rülicke-Weiler, a former member of Bertolt Brecht's theater company, the Berliner Ensemble, remarked that "of the fifty-three countries in which Brecht was staged in the ten years following his death, more than half are not in Europe but in Asia, Africa, and Latin America."[1] Brecht, generally regarded as the most influential playwright of the twentieth century, died in 1956, but his theoretical writings and dramaturgical practices shaped many of the debates—albeit to differing degrees—about the politics of culture in divided Germany throughout the politically tumultuous 1960s. The impact of his work went far beyond a German or even a narrowly defined Cold War context. He was, as this book will demonstrate, a key figure in Turkey, where a period of liberalization following the military coup of 1960 saw the emergence of a new generation of politically engaged intellectuals who sought to link culture to politics, art to life, and theater to revolutionary practice in the service of effecting societal change. I will, moreover, highlight this period's significance for Turkish-German literature, exemplified by authors such as Emine Sevgi Özdamar and Aras Ören. For decades, I will argue, Bertolt Brecht has connected two literary histories that have as a result become ever more intertwined. Studying how Brecht's thought was first interpreted by theater practitioners in Turkey, and then by Turkish writers living in Germany enhances our understanding of the intellectual interchanges that shaped the emergence of Turkish-German literature.

The Brecht-Dialog, the context for Rülicke-Weiler's remarks, was the first international Brecht conference, which was convened in East Berlin in February 1968 in honor of Brecht's seventieth birthday. With the motto "Politics at the Theater"—a phrase taken from Brecht's *Katzgraben-Notate*—it had been organized jointly by three prominent East German cultural institutions, the Berliner Ensemble, the Academy of Arts, and the Center of the International Theater Institute (ITI), which conceived of the conference as an "encounter of progressive theater practitioners and literary scholars from many countries" and placed the practicability of Brecht's working methods in differing social settings at the center of their agenda.[2] A special issue of the leading East German theater journal *Theater der Zeit*, titled "Brecht auf den Bühnen der Welt" (Brecht on the Stages of the World,

1968), included "national reports" by many of the conference's participants, in which they discussed how Brecht influenced theater in their respective countries, and whether they encountered difficulties staging Brecht.[3] While national specificities and sociopolitical realities differed across the board, contributors all insisted that their engagement with Brecht was not based on mere imitation. Instead they pointed to intersections between Brecht's dramaturgy and their respective local or national traditions (as for example in Egypt and Sri Lanka), arguing that they were adapting—rather than merely adopting—Brecht's aesthetics.[4]

Ten years later, in 1978, the Brecht-Dialog reconvened in East Berlin, in commemoration of Brecht's eightieth birthday this time, with the theme "Art and Politics" and drew participants from forty countries. Continuing the emphasis on international discussion and exchange, and including countries from all "Three Worlds" (with the Federal German Republic listed as a foreign participant), one of the colloquia organized by the Berliner Ensemble and the Brecht Center of the German Democratic Republic (GDR) was titled "Problems in the International Reception of Brecht." It was attended by theater practitioners from the GDR, Egypt, Sudan, France, Japan, and the United States, among others. As a participant in this colloquium, director Manfred Wekwerth emphasized that what was under discussion was the "Brecht Method" itself, rather than "individual results."[5] He further acknowledged an increasing interest in Brecht in "Third World" countries, while at the same time pointing to reservations about Brecht and also some rejection of his ideas in the Federal Republic of Germany (FRG). He also addressed current discussions regarding Brecht's usefulness in the GDR, as a state that resolved its "class antagonism."[6] His colleague, dramaturg Joachim Tenschert, similarly underlined the growing interest in Brecht beyond Germany and Europe noting that "in Arabic countries, sub-Saharan Africa, and in Latin American countries, for years there has been a strong, almost hungry recourse to Brecht."[7] While not in attendance in 1968, this time Turkey was represented through prominent Brechtian director and actor Genco Erkal as well as actress Zeliha Berksoy (both important figures in the Turkish reception of Brecht, but also in the context of Vasıf Öngören's theater work, to which I will turn in the first chapter).[8]

In the context of this Brecht-Dialog, representatives of the "developing countries" asked for a separate meeting, which resulted in the next Brecht-Dialog in 1980 solely focusing on Africa, Asia, and South America.[9] The reasoning behind this request, as addressed in the ensuing publication, was the perceived difference in focus: foregrounding an emphasis on the transformation of societal conditions instead of focusing on aesthetic questions, deemed central to European colleagues.[10] In his introduction to the proceedings of this event, Werner Hecht noted that "the adaptation of Brecht" was given precedence over mere "Brecht reception . . . which takes the Brecht text or Brecht source solely as stimulus or point of departure."[11] He further remarked that the "appeal of Brecht in developing countries can be traced to his method, which specifically demands the political incorporation of art into the societal process."[12] This point was reinforced by literary scholar Magdi Youssef, who directed attention to the necessity of transforming Brecht's work, even to the point of "rewriting it," to adapt it to local concerns and circumstances.[13]

In 1993 Brecht scholar Marc Silberman pointed to a "disparity in Brecht reception," addressing a "non-synchroneity" of Brecht reception in the "Three Worlds." Specifically, Silberman contrasted the canonization, professionalization, and institutionalization of Brechtian theater in Europe and North America with Brecht's role "in the so-called Third World of Central and South America, Asia and Africa" where his "work has played and continues to play a vital role in theatre for articulating the emancipatory political process of national transformation."[14] Like the participants in the Brecht-Dialog conferences, Silberman foregrounded how in the non-Western world practitioners and theorists alike stressed theater's significance for intervening in sociopolitical processes.[15] In fact, at the seventh international Brecht symposium, organized by the International Brecht Society, which was held in 1986 in Hong Kong, participants from twenty-five countries weighed in on precisely these issues, with a special focus on Africa and Asia.[16]

Why begin with this discussion of Brecht's reception outside Germany, the non-Western world in particular? In addition to the disparity with regard to the geopolitical differences in Brecht reception pointed out by Silberman, Turkey, apart from the Brecht-Dialog in 1978, seems to be absent from this international discussion—or at least in the documentation thereof. In this book I will not enter into a discussion on the changing politico-economic, ideological, or diplomatic issues regarding Turkey's position in relation to the so-called Three Worlds, nor will I attempt to discuss the usefulness and accuracy of this rhetoric.[17] However Turkey's referential status as a non-European and non-Western country located at Europe's periphery is certainly an important factor for my consideration of Turkish-German cultural exchange in the postwar period, specifically with regard to the implementation, adaptation, and transformation of Brecht in both the Turkish and Turkish-German contexts.

While the theoretical and practical conversation about Brecht reception beyond Europe and the United States has evolved, with the inclusion of Brechtian theater aesthetics in Africa, East and South Asia, South America, and the Middle East, perspectives on the reception of

Brecht in Turkey have been few and far between. In turning to address this lack—and this is one of the ambitions of the present book—we not only add Turkey to this international dialogue, as it were, but also stand to enhance our understanding of Brecht's reception in Germany itself. For while Germany's decades of division have been mirrored in scholarship on Brecht in Germany, such that discussions of Brecht's legacy have largely focused on either East or West Germany, but not both, the Turkish Brecht reception drew on discourses and practices from both East and West. This involved not only the problematization of pressing issues in Turkish politics via Brechtian theater aesthetics but also an engagement with both East German and West German theater institutions and publishing houses, with the various ways they understand Brecht, and with their diverse and distinctive visions of theater's social role. During the 1960s and 1970s Turkish theater professionals and cultural critics used Brecht adaptations, translations, and theater journals to consider intersections between epic theater, understood as the quintessential modernist theater, and traditional modes of representation on the Turkish stage. By shedding light on the Turkish reception of Brecht during this period, in this book I uncover hitherto unexamined cultural-political constellations and literary affiliations between Turkey and divided Germany, both East *and* West. Indeed, my analysis illustrates how the nascent Turkish left was open to the GDR, engaging in a cultural and intellectual exchange that transcended Cold War divisions, reimagining revolutionary aesthetics without heeding either liberal-democratic or state-socialist orthodoxies.

The 1968 Brecht-Dialog in East Berlin may have been the first international conference focusing solely on Brecht's work and methods, but it was not the first event hosted on German soil at which Brecht-inspired theater practitioners from around the world encountered one another. Founded in 1949, the Erlangen student theater festival—which ran until 1968—provided a pivotal forum, situated in West Germany, that facilitated international dialogues on political theater practices for nearly two decades.[18] Particularly in the 1960s, these dialogues proved influential for the adaptation of Brecht to the Turkish context, as Turkish theater intellectuals became a constant presence at the festival after 1954.

That the Erlangen festival played such a role was hardly inevitable. Indeed, early in the festival's history, in 1951, a dispute over a planned appearance by Brecht himself resulted in the student ensemble of the Free University of (West) Berlin withdrawing from the festival in protest against Brecht's support for the East German state. And in the mid-1950s the Erlangen event's funding—which was partially provided by the West German ministry for cultural affairs—was threatened when the festival's director, Horst Statkus, toured the GDR at the invitation of the East German cultural ministry, against the apparent wishes of West German officials.[19] Notwithstanding these early tensions, as relations between the two German states underwent periodic freezes and thaws in the later 1950s and throughout the 1960s, the Erlangen festival remained an important link between East and West, performing a kind of "cultural rapprochement" well before the détente of the early 1970s.[20]

During the sixth Erlangen festival in 1954, an international organization for the support of student theater ensembles was formed: the European Student Theater Union (ESTU).[21] Emphasizing three interlinked goals— an "international exchange of experiences," the organization of theater festivals, and the development of "new ideas for theater life" in different countries—the ESTU had thirty-three members within a year, including student ensembles from East Germany and other socialist countries.[22] This integration of theater ensembles from "behind the iron curtain" was one of its main goals from the beginning.[23] However, the participation of countries from the Eastern bloc proved increasingly difficult, both because of West Germany's entry and exit permit regulations and because of participating countries' restrictions on the outgoing travel of their own citizens.[24] Ensembles from fascist states such as Spain and Portugal, and oppressive regimes such as Turkey[25] faced similar difficulties.[26] In 1963, ESTU renamed itself the International Student Theater Union, geographically widening its appeal. During this period the festival provided a model for new festivals founded in Istanbul, Nancy, Parma, Zagreb, and Gothenburg.[27]

Turkish student theater ensembles such as the Cep Tiyatrosu, the student ensemble of Ankara University, and the Gençlik Tiyatrosu had come to Erlangen as early as 1954. Numerous individuals who later became prominent dramatists, such as Vasıf Öngören, Haldun Taner, Özdemir Nutku, and Sermet Çağan, were members of these ensembles. They came to encounter not only the work of Bertolt Brecht, but its changing interpretation and implementation in the international interchanges taking place at the festival. For Vasıf Öngören, a member of the Gençlik Tiyatrosu ensemble, the encounter with Brechtian dramaturgy in Erlangen led to an extended stay at the Berliner Ensemble, during which he shadowed Werner Wekwerth, then the Ensemble's managing director.

Until his death in 1956, Brecht's choice to settle in the GDR led to systematic campaigns against staging his work in West Germany, where he was polemically rejected as a "propaganda puppet of the East German regime."[28] Indeed, Brecht was not performed in West Berlin during his lifetime, yet throughout the rest of West Germany the boycotts were not uniformly imposed.[29] Nevertheless, the Erlangen student theater festival represented

Fig. I.1. Gençlik Tiyatrosu ensemble with Horst Statkus in Erlangen (1954). Photograph by Rudi Stümpel. Reproduced by permission from Stadtarchiv Erlangen, VIII.3146.N.1/1 30.

a notable exception with regard to the West German boycott of Brecht and his work. For the organizers, staging Brecht's works was not seen in "direct relationship to his position in the GDR," but rather perceived as a "necessary democratic contribution."[30] Such contributions were held to be particularly important at moments of crisis, such as the June workers uprising in East Berlin in 1953, the uprisings in Poland and Hungary in 1956, and the building of the Berlin Wall in 1961. Foregrounding Brecht's work as a pacifist, the Studiobühne Erlangen and the student theater festival paid particular attention to the playwright in their programs.[31] Even during these periods, as in 1953 when tensions were highest between the two German states and thunderous denunciations of West German revanchism were being delivered in print and on the airwaves, high-profile members of the Berliner Ensemble, such as Manfred Wekwerth, Hans J. Bunge, Helmut Baierl, Ekkehard Schall, Werner Hecht, and Gisela May, all came to the festival in Erlangen.[32]

During the eleventh festival in July 1961—shortly before the construction of the Berlin Wall began—the Studiobühne Erlangen performed Brecht's *Trommeln in der Nacht* (*Drums in the Night*), causing heated debate.[33] While Stuttgart's student theater ensemble had already performed the play during the 1955 festival, this Brecht play was under "quarantine" in the GDR, and would remain so until 1984.[34] Even in West Germany, including it in the international festival's program was a daring step. Concerning its inclusion in the festival program in 1955, the festival's magazine *Spotlight* commented that it was not only possible, but actually imperative to stage Brecht.[35] The 1961 festival proved particularly controversial, because the opening production was performed by an East German ensemble, the Studiobühne of East Berlin's Humboldt University. In a report on the festival in the *Berliner Zeitung*, Dieter Herrmann, one of the ensemble's actors, remarked: "For us German participants [it was] also a forum for exchanging views and establishing real contacts . . . despite all the political and ideological discrepancies."[36] In addition to the Humboldt University's ensemble, another East German ensemble, the Studentenbühne University Rostock staged Brecht's *Furcht und Elend des Dritten Reichs* (Fear and Misery of the Third Reich). Festival organizers further screened the filmed record of the Berliner Ensemble's *Mother Courage* production and organized a discussion event with Helmut Baierl, its dramaturg. This focus on Brecht and the involvement of GDR ensembles and directors led to public complaints in West German papers, and to accusations that the festival was acting "against the interest of the entire population," and that when one performed Brecht's work, one placed oneself in the service of the SED (Socialist Unity Party) regime.[37]

Turkish ensembles began to attend the festival in 1954, and one had been present nearly every year until its dissolution in 1968. By participating in the Erlangen festival and visiting East Berlin, members of these Turkish ensembles engaged with both East and West German thinkers working in the Brechtian tradition. For instance, after Vasıf Öngören and Aras Ören attended Erlangen in the late 1950s, they decided to further study Brechtian theater by attending stage rehearsals at the Berliner Ensemble in the following few years—a period during which Manfred Wekwerth, Matthias Langhoff, and Manfred Karge were there. Working later as Benno Besson's assistant at the East Berlin Volksbühne from 1976 to 1978, Emine Sevgi Özdamar met Langhoff and Karge, who also were working there. After leaving the Volksbühne, Özdamar rejoined Heiner Müller, Karge, and Langhoff in Bochum, where she worked from 1979 to 1984. Özdamar's interest in theater and Brecht developed in conversations with Öngören in West Berlin in 1965; when she returned to Istanbul to attend drama school, she joined Öngören's ensemble. First in Ankara, and later in Istanbul, she performed in his seminal Brecht adaptations before emigrating to Germany in 1976. As this short summary indicates, from these interactions a web of intersections emerged with regard to the Turkish and Turkish-German engagement with Brecht that is not linear, not teleological, and always subject to continuous renegotiation.

These discussions hardly took place in a vacuum; rather, they were profoundly influenced by the evolving reception of Brecht in divided Germany, where long-standing events such as the Erlangen student theater festival (1949–68) in the Federal Republic drew participants from nearly as many countries as the GDR's Brecht-Dialog would in the ensuing decades. At such festivals, a multiplicity of perspectives and practices were offered, and Turkish attendees at these festivals brought their own theatrical traditions and aesthetic innovations with them as well.[38] In this way, Turkish theater practice and discourse was influenced by a continuous exchange between German and Turkish contexts, stages, and ensembles.

Drawing upon original archival research and close textual analysis, in this study I reconstruct the central role of Brecht reception in Turkish theater. While the first chapter focuses on Turkey in the 1960s and explores theater programming and critical debates in literary journals in order to examine how Brechtian stage productions thematized issues in Turkish politics and cultural affairs, two additional chapters elaborate the significance of theater practice and aesthetics for Emine Sevgi Özdamar and Aras Ören. Beyond biographical similarities—both were born in Turkey, emigrated to Germany, and have become major literary figures—these two writers are linked by a shared interest and involvement in Brecht's reception in Turkey during the 1960s, and by their continued engagement with Brecht after their migration to Germany. The aim is to understand Brecht's place in the theater discourses of 1960s Turkey in order to establish a new context through which to read their later work. Indeed, in this book I move beyond the consideration of labor migration to uncover professional and cultural links between Turkish and German theatrical practices that complicate existing periodizations of the history of Turkish-German thought.

Turkish-German Texts and Contexts

The categorizations of literature written by writers of non-German descent have been based on their ethnic background, economic and legal status, or on the themes and language of their texts, evident in past labels such as *Gastarbeiterliteratur* (guestworker literature), *Ausländerliteratur* (foreigners' literature) and *Migrantenliteratur* (migrant literature). Writers themselves have intervened in these discussions, criticizing the neglect of aesthetic over thematic concerns, as well as arguing against the pigeonholing and essentializing categorizations of their literary work. In 1985 the writer, translator, and critic Yüksel Pazarkaya refused to be labeled a "Gastarbeiterautor," guestworker author, and positioned within "Gastarbeiterliteratur," guestworker literature. He explained his rejection of these categories by emphasizing that "the theme alone does not wholly determine an artwork."[39] In the same edited volume, Ören similarly argued against the ghettoization of authors' literary works through labeling or typecasting processes that focus unduly on their backgrounds.[40] In any case, the use of terms that focus on the economic or legal status of the writer to describe the work of either Emine Sevgi Özdamar or Aras Ören, the two Turkish-German writers central to this book, would factually be inaccurate, as they settled permanently in Germany not as guestworkers but as experienced theater actors. In 1985 and 1999 respectively, Ören and Özdamar received the Adelbert von Chamisso Prize, an award for authors "of non-German background" which documents "literature and language as communication between cultures," locating these works outside the German literary landscape, rather than within it, while also reducing them to a means through which to bridge cultural differences. In her acceptance speech of the Chamisso-Prize in 1999, Özdamar points to an interesting conundrum: while as a literary writer in the German language she was repeatedly asked to justify why she wrote in German, in her theater work she never faced questions about performances on German, or French stages.[41] The question of writing in German, then, seems to arise when she produces rather than performs German culture.

In her groundbreaking study *The Turkish Turn in Contemporary German Literature* (2005), Leslie A. Adelson has criticized intercultural approaches to literatures of migration that stress "dialogic communication as a process in which readers and characters engage as representatives of discrete worlds."[42] Instead she emphasizes the need for "a new critical grammar for understanding the configuration of cultural contact and Turkish presence in contemporary German literature," suggesting the need for a shift to consider the long-term effects of migration (23). Her conceptual tool "touching tales" characterizes literary texts that bring cultural and historical aspects into proximity, aspects that are "generally not thought to belong together," thus foregrounding "historical and cultural entanglements" instead of "incommensurable differences" with regard to Turkish-German encounters (22, 20). While Adelson clarifies that the literature of Turkish migration does not designate this literary corpus as written by migrants (as opposed to migrants' literature), labor migration and its enduring effects together do constitute the temporal framework at the center of her analysis. Situating literature "born of Turkish migration" within German literature, she directs our attention to how in these texts German worlds are "configured in new ways" (13). As I explore in this book, Turkish writers' engagement with Brecht—both in their own written works and on stages from Istanbul and Ankara to East Berlin and Erlangen—prompted a range of such reconfigurations.

The contributions and interventions of Turkish-German literature to German culture have been central to Adelson's work, most evident in her analytic stance against the "between two worlds" paradigm. In *The Turkish Turn*, she calls for engagement with these texts "beyond the conceptual lens that situates migrants between two worlds and national cultures" (29). Her paradigmatic intervention emerges from her focus on the effects of Turkish migration on German culture through an interpretation of literary texts written after the fall of the Wall (13). She shows how literatures of migration "involve a preponderance of interventions into and beyond national archives of twentieth-century German culture" (12). Answering this call for thinking beyond the "national archive" of German culture, I turn to the Turkish archive for evidence of the Turkish Brecht reception, itself characterized by various intersecting Turkish and German cultural practices, and reconstruct its impact on Turkish-German literature in Germany. My work centers on the mutual interaction of Turkish and German archives and their transformation in the process, thereby proposing a temporal as well as historical and geographic expansion of the archive for our consideration of Turkish-German literature.[43] Turkish theater practice and discourse throughout the 1960s was influenced by a continuous exchange between German and Turkish contexts, stages, and ensembles—an exchange that occurred outside the context of labor migration within which Turkish-German cultural exchange and literary production are customarily framed. An engagement with Aras Ören's and Emine Sevgi Özdamar's literary work after their emigration to Germany thus needs to consider their theatrical involvement in Turkey, in order to understand the full extent of "cultural contact," the "historical and cultural entanglements" between Turkish and German contexts.[44]

In this vein, my work also responds to B. Venkat Mani's argument that Turkish-German literary texts resist "the limitation of their intellectual and political affiliations to one of the two nations."[45] Anchoring his analysis in a framework of cosmopolitanism, Mani, like Adelson, focuses on novels written since 1990 that thematize various levels of interaction between Turkey and Germany. His analysis of "literary claims of multiple and simultaneous affiliations and disaffiliations" includes, in addition to works by Sten Nadolny, Emine Sevgi Özdamar, and Feridun Zaimoğlu, a novel by Orhan Pamuk, read as challenges to notions of ethnic nationhood.[46]

In addition to these interventions, a 2015 special issue of *Colloquia Germanica* titled *Turkish-German Texts and Contexts* examined the significance of the Turkish literary archive for Turkish-German studies. In his contribution to this special issue, David Gramling emphasizes some Turkish-language literary texts' stubborn resistance to classification into a single national archive, foregrounding their significance for Turkish, German, and Turkish-German studies.[47] Gramling further engages with

Turkish-language novels, including Ören's, in the line of authors who are "waiting in the lobby of German Turkish studies."[48] While he acknowledges the importance of Adelson's call for scholars to relocate Turkish-German literature within German literature, culture, and history, rather than placing it "between two worlds customarily reserved for these authors and their texts,"[49] in line with the editors of this special issue, he points to scholars' inattention to "the Turkish national archive, the Ottoman imperial archive, or indeed the transnational materials that were always too precarious to make it into an archive of any sort."[50] In the past few years, scholars have indeed increasingly turned "beyond the German archive" to include the Turkish archive, offering new insights into Turkish-German encounters.[51] Mert Bahadir Reisoğlu, for instance, has attended to Turkish literary criticism's importance for Özdamar's poetics, and Karin Yeşilada has illustrated the significance of Turkish literary traditions for Turkish-German poetry. Randall Halle has analyzed the effect of Europeanization on Turkish cinema, and its implications for Turkish-German film. Deniz Göktürk has incorporated the Turkish visual archive into discourses on German reunification, and Berna Güneli has examined intertextual references to the Turkish film genre Yeşilçam in Fatih Akın's cinematic oeuvre.[52]

Outside the realm of scholarly exchange, concerns about the cultural compatibility between Turkey and Germany have long loomed large in the German public sphere. Since the labor recruitment of the postwar period, people of Turkish descent have been at the center of attention and deemed as the group the least willing to integrate, or least capable of integrating.[53] As early as 2001, in her "Against Between—a Manifesto," which she conceived of as an intervention into political and scholarly rhetoric in Germany, Adelson challenged the persistent "notion that Turks and Germans are separated by an absolute cultural divide,"[54] a notion that continues to resonate today.[55] Frequently, as anthropologist Ruth Mandel has pointed out, "'Turk' is shown to have become a signifier of instability and anxiety in national, subnational, and transnational narrations."[56] And while people of Turkish descent have long been perceived as "ethnonational Others," Yasemin Yildiz has shown that since 2000, religion has become a factor by which Turks "have become embodiments of a differently underwritten Otherness."[57] In German usage, she argues, a locutory shift has taken place from "Turks" to "Muslims," through which the individuals in question are "situated in a new network of discursive associations," allowing for Turks to be connected to a larger community of religiously defined antagonists, and thereby linked to "large-scale, hard-to-control incidents of violence."[58]

In her recent study *Undeutsch: Die Konstruktion des Anderen in der postmigrantischen Gesellschaft* (2016), Fatima El-Tayeb also points to the persistence of "the trope of Islam as incompatible with European values" in the long history of politically expedient contrasts drawn between Turkey and Germany, emphasizing how Germany's supposedly Judeo-Christian roots have been placed in opposition to Turkey's Muslim ones.[59] Over time, she suggests, the "so-called historic 'Turk problem,' the civilizational dichotomy of Islam and Europa" has been a persistent "rhetorical construction."[60] She brings our attention to the cyclical process of perpetual othering, through which "Migrantisierte," those born and raised in Germany but denied status of Germanness, are "made other" and "externalized as un-German."[61] By using the neologism "migrantisiert" (literally translating into "made migrant") as opposed to migrant on its own, El-Tayeb draws attention to the active construction of the migrant status as a perpetual status, and thus "eternal newcomers."[62] Here she criticizes the most recent legal designator, "Bürger mit migrantischem Hintergrund." In circulation since 2005 and revised in 2016, this term literally means "citizens with a migration background" and refers to immigrants, naturalized immigrants, and the "Spätaussiedler" (ethnic German repatriates) and their descendants, prompting El-Tayeb to wonder: "When does the background become the foreground?"[63]

Rejecting such notions of "migration background" and disavowing the work of marginalization and exclusion they perform, in this book I put Turkish in "Turkish-German" center stage by studying how Turkish intellectuals actively contributed to and transformed the reception of Bertolt Brecht. Far from being a topic of marginal concern, the reception of Brecht was—in Germany and Turkey alike—a key site where the relationship between politics and aesthetics was negotiated. For in addition to being the most important German playwright of the twentieth century, Brecht was also a catalyst for the transformation of theater aesthetics in dozens of countries he never visited—countries such as Turkey, where the 1960s and 1970s saw sweeping social changes take place, with ramifications worked out not merely in newspaper editorials and formal political speech but also in books and on stages.

This book's first chapter "Intersections of Culture and Politics: Bertolt Brecht in the Turkish Context," studies the transformation of left-wing political culture in Turkey after the 1960 and 1971 military coups, carefully examining how Brechtian stage productions—understood both as productions of translations of Brecht's plays, and as productions of plays that adopted (and adapted) Brecht's theater aesthetics—thematized issues in Turkish politics and cultural affairs. Such productions were based on national and international discussions of Brecht's work, including the student festival in Erlangen and the East Berlin Brecht-Dialog conferences, as already mentioned, and provided an important setting for international dialogue on theater. Particular attention will be given in this chapter to Haldun Taner, Vasıf Öngören, Genco Erkal, and Sermet Çağan, not only because of their pioneering role in introducing and implementing Brechtian dramaturgical practices in the Turkish context, but also because of their intersecting experiences within theatrical institutions and ensembles in both Turkey and Germany, and their interlocking collaborations. In addition, they influenced Aras Ören and Emine Sevgi Özdamar. Vasıf Öngören proved particularly influential, because of his close relationship to both of them. Following this period of liberalization and democratization from the early to mid-1960s, the Turkish military intervened once again in 1971, nullifying the basic democratic rights and freedoms that had been extended in 1960. In the process thousands of democrats and socialists were imprisoned, and the Turkish Workers' Party (TIP) was banned along with oppositional newspapers, magazines, and publishing houses. In the face of this growing oppression and persecution of the left, Aras Ören and Emine Sevgi Özdamar left Turkey for Germany. This chapter reconstructs the major arguments in the politicization of Turkish theater during this time of upheaval, foreshadowing their significance for Ören's and Özdamar's oeuvre after their emigration to Germany.

At the center of the second chapter, "Didactic Realism: Aras Ören and Working-Class Culture" is Aras Ören's so-called Berlin trilogy (1973–80), a cycle of narrative poems, and the unpublished learning play "Lehrstück für türkische Arbeiter" (Learning Play for Turkish Workers, 1970). Ören was one of the earliest and most significant Turkish-German writers to emerge in Germany. In his view, Turkish guestworkers integrated themselves into Germany's labor movement by engaging with its existing legacies of working-class struggle and solidarity and actively adapting them to the socioeconomic and political circumstances of West Germany in the 1970s. Through his literary work, Ören stimulated forms of collectivity across national borders. Meanwhile, in his activist editorial work as a member of the artist organization Die Rote Nelke, he modeled ways to disseminate his works—poetic, prose, and dramatic—and foster further transnational, literary-political expression and action. Based on a variety of previously unexamined archival sources, this chapter offers a rereading of Ören's early writings in the context of a larger politicization of German literature at the time. My close reading of Ören's trilogy and the learning play pays special attention to the representation of workers' solidarity and of Turkish participation in the German workers' movement, showing how Ören represents Turkish workers as subjects, not objects, of German labor history. Ören models a praxis of realism and artistic social responsibility that displays the marked influence of Brecht's theoretical approach and aesthetic practices. This chapter illustrates how central Brecht's legacy is to Ören's work, focusing specifically on his conceptualization of art as a political tool and his realist aesthetics. My reading moves beyond the classification of Ören's work within restrictive ethnicity-based categorizations of literature by minorities that locates their contributions outside the German national canon; instead it places him more broadly within West Berlin's working-class culture, leftist protest, and transnational solidarity movements.[64]

The third chapter, "Staged Pasts: Emine Sevgi Özdamar's Dramatic Aesthetic" focuses on the significance of Brechtian theater and strategies of staging in Özdamar's novel *Seltsame Sterne starren zur Erde* (2003). In this chapter I engage with her extensive theatrical experience in East and West Germany and the Turkish adaptation and transformation of Brecht's work connected with it—processes in which she herself was a participant. Like Ören's engagement with Brecht, Özdamar's spans multiple contexts; and as my analysis shows, they are interlinked; there are continuities between the Volksbühne and the Bochumer Schauspielhaus, but also with the Turkish Brecht reception, which provided the impetus for her theatrical career. While scholars have paid some attention to her theatrical involvement in both East and West Germany, less has been said about the degree to which her East and West German theatrical activity were linked not only to one another but to her work with Turkish Brechtian ensembles and directors as well.

At the core of my analysis of the 2003 novel will thus be the significance of theater for Özdamar's prose, which, I argue, draws on her multifaceted encounters with Brecht. By employing literary montage as a structural principle for the staging of divided Berlin in *Seltsame Sterne*, Özdamar, like Brecht, draws attention to the unfolding of social, historical, and political processes. Music serves as a means of linking different city spaces and temporalities to one another: East to West Berlin, and both parts of Berlin to Istanbul. Furthermore, the transitions between multiple places and temporalities, as well as between tradition(s) and their renewal are ultimately and intrinsically connected to the Brechtian development of art as political act. My reading reframes her work as underpinned by a continuous engagement with theater in Turkey and divided Germany, foregrounding continuities between Turkish and German contexts, rather than ruptures. Theater also serves as a basis for linking East and West Berlin to Istanbul. Özdamar's text thus invites us to reconsider the cultural topography of Cold War Berlin, and the role of Turkish migrants in the public discourse of the city's present and past.

Brecht, Turkish Theater, and Turkish-German Literature illuminates the inextricability of Turkish and German literary histories in the second half of the twentieth century by considering the significance of a Turkish archive that had itself been strongly impacted by Brechtian theory and practice. More than that, it offers a detailed account not only of the cultural effects of Turkish immigration and inscription of Turkish subjects into German discourses of working-class culture and literary politics beyond ethnicity and nationality in divided Germany, but also of the vital role Brecht's thought played in the process. The developments in Turkish theater, especially its politicization throughout the 1960s and 1970s, were of great significance for the Turkish writers and intellectuals who left Turkey for West Germany in the face of growing oppression in the late 1970s. A variety of theaters and ensembles, such as Öngören's Kollektiv Theater, formerly Birlik Sahnesi in Istanbul, continued working in Germany, emphasizing the need for cultural rapprochement and exchange.

Transnational cultural practices are never unidirectional, as the Turkish and the Turkish-German encounter with Brecht central to this study shows: I engage not only with the impact of Brecht on Turkey but also with the role Turkish intellectuals played in engaging with Brechtian methods after their move to Germany. Consequently, both the significance of Turkish-German cultural practices for Berlin and the centrality of Brechtian aesthetics for literary and theoretical innovations in Turkey figure centrally in this book. Spanning sources in multiple languages (Turkish, German, and English) and multiple genres, this interdisciplinary project contributes to the growing body of work on transnationalism, studying the anchoring of aesthetic exchange in political endeavors, and further situating artists' alliances and aesthetic affinities with respect to the Cold War geopolitical contexts within which they took shape. By examining how this varied body of Turkish-German literature attests to a shared history of cultural innovation that spans the Turkish and (East and West) German contexts, and paying close attention to those contexts' transformation by, and portrayal within, these texts, this book recovers, and reasserts, the significance of Turkish-German literary encounters in discourses on German culture and history.

1: Intersections of Politics and Aesthetics: Bertolt Brecht in the Turkish Context

IN A LETTER TO HANNS EISLER, sent from exile in Helsinki in March 1941, Bertolt Brecht wrote the following: "I did not hear anything about a new route, maybe we can travel through Turkey, but it's not at all sure."[1] In the end, Brecht never went to Turkey; his journey to California instead led him through Moscow, Leningrad, and Vladivostok. But Brecht could have traveled through Turkey, and engaged with Turkish intellectuals, academics, and institutions—as Leo Spitzer, Ernst Reuter, and Erich Auerbach did.[2] For in addition to taking in refugees who had been victimized by Nazi persecution—professors, teachers, attorneys, artists deemed unreliable—Turkey was an important transit country for Jewish emigrants.[3] While Brecht's own journey took a different path, his theatrical practices found their way into Turkish literary and political life, starting in the mid-1950s with the international success of *Mutter Courage und ihre Kinder* (*Mother Courage and Her Children*, 1939) in guest productions in Paris in 1954 and London in 1956. The reception of Brecht in Africa and South America, Asia, and the Middle East has been the topic of past conferences and publications.[4] However, despite continuous and intensive engagement with Brecht by Turkish academics, intellectuals, dramatists, and directors,[5] almost no scholarly attention has been paid to the reception of Brecht in Turkey. This is the case within both Brecht studies and German studies.[6] The history of Turkish theater in the twentieth century is marked by continuous exchange between Germany and Turkey—an exchange that, to be sure, extends beyond Brecht. Muhsin Ertuğrul (1892–1979), for example, considered the leading figure or 'father' of modern Turkish theater,[7] regularly went to Berlin as early as 1916 (Lessing Theater and Deutsches Künstlertheater) to "deepen his technical skills,"[8] returning decades later to Munich and Bochum in 1966 to research "theater education methods."[9] At the invitation of the Turkish government, the German composer Paul Hindemith came to Turkey to establish the State Conservatory for Music and Drama in Ankara in 1936, while at the same time serving as adviser to the Turkish government on issues pertaining to culture and music. The Conservatory's drama and opera section was established and run by German actor and director Carl Ebert, who made what the theater critic Metin And has described as an immense "contribution to the development of the State Conservatory and national theater."[10]

The Turkish-German theatrical exchange manifested itself not only in the involvement of German dramatists in reforms of Turkish theater, but also in Turkish dramatists' experiences in Germany. Haldun Taner studied drama in Vienna in the mid-1950s, during which time he encountered Brecht's work at the Kammerspiele in Munich for the first time. Dramatist and literary critic Özdemir Nutku's engagement with Brecht, and the German theatrical canon, occurred during his time in Göttingen, in the Georg August University's drama department, where he received his PhD in the late 1950s. The Berliner Ensemble, in particular, played a key role, as a number of significant figures in Turkish theater history such as Mehmet Ulusoy (1942–2005), Vasıf Öngören (1938–84) and Genco Erkal (1938–) went to East Berlin to study Brechtian theater. Moreover, two student theater festivals, in Istanbul and Erlangen, provided a forum for exchange and collaboration between Turkish and German directors, artists, and ensembles.

In this chapter I focus on the beginning of an increased Turkish engagement with Brecht's plays and writings on theater in the early 1960s, surveying translations of Brecht's writings on theater into Turkish, the journals that familiarized Turkish audiences with Brecht's dramaturgical precepts, the theater festivals that served as forums for exchange, and Turkish dramatists' interpretations of Brecht and their collaborative efforts. While some attention will be paid to individual Turkish stage adaptations of Brecht's plays, I will primarily focus on Turkish dramatists' adaptation and transformation of Brechtian dramaturgical concepts and practices in the creation of a progressive national Turkish theater. Reconstructing how a Turkish Brechtian discourse on the theory and practice of theater emerged reveals the crucial influence of Brecht's own writing. Particularly central to this discourse's emergence were Haldun Taner, Vasıf Öngören, Genco Erkal, and Sermet Çağan, not only because of their pioneering role regarding the introduction and implementation of Brechtian dramaturgical practices, but also because of their various intersecting experiences within theatrical institutions and ensembles, and their multiple instances of collaboration. Of these intellectuals, Vasıf Öngören was particularly influential, because of his close relationship to both Aras Ören and Emine Sevgi Özdamar, whose work is explored at length in the second and third chapters of this book respectively.

Aesthetics and Politics: Literary Debates and Theatrical Practice in 1960s Turkey

In the aftermath of the 1960 military coup, parliamentary democracy was established in Turkey and a new, progressive constitution ensured freedom of expression and thought, political activity, organization, and demonstration. A number of constitutional changes affected the press, publishing, and the governance of universities, in particular by introducing new liberties. The freedom of thought and from censorship regulations was declared in articles 20, 21, and 22. For the first time, political ideas that had previously been prohibited now entered public and political discussion, as well as organizations.[11] A political left was now able to openly formulate and debate their opinions in new journals and newspapers, and constitutional changes now legitimized the legal existence of Marxist movements, which, as historian Özgür Ulus writes, are "generally referred to as the left or extreme left," and which "expanded and diversified during the 1960s."[12]

This is not to say that the persecution of the left ceased during the 1960s. Particularly under the rule of Prime Minister Süleyman Demirel and his Justice party, which won a parliamentary majority in 1965, the leftist intelligentsia became a principal target, with radical writers and artists being constantly harassed. Many of them were prosecuted under articles 141 and 142 of the penal code for disseminating communist propaganda. Nevertheless, at the beginning of the decade, "a legal movement of the left arose in Turkey within which diverse leftists, left-wing radicals, social democrats, trade unionists, and Marxists were active, styling themselves and the movement as socialist."[13]

Changes in censorship resulted in the translation of previously prohibited texts, providing new opportunities for exchange and discussion of formerly inaccessible sources. While the ban on communist activity remained in effect, Marxist literature could now be translated into Turkish and legally distributed.[14] Here changes made in the section of the constitution titled "The Rights and Freedoms of Thought and Belief" are of particular significance with regard to freedom of thought, speech and the press. Newly introduced Article 20 in this section now guaranteed "freedom of thought and opinion," and the right to circulate and disseminate ideas in speech, writing, or image.[15] Furthermore, article 21 implemented the right for everyone "to learn and teach, state and publicize" in the area of science and art.[16] It further stipulated universities' autonomy in terms of self-governance (independence from state control) and articulated for its members the right to "freely" research and publish.[17] Article 22 stipulated: "The press is free, it cannot be censored."[18] In this section, further articles now introduced the right to publish journals, newspapers, books, and brochures without prior state consent and free from censorship.[19]

These changes had far-reaching and visible effects with regard to Turkish theater, resulting in an increase in the number of private theater ensembles, which doubled after 1965, and the (re)opening of higher education's first theater department in 1964, the Ankara University Theater Institute.[20] In response to all this activity, Talat S. Halman notes, "the most remarkable development in Turkish culture in the 1960s was the explosion of theatrical activity."[21] Dramatist and actor Genco Erkal refers to this time as the "renaissance period" for theater in Turkey, while also foregrounding in the process that it was the period in which "Brecht came to Turkey."[22] This theatrical renaissance manifested itself in the founding of multiple progressive theater companies, such as the Gülriz Sururi-Engin Cezzar Tiyatrosu and Arena Tiyatrosu in 1962, its successor Ankara Sanat Tiyatrosu (AST) in 1963, Halk Oyuncuları in 1967, Dostlar Tiyatrosu in 1969 and the Ankara Birliği Sahnesi in 1970.[23]

Alongside the constitutional changes regarding censorship, sociopolitical changes also had an impact on public readership and intellectual productivity. Between 1960 and 1970 the number of libraries almost doubled to 327, the number of library users tripled to almost 4 million, and the number of foreign books translated into Turkish doubled from 400 in 1961 to 800 in 1971; moreover, fifty-six new journals appeared.[24] Socialist-oriented journals, of which *Yön* and *Ant* are just two examples, began to be published in Turkey as well. *Yön,* a weekly, appeared in Ankara from 1961 to 1967, and was the most widely read journal among students.[25] For the *Yön* circle, the main goal was a fundamental reform in the socioeconomic sector; in an effort to combat imperialism and feudalism, they advocated economic and political independence from the United States and suggested that land reform would prevent the bourgeoisie from maintaining its hegemony. *Ant,* "*Yön*'s more extremist heir," started to appear in Istanbul in 1967, and quickly became a forum for left-wing socialists to freely express and exchange ideas in support of socialism as well as the anti-imperialist struggle.[26] *Ant* "preached a combination of revolutionary theory and practice."[27] In addition to the translation, circulation, and discussion of political texts by Marx, Lenin, Minh, Guevara, and Mao, and the examination of current political affairs and economic conditions in Turkey and abroad, these two journals regularly included translations of Brecht's writings in their arts sections.

Journals devoted specifically to the arts and theater aesthetics also began to appear increasingly throughout the 1960s. Here, *Oyun* is worthy of mention, a journal that regularly published contributions by contemporary theater critics and academics, including Özdemir Nutku, Hayati Asılyazıcı, and

Metin And. In support of the formation of a socialist Turkish theater, *Oyun* showed a particular interest in the works of Nazım Hikmet, Aziz Nesin, and Haldun Taner. Moreover, until its discontinuation in 1966, *Oyun,* in addition to promoting Turkish playwrights, was a leading force in introducing Brecht's plays and theories on theater to Turkish readers.[28] In 1963, for example, *Oyun* published a series titled "Brecht: Writings on Theater," which comprised a selection of Turkish translations from Suhrkamp Verlag's *Schriften zum Theater* (Writings on Theater, 1963–64)[29] by the prominent Brecht translators Adalet Cimcoz and Teoman Aktürel. Both are important not only for championing Brecht's theoretical writings but also for their efforts at translating Brecht's plays, *Der gute Mensch von Sezuan* (*The Good Person of Szechwan*) being the first one published in 1956 followed by *Die Gewehre der Frau Carrar* (*Senora Carrar's Rifles*) and *Leben des Galilei* (*Life of Galileo*) in 1963. *Oyun*'s first issue appeared on November 1, 1963, with Nurten Akarsu and Günay Akarsu, himself a frequent contributor, on its editorial board. Günay Akarsu is also the founder of Izlem Yayınevi, one of the main publishing houses to publish Brecht's plays in Turkish translation, including those mentioned above, but also publisher of the theater journal *Oyun* and its successor *Tiyatro*. The latter began appearing in 1970 and was conceived as a "developed continuation" of *Oyun,* "address[ing] the problems of Turkish theater in the context of Turkish society," and providing a regular discussion platform for dramatists, critics, and academics.[30] Moreover it regularly reported on theater—national and international—and published foreign plays in translation. In *Tiyatro*, two of Brecht's learning plays, *Der Jasager und der Neinsager* (*The Yes-Sayer and the No-Sayer*) and *Das Badener Lehrstück vom Einverständnis* (*The Baden-Baden Lesson on Consent*), were first published in Turkish translation by the writer and journalist Engin Ardıç as *Evet diyenlerle Hayır diyenler* and *Baden-Baden Didaktik Oyunu* in 1970 and 1971 respectively. In addition to *Oyun* and *Tiyatro*, various literary journals such as *Ataç, Yeni Dergi, Cep Dergisi, Papirüs,* and *Dost* published translations of Brecht's poetry, plays, and writings on theater throughout the 1960s. Along with these journals, theater ensembles and institutions such as the Istanbul Şehir Tiyatrosu, the Dormen Tiyatrosu, the Ankara Birliği Sahnesi, and AST published their own journals—including brochures of their repertoire—which featured critical essays and translations on theater. When Brecht adaptations were staged by these ensembles, special issues of their journals focused extensively on Brecht and on his life, plays, and dramaturgy.[31]

Together, these new journals and other publications constituted a forum in which new forms for a progressive Turkish theater could be proposed and debated. The discussion and dissemination of Brecht's work played a key role in this process, as Turkish intellectuals and dramatists drew upon the German playwright's ideas and practice, while emphasizing the need to adapt (and thus transform) Brechtian dramatic techniques to reflect Turkish sociopolitical realities. They did so even as they foregrounded intersections between epic theater and traditional Turkish folk theater, thus striving for a synthesis between the two.[32]

The "Brecht Incident"

While the earliest Turkish translation of a Brecht play dates back to 1956, the increased engagement with Brecht in the mid-1960s occurred in the context of and aftermath of the so-called "Brecht incident" of 1964. On March 22, 1964, the performance of *Sezuanın iyi insanı* (*The Good Person of Szechwan*) at the Dram Tiyatro, one of six Istanbul Municipal Theaters under the directorship of Muhsin Ertuğrul, was interrupted by protests. As the newspaper and journal articles reported the next day, between 150 and 200 "reactionaries" disrupted the performance.[33] The majority, it seemed, were students of *Imam Hatip Schools*, schools of prayer leaders and preachers,[34] as well as *Nurists*,[35] "whose aim was to bring together all Turkish Muslims in opposition to the doctrine of secularism in order to

Fig. 1.1. Ayla Algan as Shen Te/Shui Ta in *The Good Person of Szechwan*, Istanbul, 1964. Reproduced by permission from Akademie der Künste, Berlin, Bertolt-Brecht-Archiv Theaterdokumentation 2561/023.

Fig. 1.2. Mete Sezer, Ertuğrul Bilda, and Kayhan Yıldızoğlu as
three gods in *The Good Person of Szechwan*, Istanbul, 1964.
Reproduced by permission from Akademie der Künste, Berlin,
Bertolt-Brecht-Archiv Theaterdokumentation 2561/010.

restore the Islamic State."[36] After the first curtain fell, they first went to
the foyer, protesting loudly, and then raided the stage. They threatened a
number of actors, tore up and burned posters, and shouted anti-commu-
nist slogans such as "down with the leftists" and "down with the communists."[37] They brandished a copy of Brecht's *Szechwan*, saying "This writer
is the servant of Moscow, he won the Stalin prize, how come this play can
be read and staged here in Turkey?"[38] Actress Ayla Algan, who appeared
in the role of Shen Te, was physically threatened. In addition to the police,
military forces had to come to the theater to put an end to the turmoil.[39]
Seven suspects, among them a magazine owner, a food sector union leader
and secretary general, a teacher, and lawyers were taken into custody but
released a day later.[40]

The "Brecht incident" made national and international news, with a
variety of journals and newspapers reporting on the details of the incident

Fig. 1.3. Trial scene, *The Good Person of Szechwan*, Istanbul, 1964.
Reproduced by permission from Akademie der Künste, Berlin,
Bertolt-Brecht-Archiv Theaterdokumentation 2561/046

and the events that followed. The *Jerusalem Post, Aufbau, Le Monde,* and the *Frankfurter Rundschau* reported on the incident abroad, while the Turkish dailies *Hürriyet* and *Cumhuriyet* printed detailed accounts at home. As an immediate result of the incident, Brecht's play was temporarily banned from being performed and an expert committee was convened to judge the content of the play based on a special performance at the Dram Tiyatro the day after the incident. The theater was heavily guarded by armed forces and the police, while the committee of experts, including academics such as history professor Cemal Tukin, professor of criminal law Sulhi Dönmezer, and lecturer Ayhan Önder watched the play. M. Oğuz Berutçioğlu, a lawyer for press-related affairs, and M. Kadri Ilkay, the deputy mayor of Istanbul, rounded out the committee. Together, they were charged with making an informed decision about the play's alleged communist content. Shortly after the panel convened, it made a public statement that was based on article 142 of the penal code,[41] which prohibited communism: no communist propaganda was detected in the play.[42]

The weekly news journal *Akis* announced it as a "victory for the good persons of Szechwan."[43] On March 24, 1964, two days after the incident itself, a press conference was held at the theater by a number of actors and representatives from private theaters such as the Dormen Tiyatrosu, Kent Oyuncuları, Küçük Sahne, Grup 6, and Şehir Tiyatrosu, as well as the actors of the play. The participation of Grup 6, an amateur ensemble in Istanbul, is notable, because two months prior to the Dram Tiyatro's *Szechwan* production, it staged the first Turkish Brecht adaptation, *Carrar Ana'nın Silahları* (*Senora Carrar's Rifles*), which was based on Teoman Aktürel's translation of 1963.[44] In addition to well-known actors Yıldız Kenter and Haldun Dormen, director Genco Erkal participated in the press conference, stating, "the incident was not against the play but against art."[45] Public condemnation of the incident not only occurred in the press and in the context of this press conference, but theaters throughout the city also showed their support for the Dram Tiyatro by displaying placards and signs at their doors and display windows. These bore slogans condemning the interruption of the performance and the ensuing performance ban: "This country is managed by reactionaries"; "What time are we in?"; "This is not fascist Spain"; and "Istanbul's bad person silenced the good person of Szechwan."[46] Writer and theater critic Hayati Asılyazıcı was in the audience on the night of the performance, and wrote about his impressions for *Oyun*, perceiving it as a "blow" to Turkish theater.[47] In the same issue, the legal theorist and journalist Çetin Özek also commented on the incident in his article "Mutsuz Sezuan," where he stated that it was no one's right to turn Turkey into an "Unhappy Szechwan" by instilling fear in audiences.[48] While the incident and ensuing discussion can be read as an indication of the growing anti-communism that left-wing theater companies would face in the following years, the "Brecht incident" also prompted, as we have seen, extended public, cultural, and academic discussions about Brecht and the role of theater in Turkey. The "Brecht incident" was also not without its commercial effects: while performances of *Szechwan* at the Dram Tiyatro that preceded the incident were only attended at half occupancy, this changed drastically in the aftermath of the incident.[49]

The Dram Tiyatro production of *Szechwan* was based on Adalet Cimcoz's translation. This translation had already had to undergo state censorship procedures years before the incident, and a 1958 judicial decision deemed it a safe piece that did not disseminate communist propaganda. *Sezuanın iyi insanı* was in fact scheduled to be performed during the 1957–58 season at the Istanbul Şehir Tiyatroları, the Istanbul Municipal Theaters, with Max Meinecke as its director, but it was cancelled after rehearsals. In Adalet Cimcoz's published biography, she reports that she had attended the stage rehearsals regularly. On the day of final rehearsals, she received a phone call, letting her know that the civil police had come and prohibited the staging of the play.[50] Notwithstanding the legal decision about its non-propagandistic nature, it was taken off the program two days prior to its premiere for unspecified reasons, as reported by the Istanbul Municipal Theaters's stage manager Kemal Tözer in the press coverage of the "Brecht incident."[51]

Even as it prompted public discussions and advanced the Turkish engagement with Brecht into a broader and more public realm, the incident also had serious consequences with regard to Turkish theater. Muhsin Ertuğrul was being pressured to resign as head of the Istanbul Municipal Theaters over disputes with the right-wing-dominated municipal council, which wrote a new constitution for theater in the aftermath of the "Brecht incident."[52] As already stated, he was one of the most important figures in Turkish theater history, under whose aegis the work of Turkish playwrights was presented in theaters throughout Turkey, thus encouraging Turkish playwriting, especially supporting and promoting young talent.[53] In the early 1960s Ertuğrul expanded the Istanbul Municipal Theaters from a three-theater company, the Dram Tiyatrosu being one of them, into a complex of six theaters in different parts of the city.[54] Further, in his efforts to reach the broadest audience possible, he adjusted ticket prices in poorer sections of the city, provided transportation to and from the theaters, and in addition to the performance at 9:00 p.m. he introduced one at 6:00 p.m. to accommodate workers.[55] In response to his persistent pressure, theater's significance as an academic discipline was acknowledged when in 1958 the first theater institute was founded at the University of Ankara. This institute, the *Ankara Üniversitesi Dil ve Tarih—Coğrafya Fakültesi Tiyatro Enstitüsü*, defined its primary mission as the establishing of an archive and theater education. It was closed in 1962, in order to make the changes necessary for its transformation into a degree-granting department, and reopened in 1964 with a fully operative drama section.[56] Theater critics and directors Özdemir Nutku, Haldun Taner, Metin And, and Sevda Şener all served as professors of drama there.[57] Ertuğrul was the executive director of the Istanbul Municipal Theaters from 1958 until his dismissal in 1966, when the position was cut. This drew a lot of criticism by various ensembles, dramatists, and actors, which culminated in the public reading of a protest statement for a week prior to each performance at the theater. This statement described Ertuğrul as the person responsible for the fact that up to fifty theaters could "open their curtains" throughout the country.[58]

Many prominent theater professionals, including Asaf Çıyıltepe (founder of AST), Genco Erkal, and Güngör Dilmen, among others, were in the early stages of their careers affiliated with the Istanbul Municipal Theater under Ertuğrul's leadership. Following Ertuğrul's dismissal he went abroad, to Germany, the United States, and France, returning to Istanbul in 1967 and becoming the administrative head of the first privately owned theater conservatory in Turkey, the LCC (Language and Culture Center). The LCC is the theater school where Emine Sevgi Özdamar took acting classes from 1967 to 1970. In addition to studying with Haldun Taner and Muhsin Ertuğrul, she also took classes with Beklan Algan, the director of the *Szechwan* performance at the Dram Tiyatro in 1964.

Genco Erkal, Haldun Taner, and Vasıf Öngören: Brechtian Dialectics

Out of these energetic debates there emerged collaboration and exchange between the Turkish Brechtian dramatists Genco Erkal, Haldun Taner, Sermet Çağan, and Vasıf Öngören. I will begin with Genco Erkal, whose engagement with Brecht has spanned more than half a century. His stage career as a dramatist and actor began in the mid-1950s at the Genç Oyuncular (which he cofounded in 1957). Until 1969, when he cofounded the Brechtian ensemble the Dostlar Tiyatrosu together with Mehmet Akan, Şevket Altuğ, Arif Erkin and Ali Tahsin, he was a member of various progressive theater ensembles including the Arena Tiyatrosu (1962) and the AST. In addition, as director, Genco Erkal staged Haldun Taner's *Keşanlı Ali Destanı* (*The Ballad of Ali Keshan*, 1962), first performed in March 1964, and Öngören's epic play *Asiye nasıl kurtulur?* (How can Asiye be saved?, 1968), performed by the Dostlar Tiyatrosu ensemble during the 1970–71 season, both significant with regard to the Turkish adaptation of epic theater.

Brecht has been an important influence for Erkal and the Dostlar Tiyatrosu ensemble's theatrical activity from the beginning. Members of the ensemble emphasize their efforts to provide thought-provoking stimuli for the audience, and to create "a discussion-oriented theatrical medium . . ., having given Brecht's work particular importance."[59] Furthermore, on their website all productions are presented as "deneme" (experiments), establishing yet another connection to Brecht, who conceptualized his own writing for the theater as "Versuche" which had to be continued.[60] This emphasis on openness attests to Brecht's understanding of his theoretical work and thus dramaturgical practice as work-in-progress. Indeed, in Brecht's own words, art has to adapt to changes, to what is new in the world around us. Thus Brecht called for continued expansion, revision, and development.[61]

Precisely this emphasis on continuous experimentation, with regard to both performance practice and the implementation of Brechtian dramatic theory in the Turkish context, is at the core of Erkal's interpretation of

Brecht's theater aesthetics.[62] For Erkal, Brecht "will always be open to new interpretations," a view that warns against a "narrow-minded" approach. Because Brecht developed his theory on and in a changing—and changeable—world, Erkal believed that "to lock him up in molds . . . to accept him as unchanging" would "fossilize him."[63]

The Dostlar Tiyatrosu ensemble's repertoire included adaptations of works by Peter Weiss, Jean-Paul Sartre, John Steinbeck, Samuel Beckett, Maxim Gorki, Václav Havel, and Nikolai Gogol, alongside the works of the Turkish writers Aziz Nesin, Nazım Hikmet, Can Yücel, and Yaşar Kemal. Additionally, Erkal directed three Turkish Brechtian plays: first and foremost, Haldun Taner's internationally acclaimed *The Ballad of Ali Keshan*, acknowledged as the first Turkish epic play in a Brechtian mode, and even dubbed the Turkish *Threepenny Opera* by reviewers.[64] Erkal directed Taner's play, which was staged by the Gülriz Sururi-Engin Cezzar Tiyatrosu ensemble during the 1963–64 season, and premiered on March 31, shortly after the "Brecht incident." The play was a tremendous success, with Taner referring to it as a "tiyatro olayı" (theater event),[65] a perception shared by various reviewers. For example, in the Turkish newspaper *Tercüman*, a reviewer announced "The Germans have had their *Threepenny Opera*, the British their *My Fair Lady*, the Americans their *Porgy and Bess*, the French their *Irma la Douce*. Now we have our *Ballad of Ali of Keshan*."[66] Özdemir Nutku, despite directing some criticism at Taner's implementation of epic elements, nevertheless draws a direct parallel between Taner and Brecht in his elaborate review of the play: "In *The Good Person of Szechwan* the narrator is the water seller Wang. Here it is Şerif Abla."[67] Both Brecht's Wang and Taner's Şerif Abla address their audiences, and through their performance they interrupt the narrative flow, in Şerif Abla's case specifically through songs, in Wang's case as part of the interludes. By 1970 Taner's play had been performed more than four hundred times on Turkish stages, and at the invitation of the West German government, even toured the Federal Republic of Germany in 1966.[68] It premiered in Bonn, and was then taken on tour for Turkish workers in Cologne, Stuttgart, Frankfurt, Munich, and Nuremberg.[69] Eventually translated into German, English, Arabic, Bulgarian, Russian, and Czech, and entering the international canon of 1960s theater, Taner's play paved the way for epic theater in Turkey, specifically with regard to the formation of "musical epic plays," as Ayşegül Yüksel notes in her monograph on his dramatic work.[70] For his part, Taner, alongside Adalet Cimcoz, Teoman Aktürel, and Özdemir Nutku, had led efforts to translate Brecht's writings and plays as early as 1955,[71] and had long sought to synthesize epic theater with Turkish folk theatrical traditions.[72] On this point, in an interview with the leading East German journal *Sinn und Form*, Taner explained his work with Turkish traditional theatrical forms such as *Karagöz* (shadow theater) and *Orta Oyunu* (Turkish *commedia dell'arte*[73]) as follows: "I used anti-illusionist elements of Turkish folk theater and combined them in synthesis with modern epic theater."[74] In an earlier interview with the Turkish literary journal *Varlık* in 1964, Taner had already elaborated on the intersections between epic theater and anti-illusionist elements rooted in the Turkish folk traditions *Orta Oyunu* and *Karagöz*,[75] long considered interrelated by reason of their dramaturgical structures and character constellations.[76] Here he specifically mentioned the similarities between the figure of the story-teller and that of the *meddah* (public storyteller and mimic), prologues and epilogues, actors addressing the audience, songs, projections and placards, minimal stage décor and props—all elements he included in his *Ballad*.[77]

The epic structure was not just a formal matter for Taner. While highlighting the intersection of formal elements between epic theater and Turkish (non-illusionistic) folk traditions, Taner had criticized the "lack of any progressive content" in the latter.[78] Thus the Turkish folk performance traditions would need modification to gain new political currency. Similarly, in his discussion of the *Karagöz* tradition, the writer and translator Yüksel Pazarkaya pointed to the lack of audience engagement beyond the play, while highlighting that even those elements in traditional performance which one might regard as enacting *Verfremdung*[79] were merely used for their own sake, as "a purpose unto itself," as opposed to Brecht's "purposeful-ness."[80] Furthermore, despite its socio-critical elements, traditional Turkish folk theater retained its "comedy character."[81] While taking full advantage of the similarities in formal elements between Turkish theater and epic the-ater, Taner, in an effort to more effectively synthesize the two, emphasized the need to re-conceptualize theater as a didactic instrument and sociopo-litical tool, presenting the dialectical processes within the play, and between art and society at large.[82]

By choosing to perform Taner's work, then, Erkal was selecting material at the cutting edge of the theoretical and practical transformations of drama that were taking place in the 1960s in Turkey. Moreover, it becomes evident that in addition to examining productions of Brecht's plays, Turkish drama-tists such as Taner and Erkal drew on elements of Brecht's epic theater and critical dramaturgy in creating a new aesthetic of political theater, emphasiz-ing the need to adapt Brechtian concepts to pressing national concerns, and to place them in dialogue with Turkish aesthetic traditions.

But Haldun Taner was not the only writer whose work Erkal empha-sized. In addition to Taner's play, Erkal codirected *Feleknaz Hatun ile Gülüzar Kızın Analık Davası* (Mrs. Feleknaz and Miss Gülüzar's Maternity Case, 1972) by Mehmet Akan, one of the cofounders of the Dostlar

Tiyatrosu, who based his play on Brecht's *Der kaukasische Kreidekreis* (*The Caucasian Chalk Circle*, 1949). Erkal also directed Vasıf Öngören's How can Asiye be saved?, which was performed more than a thousand times during the 1970–71 season by the Dostlar Tiyatrosu ensemble.[83] Öngören is one of the main dramatists introducing Brechtian theater to the Turkish context; for him, "the epic system was the only Marxist theater system for a revolutionary purpose."[84]

Parallel to his role on and behind the stage, Öngören gave various interviews on this understanding of theater, and specifically with regard to the adaptation of epic theater in the Turkish context, elaborating on his theoretical and aesthetic inclinations. His interest in Brecht was sparked by the Turkish translation of the *The Good Person of Szechwan* by Adalet Cimcoz in 1957, which included a foreword on epic theater written by Haldun Taner.[85] This translation was also the basis for the *Szechwan* production at the Dram Tiyatro, the setting of the aforementioned "Brecht incident." Öngören's career in theater began in 1959 when he joined the Gençlik Tiyatrosu ensemble, of which he was a member until 1962. Among his colleagues in this ensemble was Aras Ören, whose engagement with and interpretation of Brecht will be discussed in the next chapter. At the Gençlik Tiyatrosu, Öngören participated in the capacity of actor and director and traveled with the ensemble to Erlangen, West Germany, in 1960. There, he took part in two performances: Iskerleç's *Pabuçcu Ahmet'in Garip Maceraları* (The Strange Adventures of Ahmet the Cobbler, 1809) and Güngör Dilmen's *Midas'ın Kulakları* (Midas's Ears, 1959).[86] His participation in the Erlangen student theater festival, to which I will turn later in this chapter, strengthened his interest in Brecht, resulting in his move to Berlin to study Brechtian theater. From 1962 to 1966 he, together with Aras Ören,[87] regularly attended stage rehearsals in East Berlin at the Berliner Ensemble and conducted research in its archive, while being enrolled in the Free University's theater department in West Berlin.[88] During this time Öngören began working on his first play, *Almanya Defteri* (The Germany Notebook, 1971), which he first wrote under the title *Göç* (Migration, 1965). Upon his return to Turkey in 1966, the piece was performed by the Gençlik Tiyatrosu ensemble at the international student theater festival in Istanbul, organized by the Milli Talebe Federasyonu, Istanbul University's National Student Association; there, it won second place. During his military service in the following two years, Öngören wrote How can Asiye be saved? which he subtitled "tartışmalı oyun" (controversial play). In 1969 he joined the Halk Oyuncuları as an actor, but upon realizing that he would not be able to implement his views on theater, he left them the same year with his colleagues, Mustafa Alabora, Halil Ergün, and Erdoğan Akduman, in order to found the Ankara Birliği

Sahnesi. Like Erkal's theater ensemble, the Ankara Birliği Sahnesi advocated for epic theater and an "antifascist agenda."[89] The first performance of this ensemble, Öngören's play *Asiye* in 1970, featured Emine Sevgi Özdamar in one of the female roles. This performance was followed by Öngören's first Brecht adaptation, *Adam Adamdır* (*Man Equals Man*), for which he provided the translation, again with Özdamar as member of the cast.

The ensemble published a monthly journal, *Ankara Birliği Sahnesi Dergisi*, whose first issue appeared in January 1970 and included two separate manifestos in which members of the ensemble announced their participation in the anti-imperialist and anti-feudal cultural-political struggle. Setting the formation of a "national revolutionary theater" as their goal, they acknowledged that achieving this would be "impossible without starting from a proletarian ideological understanding of theater."[90] They further highlighted their understanding of culture as "weapon," and in relationship to theater the ensemble proclaimed, "without being grounded in class, a national theater would not be realized."[91] In their view, theater is seen as "a social force" and should thus be used as a means to change the audience by "raising an awareness," and by "showing the changeability of the world, [and] presenting it to the audience for their criticism."[92] This can only be accomplished through the epic method, the only "contemporary progressive method."[93] In addition to the manifestos, this first issue includes an article by Öngören on national revolutionary theater, as well as translated excerpts from Brecht's *Short Organon* (presented as his "manifesto") and from his outline on epic theater (which Brecht included in his notes to *Rise and Fall of the City of Mahagonny*). In his contribution to this first issue, Öngören reiterates the ensemble's manifestos' emphasis on the role of culture within the fight against imperial and feudal oppression, while elaborating that this can only occur through a "working-class view of culture" with the "guidance of socialist ideology."[94] Öngören criticizes the Stanislavsky method, which he perceives as relying on the technique of illusion and on catharsis. Such criticism of Stanislavsky formed a two-pronged polemic, aimed at both Soviet theater, with its reliance on "classic" plays to provide models of ethical behavior, and at the US-based interest in method acting in the cinema, developed from Stanislavsky's teachings. Furthermore, Öngören considered Stanislavsky's work not suited to the working class, because in order to bring about change, class society's illusions need to be destroyed by use of the epic method, which replaces illusion with criticism.[95]

For Öngören, it is the writer's responsibility to "speak of reality," while emphasizing that there are different views about reality. In his case, he "forged a dialectical link between peoples' fates and social events."[96] The role of the writer, therefore, is not to teach materialist dialectics but to employ it as a method to show that reality is changing and changeable. The writer, according to Öngören, "cannot teach more than that reality is changeable."[97] Here he again foregrounds the significance of Bertolt Brecht in this realization; indeed, "Brecht was the first person to use dialectical materialism to understand reality and to represent reality through art."[98]

In an interview with the journal *Militan* in 1975 Öngören pointed out that "old tools" would not be useful for new purposes, emphasizing that it is through dialectics that theater becomes a weapon.[99] For Öngören, the artistic tool of materialist dialectics is *Verfremdung*, through which theater's function can be changed (50). The benefits of this approach include an audience that is faced not with the totality of social conditions as a *fait accompli* but instead with the process of their formation, thus unveiling the dialectic underlying Öngören's play and life itself. After citing Brecht's "Dialektik und Verfremdung" at length, Öngören presents the following "practical outcomes" through the use of *Verfremdung*: representing society as changeable, showing humans as capable of changing their surroundings, foregrounding that human nature is tied to class status, and staging the dramatic conflict as the result of societal conflicts (50–51). Furthermore, for Öngören, the theater must represent only characters with real conflicts, disrupt narratives through a lack of coherence, and include a dialectical perspective made entertaining. Accordingly, revolution must first take place within art in order to make revolutionary art. For years theaters, according to Öngören, evolved for the sake of the ruling classes, and it is now the role and duty of the revolutionary artist to return art to the masses. In Öngören's view, the "revolutionary theater is Brecht's theater" (51). On the question of whether his own plays reach the desired audience, Öngören reiterates his statement that "first the stage has to change, so that those watching it can change" and identifies this change as one that enables the "working class's use of a revolutionary aesthetic" (53–54). According to Öngören, turning a bourgeois stage into a revolutionary stage is dependent upon forming an organic whole with the working class and the working masses. A stage that does not equip itself with the working class's aesthetic views cannot achieve this organic whole.[100]

The ensemble's efforts were interrupted in 1972 when Öngören and his colleagues were arrested for founding a secret underground movement at the theater, which was subsequently shut down under the penal code's article 141. Two years after his release from prison following a general amnesty in 1974, Öngören reopened his theater in 1976, this time in Istanbul. This event has to be viewed in the context of the aftermath of the second military coup on March 12, 1971, which nullified the basic democratic rights and freedoms that had been extended in 1960, leading to the imprisonment of thousands of democrats and socialists, including Öngören and his colleagues. The Turkish Workers' Party (TIP) was banned, along with oppositional newspapers, magazines, and publishing houses. Öngören's ensemble, called Birlik Sahnesi both in Ankara and now in Istanbul, was already underlining two things. In choosing to name themselves "sahne"—stage, rather than the-ater—they emphasized that "change in theater had to begin at the stage."[101] "Birlik," meaning solidarity, emphasized collaborative work and coopera-tion. In an interview on the reestablishment of his ensemble as the Birlik Sahnesi, Öngören reaffirmed the "cooperative" nature of their ensemble, which from its inception was seen as collaborative, and expressed its inten-tion to work with other ensembles. He further reiterated Brecht's continued significance for the ensemble's theatrical endeavors. He stated that Brecht's theater realized "Marxist aesthetics' most important experiments and pro-cesses" and that the "working-class projection of aesthetics passes through Brecht."[102] As outlined in the ensemble's manifesto a few years earlier, the changeability of the world remained a main premise. The first play of the Birlik Sahnesi in 1976 in Istanbul was Brecht's *Furcht und Elend des Dritten Reiches* (*Fear and Misery of the Third Reich*, 1938), a selection that Öngören saw as responding to the "increasing danger of fascism in Turkey."[103] Writer and translator Hasan Izzettin Dinamo, in his review of this production, perceived Brecht as an ally in the fight against fascism.[104] While addressing the rise of fascism in Turkey, Öngören also conceived of his adaptation of Brecht's play as an "araştırma oyunu,"[105] a research play that examined who fascism's beneficiaries are and how it gains critical mass. For Öngören, the-ater had to contribute to the antifascist front, to which he, in addition to his Brecht adaptation, contributed with his own play *Zengin Mutfağı* (The Kitchen of the Rich, 1977).[106] Öngören contexualized his play by tying it to the rise of the far-right Nationalist Action Party (MHP), which had won sixteen seats in parliament. It was staged during the 1976–77 season by the Birlik Sahnesi and in 1977 received the play of the year award from the the-ater journal *Tiyatro*, which perceived it as the "most constructive play for the dialectic development of Turkey's current phase."[107] Making contemporary references through his plays' settings, both of his own scripts as well as of adaptations, is a method Öngören had practiced from the ensemble's incep-tion. For example, their production of *Adam Adamdır*[108] in 1970, directed by Öngören, was "adapted to Vietnam."[109] Özdemir Nutku, in his review of the play, describes the text as "montaged on Vietnam" and therefore made "contemporary" through the projection of photographs.[110] In the face of growing oppression and persecution of the left, and after the bombing of his theater by fascists in the late 1970s, Öngören left Turkey for West Berlin in 1980, where he reestablished the Birlik Sahnesi as the Kollektiv Theater until his move to the Netherlands in 1982.[111]

International Student Theater Festivals: Turkish-German Exchange at the Erlangen Festival and Beyond

An important factor in the theatrical exchange between Turkey and Germany were the student theater festivals in Erlangen and Istanbul. The international student theater festival in Erlangen is significant not only because of the regular participation of Turkish student theater ensembles, but also because of its emphasis and focus on Brecht, which contemporaries called the "Brechtlastigkeit," or "Brecht-burden," of the program. In a short dictionary entry on the festival, Wolfgang von Rimscha, a long-term member of the Studiobühne Erlangen, refers to Brecht as its "Säulenheiliger,"[112] its pillar-saint or stylite, to point to the central symbolic position he occupied for its programmers.[113] This international theater festival was also an important platform for exchange among participating ensembles. In addition to the performance of various plays, with lectures, panels, and roundtable discussions, the aim of the festival was understood as an "Arbeitstreffen," providing a venue for critical discussions of the performances and plays, of dramaturgical practices, and more generally about the intersection between theater and politics.[114] Early performances of Brecht, Peter Weiss, and Peter Handke attest to its increasing politicization, with particular significance assigned to Brecht, as is evident also in the conceptualization of the student theater as a space to "test" and "develop" Brecht's epic theater, in accordance with the demand for theater to be a "dialectical institution."[115]

The Erlanger Studententheaterwoche was initiated by the student theater ensemble Studiobühne Erlangen in 1949. It took place seventeen times between 1949 and 1968,[116] with participants from West and East Germany, among them Hans Bunge (East German theater intellectual and Brecht scholar), members of the Berliner Ensemble, West German writers Hans-Magnus Enzensberger, Günter Grass, and Martin Walser, as well as theater directors Peter Stein and Claus Peymann.[117] Looking back, Claus Peymann in an interview referred to the festival as a "nucleus of that which seized theater institutions ten years later,"[118] pointing to the significance of the festival in terms of the later development of the German theater scene.

In the largely conservative cultural climate in West Germany during the 1950s, the Studiobühne Erlangen occupied a crucial and oftentimes controversial position. Some flashpoints were the cancellation of the invitation extended to Brecht in 1951 (under pressure from West Berlin's Free University's student stage), the festivals' opening with a student ensemble from East Berlin in 1961, and the events surrounding the performance, also in 1961, of Brecht's *Trommeln in der Nacht* (*Drums in the Night*, 1923) in face of the West German Brecht boycott, which resulted in the organizers being summoned before the state commission of Bavaria and suffering financial pressure thereafter from the state.[119] Moreover, because of the participation by members of the Berliner Ensemble in 1963, two agents from the Federal Office for the Protection of the Constitution attended the festival. The tenth festival in 1960 marked the beginning of the debate between proponents of epic theater and the theater of the absurd; these took place in a panel discussion between Hans Bunge, Günter Grass, and Hans-Magnus Enzensberger (among others).[120] However, subsequent festival programs attest to an increased focus on Brecht, such as the festival in 1961, and the 1963 festival was held "entirely under the sign of Brecht."[121] Indeed, in addition to two Brecht adaptations, the festival program included a performance of "Bertolt Brecht: Szenen und Songs" by members of the Berliner Ensemble, an in-house production by Gisela May, Ekkehard Schall, and Werner Hecht, and scholarly lectures on Brecht's poetics.[122]

Turkish student ensembles participated in the festival as early as 1954, with the prominent Istanbul Gençlik Tiyatrosu, founded in 1952 by the Istanbul Üniversitesi Talebe Birliği (Istanbul University Student Association), becoming a regular participant, with six more appearances at the festival in subsequent years.[123] In addition to the Gençlik Tiyatrosu ensemble, the Istanbul Cep Tiyatrosu ensemble (founded by Haldun Dormen in 1954) and the Ankara University student ensemble also performed in Erlangen. The Gençlik Tiyatrosu ensemble, and its participation in Erlangen, is of particular significance for the Turkish reception of Brecht. In an interview Öngören gave in *Tiyatro* in 1977, he further underlined the importance of the Gençlik Tiyatrosu ensemble for his own career in theater, describing it as a unique place for theater training and education with no other comparable theater in existence at that time.[124] Öngören further assigns the festival, which he attended multiple times as member of this ensemble, particular significance in the context of his interest in and encounter with Brechtian dramaturgy. Aras Ören, whom I will discuss in the next chapter, joined the Gençlik Tiyatrosu ensemble as an actor the same year as Öngören, in 1959, participating in Erlangen multiple times during the 1960s.

Particularly illuminating with respect to the Turkish-German theatrical exchange are the fourteenth and fifteenth festivals of 1964 and 1965 respectively. Extensive reports on these were published in *Oyun* by

Yüksel Pazarkaya, a pioneer of Turkish-German theater, who cofounded the Studiobühne Stuttgart in 1961. During these two festivals, Sermet Çağan's and Haldun Taner's Brechtian plays were performed. In addition to the performance of Turkish plays in the Brechtian mode, the discussions taking place at the festival in these years were of particular significance. Yüksel Pazarkaya specifically mentions Hans Bunge's talk "The Social Function of Theater—the Example of Brecht" at the fourteenth festival in 1964.[125] Pazarkaya further reported that during this festival discussions were taking place in four languages, confirming the festival's emphasis on providing a forum for exchange among its various participants and guests.[126] The 1964 festival is considered the highpoint in the history of the Studententheaterwoche, with seventeen international ensembles (out of twenty-two) participating. It was also this year that Sermet Çağan's *Ayak Bacak Fabrikası* (Foot and Leg Factory, 1964), directed by Cüneyt Türel, was premiered there by the Gençlik Tiyatrosu ensemble, winning fourth prize. Set in a nameless country and based on real events, as for example a report published in a *Yön* article in 1962, Çağan's play focused on systems of exploitation by juxtaposing exploiters and exploited, and on economics as defining all human relations, thus presenting a model of the capitalist profit system, which through corruption makes the rich richer and the poor poorer. The playwright Çağan's career in theater had begun more than a decade earlier, in 1951, at an ensemble he cofounded, the Ankara Players, which performed English-language plays. After one year in this ensemble, he began working as stage designer and technical director at Ankara's Devlet Tiyatrosu in 1952, which was directed by Muhsin Ertuğrul.[127] Çağan joined the Gençlik Tiyatrosu ensemble as director in 1964.[128]

At the festival, Manfred Wekwerth, head of the jury and director of the Berliner Ensemble at the time, led the discussion of the play.[129] The play's success continued in Turkey through a staging at AST in the 1965 season, where it became the most-produced play in the history of this theater.[130] Çağan's play would gain even further significance through TÖS, the Turkish Teachers' Union, which was established in 1965.[131] The Teachers' Union perceived itself as anti-imperialist, national, and pro-labor. Prominent writer Fakir Baykurt, who settled permanently in the Ruhr area in West Germany in 1979, became its first chair.[132] Art and culture were significant components of the Union's program, and under the motto of "taking theater to the people"[133] TÖS founded the TÖS Theater in 1966, with Çağan as its director. This project was conceptualized as a "gezici tiyatro" (traveling theater), with the stated aim of, among other things, providing "theoretical education."[134] Foot and Leg Factory was the first play the TÖS Theater produced. Between October and December 1966 it was staged seventy-four times in fifty-two regions in Turkey.[135] Its twenty-two-member ensemble was made up of members of AST, Arena Tiyatro, and Gençlik Tiyatrosu, and included director and actor Mehmet Ulusoy.[136]

In the following year, 1965, the Erlangen festival showed a strong emphasis on its conception as "Arbeitstreffen," with a series of seminars, presentations, and film screenings being offered as a response to accusations that the festival had become "outdated" and "uncommitted."[137] Among the various seminars, the Turkish participants offered "The Social Function of Student Theaters in Turkey" convened by Özdemir Nutku, Yüksel Pazarkaya, Vasıf Öngören, and Yurdaer Ersan.[138] In addition to this seminar, the festival included performances of Taner's *Ballad* and Çağan's *Savaş Oyunu* (War Play, 1965) by the student theater ensemble of the University of Ankara (DTFC[139]). Çağan's play became the "festival's sensation" and was the "most applauded."[140] A review of Çağan's play that appeared in *Spotlight*, the festival's official magazine, was circulated in the Turkish press.[141] *Spotlight* appeared for the first time in 1953 during the fifth festival and was published daily during the festivals, providing introductions to ensembles and reports on performances, as well as ensuing discussions by a succession of different editors. Among them were Hans-Magnus Enszensberger, Karl-Heinz Braun, Reinhold Grimm, Elisabeth Stöhr, Irmgard Hartig, Claus Peymann, Horst-Dieter C. Ebert, and Joachim Lucchesi.[142] *Spotlight* was essential, as it provided synopses of all plays in French, German, and English. Sometimes the discussion and reviews of performances were multilingual, as for example Pazarkaya's critical review of Gençlik Tiyatrosu's performance of Taner's *Ballad*, which was printed in German and Turkish.[143] Starting in 1962 the *Spotlight* editorial introduced the "spotlight hit parade" nominating the three best ensembles based on direction, stage design, play selection, and overall performance.[144] Of Çağan's play a *Spotlight* contributing editor wrote that the play was one of two with "global relevance."[145] Further, prominent literary critic Darko Suvin, in his review of the festival for the Swiss weekly *Die Weltwoche*, singled out Çağan's play as a "pacifist-humanist play" that "could be called a model for today's student theater."[146]

Initially Çağan had written it as a radio play titled *Öyle Bir Oyun* (Such a story, 1964). This piece, when it aired in 1964 on Ankara Radyo,[147] drew the attention of the dramatist and director Özdemir Nutku. With Nutku, Çağan revised and published it as *Savaş Oyunu*; this publication won the *Regiepreis*, the award for directing, at Erlangen. Nutku summarizes the content of the play as a report on "economic reasons for war, and human behaviors that support it."[148] As a result of its success at the festival, Çağan was invited to stage the play in Würzburg, Berlin, Cologne, Munich, and in Turku in Finland. Further, he was offered the opportunity to have it translated into Finnish and German; the German translation appeared in 1967 with Theaterverlag, translated by Max Fisch, whose production notes remark on the play's universality: "This play takes place nowhere and everywhere."[149] The play itself incorporated poems by Nazım Hikmet and an excerpt from the first section of Brecht's *Svendborg Poems* titled "Deutsche Kriegsfibel" (German War Primer, 1937): "General your tank is a powerful vehicle." One of the poems by Hikmet, sung by a choir in the play, was recorded to air on German radio.

The Istanbul-based Milletlerarasi üniversite tiyatroları festivali, International University Theaters Festival, organized by the Istanbul University's National Student Association (TMTF) and founded in 1948, represented a significant counterpart to the theater festivals in Erlangen. The West German student ensembles Studiobühne Erlangen and Neue Bühne Frankfurt were regular participants at this event,[150] and the first international student theater festival in Istanbul took place in 1954.[151] On its organizational committee were prominent figures, including Haldun Taner, writer Melih Cevdet Anday, Max Meinecke (director of the Istanbul Municipal Theaters when Brecht's *Szechwan* was planned to be first staged during the 1956–57 season), and poet Ahmet Kutsi Tecer.[152] Both festivals, the one in Istanbul and the one in Erlangen, show how extensive and manifold Turkish-German connections and exchanges were over the decades. For example, after becoming a success in Erlangen in 1965, Cağan's *Savaş Oyunu* was performed by the Ankara Deneme Sahnesi two weeks later at the tenth Istanbul festival.[153] In Ören's case, his participation in Erlangen led to an involvement with the Neue Bühne Frankfurt, which he joined as an actor in 1962. At the festival in Istanbul in 1963, it was the Neue Bühne Frankfurt that brought the first Brecht performance to a professional Turkish stage, performing his learning play *Kuralla Kural Dışı* (*The Exception and the Rule*) with Aras Ören as one of the actors.[154]

Conclusion

In this chapter I have shown that the Turkish Brecht reception emerged from many different intersections between dramatists, ensembles, and institutions in Turkey and both Germanies. The 1960s and early 1970s witnessed the emergence of new progressive theaters, which, like Erkal's Dostlar Tiyatrosu ensemble in Istanbul and Öngören's Birlik Sahnesi in Ankara and Istanbul, understood Brecht's epic theater as providing tools for fashioning a political consciousness in Turkish drama. Brecht's theater practices were central and functioned as a catalyst for political reflection, opposition, and action — all without abandoning Turkish elements in the process.

The story of Brecht in Turkey in the 1960s and 1970s is one of a network of various collaborators and institutions, dramatic, cultural, and academic. The Gençlik Tiyatrosu ensemble represented the starting point for many actors, both in their careers and with regard to their encounter with Brecht. The various theater festivals, especially in Erlangen and Istanbul, served as a forum for discussion and exchange in which Brecht took center stage. In addition to providing a platform for extensive international exchange, they were also a performance venue in which German dramatists encountered, discussed, and engaged with Turkish political plays. Moreover, the performances in Erlangen, as we saw in the cases of Taner and Çağan, led to the translation of their plays into German and resulted in additional performances throughout Germany. For Öngören, his participation in Erlangen directly influenced his decision to go to the Berliner Ensemble to further study Brecht.

In addition to the significance of the student theater festivals, which provided a platform for a discussion of working methods, changes regarding censorship and freedom of thought and expression, introduced with the 1961 constitution, resulted in the translation and rigorous discussion of Brecht's epic theater within newly formed journals. Key figures in these debates and in debates about the adaptation of epic theater to the Turkish context included Vasıf Öngören, Özdemir Nutku, Haldun Taner, and Sermet Çağan, all of whose paths routinely crossed; Aras Ören and Emine Sevgi Özdamar, too, moved within these circles. Öngören was Ören's colleague at the student theater ensemble Gençlik Tiyatrosu, their joint participation in the Erlangen and Istanbul festivals, their research at the Berliner Ensemble, and their continued exchange of ideas on theater occurred over distances and years (to which letters in the archive attest). Ören also performed in various plays directed by Sermet Çağan. With regard to Özdamar, Öngören is the person who introduced Brecht to her while both were in Germany in 1966, at the dorm where she lived, and where he was the warden. Upon her return to Turkey, she moved in theater circles, through her attendance at LCC, where Ertuğrul and Taner were among her teachers, and performed as an actress in its ensemble. Özdamar was also close to Sermet Çağan, with whom she traveled to Ankara to perform as Frau Carrar in Çağan's adaptation of Brecht's *Die Gewehre der Frau Carrar* at the Yenişehir Tiyatrosu.[155] All these developments in Turkish theater, especially its politicization throughout the 1960s and 1970s, were of great significance for Turkish writers and intellectuals, such as Aras Ören and Emine Sevgi Özdamar, who left Turkey for West Germany in the face of growing oppression in the late 1960s and 1970s, as the next chapters will illustrate.

2: Didactic Realism: Aras Ören and Working-Class Culture

IN THE SECOND INSTALLMENT of Aras Ören's narrative poems constituting the Berlin trilogy (1973–80), we encounter a two-line reference to the Dram Tiyatro, the oldest theater in Istanbul.[1] Apart from being the location of an encounter between two characters in the story, and the mentioned detail of torn Brecht posters in front of it, this passage appears in the narrative poem without being supplemented by additional references to its historic, cultural, and political significance. The Dram Tiyatro has a special place in Turkish theater history, in particular with regard to Brecht. Indeed, the "Brecht incident" discussed at length in the previous chapter made the Dram Tiyatro not merely the center of Turkish debates on the politics and possibilities of a revolutionary theater, but also the site to which an international discussion of Turkish cultural politics referred. These public discussions led to an increased interest in Brecht and an intensive engagement with Brecht's writings on epic theater, and Haldun Taner's success with his play *The Ballad of Ali Keshan*, which employs a Brechtian epic mode and premiered on March 31 of the same year, further intensified the interest in Brecht's dramatic theory and practice.

The transformation and politicization of Turkish theater throughout the 1960s constitutes an important context for Ören's oeuvre after his emigration to Germany—a period during which he has said he "looked for a home in political theories as well as on theater stages."[2] Indeed, during the 1960s Ören worked as an actor and dramaturg with different theaters in Istanbul, West Berlin, and Frankfurt am Main. His engagement in theater began in Istanbul at the Gençlik Tiyatrosu in 1959. By invitation of the Goethe University's student theater Neue Bühne in Frankfurt/Main, he participated as an actor in two productions in 1962, Nelly Sachs's *Eli* (1950) and Bertolt Brecht's *Die Ausnahme und die Regel* (*The Exception and the Rule*). The latter production even toured Turkey, with performances in Istanbul, for the international student theater festival, as well as in Ankara and Ordu.[3] Besides working closely with Öngören in various plays with the Gençlik Tiyatrosu ensemble, Ören further collaborated on multiple occasions with Sermet Çağan as a member of the Gen-Ar Tiyatrosu ensemble (founded in 1963)[4] and the TÖS Theater discussed in the previous chapter.[5]

Fig. 2.1. Aras Ören as member of Gençlik Tiyatrosu in *Midasın Kulakları* (Midas' Ears) Erlangen (1960). Reproduced by permission from Akademie der Künste, Berlin, Aras-Ören-Archiv.

Fig. 2.2. Aras Ören as member of Gençlik Tiyatrosu *Kafes Arkasında*
(Behind the Lattice) Erlangen (1962). Reproduced by permission
from Akademie der Künste, Berlin, Aras-Ören-Archiv.

In addition to working as an actor, Ören adapted Brecht plays such as
Der gute Mensch von Sezuan for the Turkish stage, and wrote several plays
in Turkish, for example *Kör Oidipus* (Blind Oedipus, 1980), which was
published in installments in the theater journal *Tiyatro*.[6] Between 1962
and 1966 Ören, together with his colleague and friend Vasıf Öngören, regularly attended stage rehearsals at the Berliner Ensemble, during a period
when Brecht's creative legacy was being negotiated between a number
of different stakeholders, including Brecht's widow (Helene Weigel, the
manager of the Berliner Ensemble), Brecht's students and protégés, and
the ruling Socialist Unity Party of East Germany. Brecht therefore was
an important interlocutor for Ören's dramaturgical practice and literary
poetics. As a result of Ören's creative practices and travel between Turkey
and Germany, there were a number of contexts in which he encountered
Brecht's thought.

While Ören's theatrical practice in Germany and Turkey was of crucial
importance for his engagement with Brecht's aesthetics, he also engaged with
Brecht's thought at a theoretical level. Principally drawn from Suhrkamp

Fig. 2.3. Aras Ören as member of Gen-Ar Tiyatrosu in Sławomir Mrożek's
The Police, directed by Sermet Çağan (1967). Reproduced by permission from
Akademie der Künste, Berlin, Aras-Ören-Archiv.

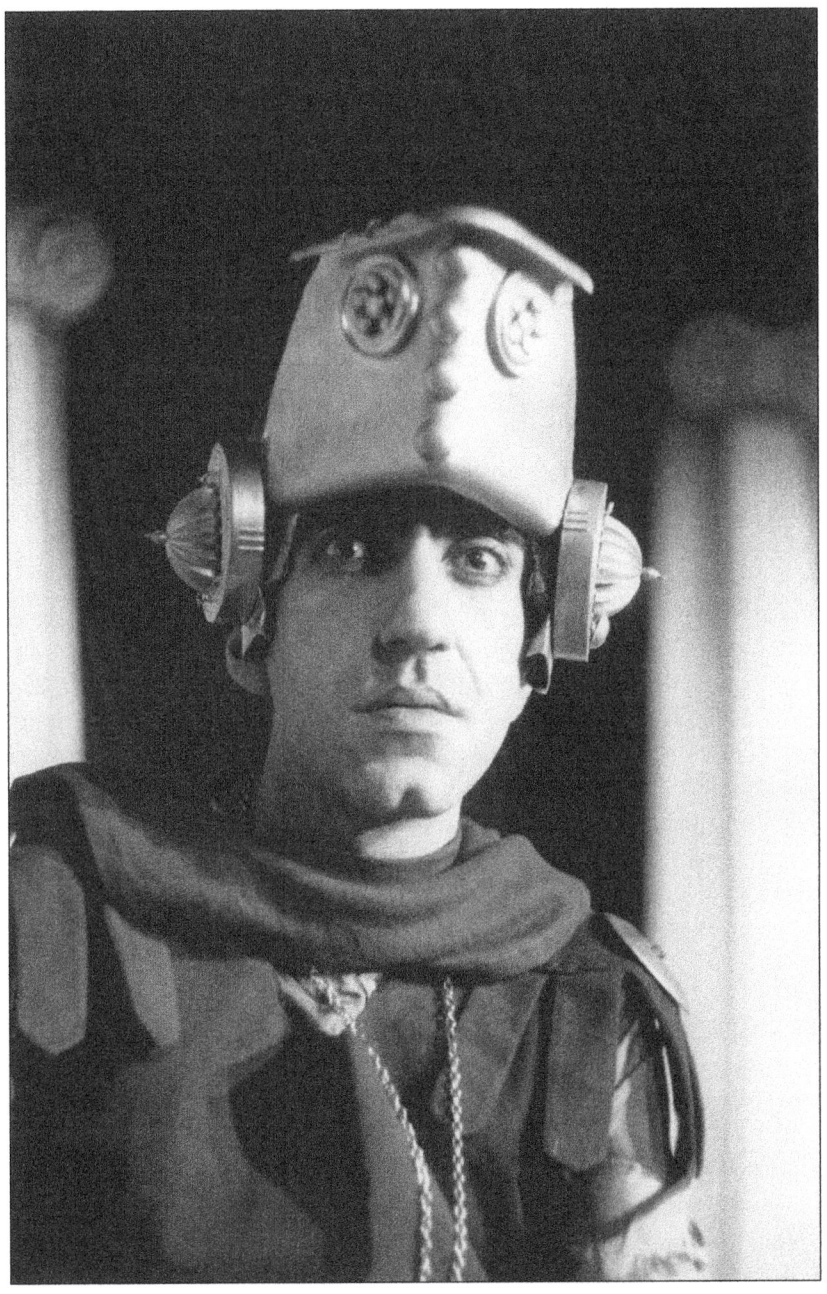

Fig. 2.4. Aras Ören as member of Gen-Ar Tiyatrosu in Gyula Háy's
The Horse directed by Ege Ernart (1968). Reproduced by permission
from Akademie der Künste, Berlin, Aras-Ören-Archiv.

Verlag's *Schriften zum Theater* (1957), and John Willett's *Brecht on Theater* (1964), translations of Brecht's thought into Turkish began appearing in publications such as the theater journal *Oyun* (of which Ören was an avid reader) in the late 1950s.[7] As a result of these careful translations of Brecht's thought into Turkish,[8] Ören—like many other Turkish intellectuals in this period—was able to engage with Brecht's thought, in translation, as a comprehensive corpus of theater theory from which he could then draw specific, context-appropriate insights.[9]

As a reader, Ören was able to conceive of Brecht's thoughts on theater as a unified body of knowledge and a life's work full of sometimes contradictory moments, rather than as an ongoing series of context-specific remarks that are not meant to constitute an overall systematic aesthetics. His engagement with Brechtian theater in a variety of contexts spanned more than a decade, and it therefore comes as no surprise that this theater aesthetic manifests itself in complex ways in his literary poetics. Indeed, as I illustrate, his didactic realism, a dialectical concept of literary aesthetics, draws on dramatic elements and techniques of Brecht's epic theater in order to produce a dialectical relationship between the text and the audience. Specifically, as my readings of Ören's narrative poems from the Berlin trilogy and of his unpublished didactic play "Lehrstück für türkische Arbeiter" (Learning Play for Turkish Workers, 1971) show, Ören adapted Brechtian dramaturgical practices, using V-effects in order to break away from the bourgeois pleasure principle and create the collective consciousness necessary for social change. Reading these literary works alongside his writings on literary poetics, and reconstructing how Ören's work was shaped by his cultural-activist engagement in the communist artist organization Die Rote Nelke and by West German discussions about the politicization of literature in the late 1960s and early 1970s, I show how Ören established Turkish immigrants as agents in the German present and thus as part of historical processes, while writing them into German discourses of labor protest and engaged literature.

On both the formal and thematic levels, Ören's writings are strongly tied to one another. This becomes evident not only through the incorporations of his early poems into the Berlin trilogy, and his interpolation of a section of the 1971 "Lehrstück" into his later novel *Manege* (1984), but also in the degree to which his various literary texts engage in dialogue with one another. This mutual interaction of his works with one another bespeaks Ören's conception of Brechtian dialectics as a practice that, while foregrounding the independence of various parts within a whole, also emphasizes that the interaction of disparate elements within a whole allows for "another meaning" to emerge, where "one [element] is understood through the other."[10] This results, in particular, from Ören's employment of a cyclical structure in his works, such that characters, settings, motifs, and themes recur. His work is thus composed of different parts that while independent, relate to each other; viewed over time, they constantly generate new meanings and suggest new possibilities for collective action, even as historical events require their readjustment to new predicaments and configurations of class inequality.

Realism, Dialectics, and Immigration

In his various essays, interviews, and even to some extent in his literary oeuvre, Ören has explicitly formulated his poetics. He points repeatedly to the significance of grasping historical conditions—especially Turkish immigration to postwar Germany—as processes. In a 1999 lecture on his poetics in Tübingen, Ören states: "Everything I ever wrote is a testimony of times, times that I shaped and temporalities whose witness I am."[11] Identifying himself as a kind of literary archivist, Ören indicates his work's evocation of multiple and changing temporalities and highlights his role in shaping them. Ören's "poetisches Denken,"[12] his poetics, as he further elaborates, is marked by a dynamic relationship between various temporalities, which is evidenced by his literary practice of "planting" images from his Turkish past into later different "temporalities" of his German present. When brought "into new relationships," Ören says, these "create new tensions and acquire a new veracity" (12). It is through this literary method that he establishes connections between Turkish and German temporalities, histories, and contexts in order to reflect on the Turkish-German present.

At the same time, Ören perceives literary representation as an "intervention of the author in reality" (6). This stance attests to his understanding of the reciprocal influence between literature and reality, and to his rejection of aesthetic autonomy or apolitical art. By way of such interventions, he says, writers are able to take "revenge on history" (6). What Ören refers to as revenge here amounts to a literary intervention into official German historical narratives, especially those concerning the Turkish presence in divided Germany, and specifically in Berlin. As he states, "In order to complete the picture, a new social class in the demographic panorama of the divided city needs to be integrated, a class that despite its presence is not perceived to be in existence, one that produced without consuming."[13]

This becomes particularly significant for Ören's writing, as he maintains, in light of the West German public's refusal to perceive immigrants as part of German society, despite their "having changed and continuing to change it."[14] Given his dual role as "participant" and "witness" with regard to Turkish migration to Germany, immigration constituted an important impetus for and topic in his writing. According to Ören, through the process of immigration, a "different time" is introduced to the city through which new "societal structures emerge."[15] For him, West Berlin—a "half-city" and "product of the Cold War"—was profoundly changed as immigrants and immigration provided a new driving force.[16]

In 1985 Ören, together with Syrian-German writer Rafik Schami, was the first recipient of the Adelbert von Chamisso Prize, awarded by the Robert Bosch Foundation for writers writing in German "whose work is characterized by a cultural change."[17] In his acceptance speech Ören characterized the goal of his writing as "to look out for uncharted territory, break new ground and to cultivate it ... to redefine the role of literature. ... An important impetus, I am convinced of this, can come from us foreigners in German literature, and we stand by this task."[18] Here he points to the catalytic function of writers of non-German ethnicities[19] within German literature, with an emphasis on contributing to and transforming it. In Ören's writings on literature he repeatedly emphasizes an engagement with German literature and literary traditions, arguing against the "ghettoization" of works by writers of non-German ethnicities through the use of terms like *Ausländer-* or *Gastarbeiterliteratur*, with which a literary text is categorized based on the author's ethnic background or economic status.[20] Specifically, Ören perceives literature written in Turkish in Germany "as an integrated and autonomous part of German literature in the Federal Republic and West-Berlin. ... [It] engages both with its own Turkish traditions, but also with German ones."[21] In this way, multiple literary-historical temporalities—the sweep of both Turkish and German cultural history and the countries' intertwined economic and political histories after the Second World War—come into view as the backdrop of his literary interventions. In this context, it is no surprise that Brecht reception in both Turkey and Germany continued to be formative for Ören's literary productivity even after he had immigrated to Germany.

In addition to this vital role assigned to writers of non-German ethnicities by Ören, Turkish immigration to Germany, including his own move, is closely tied to his writing. Both developments "ran parallel to" and "illuminated" one another, suggesting that Ören apprehended a reciprocal relationship between his literary oeuvre and historical processes.[22] For Ören, immigrants, who figure predominantly as subjects in his early works and also constitute a significant topic in his poetics, are perceived as a "Triebkraft,"[23] a driving force, just as writers of non-German ethnicities provide a new impetus within the German literary landscape. This is a point he continually reiterates, resulting in a thematic focus on workers and the working class in his early works. Here he stresses: "while narrating the relationship of the worker to the welfare state, narrating his problems with this society, you illuminate society's issues: the two cannot be separated."[24] Through his literary representation of human interactions within their social contexts, and of the conditions of labor, Ören therefore reflects on the sociopolitical reality in German society at the time, and on its relationship to immigration.

This concept of social transformation also influenced Ören's understanding of his audience. In a 1974 radio interview with the West German public broadcasting institution SWF Ören stated: "I write more for the Germans than I write for the Turks. I want to show the Germans that Turks have their own past and history.... I don't understand solidarity in the sense that a group dissolves in the foreign society and gets lost in it and identifies with it 100%."[25] Here again we see an emphasis on immigration as a process through which new contexts and histories are introduced, emphasizing the significance of Turkish past(s) for the German present and future. With his literary work, Ören therefore sought to "bring newcomers ... together with the Berliners ... to translate their perception of their temporality ... [by] taking on the role of a translator."[26] He further stressed the bidirectionality of this process, pointing to the need for rapprochement on both sides, Turkish and German. This rapprochement can be facilitated by what he writes: "The shared interests of German and Turkish workers imply the necessity of solidarity. This solidarity can only exist through coherence between both groups.... For this, it is necessary that both sides get to know each other, understand each other, and know each other's past. What I write may be helpful."[27]

In the process of familiarizing the German audience with Turkish contexts, literature also becomes a means to countering public images of Turks, who according to Ören were expected "to take the bottom seat in the societal pyramid."[28] Ören's literary work confronts the dehumanization of Turkish guestworkers in West Germany, presenting their (hi)stories in order to challenge the established official narratives, which reinforce a division within the working class on the basis of ethnicity. His main impulse to write comes from "... humans. Humans as they grapple with their environment each day, their struggle in society, the visible class-character. For me there are no abstract humans, just class humans. Looking at humans from this perspective, there is no absolute life form: when societal structures have changed ... then characters change too."[29]

Two points are significant to consider here: first, that class identity emerges out of societal structures, and, second, that class subjects have a role in changing established hierarchies. For Ören, understanding class identity is necessary for understanding the possibilities of challenging and changing not only the roles that German society assigns to Turkish newcomers but

German society itself. The interaction between workers as exploited class subjects and their new environment is central to Ören's writing, because, as he puts it,

> people coming from Turkey, no matter where they came from and which class they belonged to, they now were part of a historical process, they were new members of the working class in Germany. . . . I had the expectation that they would take on the legacy of the German labor movement. That they would appropriate this legacy and carry it into the future.[30]

In Ören's view, Turkish guestworkers immigrated and—despite their differing backgrounds—integrated themselves into Germany's labor movement by continuing its existing legacies of working-class struggle and solidarity as participants, not as outsiders, in the shaping of German history. For Ören, the guestworkers provided the impetus for solidarity and for labor conditions to change.

Discussing the first part of the Berlin trilogy, Rita Chin has argued that "Ören's narrative . . . giv[es] [the guestworkers] agency even as it documents their exploitation—and envisions a radical transformation of society emerging from below in the form of a united Turkish-German proletariat."[31] The exploitation that Turkish guestworkers face becomes visible through highlighting the alienation—in the strict Marxist sense—at the center of their experience, which is to be overcome by representing the experience of alienation, through the use of Brechtian V-effects, as one that is shared among both Turkish and German workers in the German context. Ören therefore strives to represent existing divides between German and Turkish workers, while at the same time bridging this divide by showing them all to be victims of exploitation, thus revealing the underlying collective struggle of workers—beyond race and ethnicity. "By juxtaposing the economic concerns of Germans with those of the Turks" as Bala Venkat Mani argues, Ören "brings mutually exclusive communities together."[32]

Brecht had emphasized that the relation between writers and surroundings is never passive, foregrounding the effect of the writer's work on society and conceiving of poetry as a catalyst for change. Ören understands the relationship between the poet and his surroundings in similarly dynamic terms. He underlines the interaction of the poet (himself) with his surroundings (Berlin), while inscribing himself into the city's traditions, by which the oppressed classes conduct their fight against hegemonic forces. Through his repeated emphasis on his role as witness and translator, he presents himself as a collective autobiographer, an archivist of Berlin's broader history, and an intellectual activist, constantly reflecting on how the course of that history might be changed.

Ören's literary engagement with the working class developed in tandem with his theatrical activities and his work as an actor in Turkey and Germany during the 1960s. Writing in 1969, he attributed particular importance to the theater: "In service of those who would change and constitute the world anew, theater would reach new functions."[33] Like Brecht before him, then, Ören advocated changing the function of theater in society, and the role of art more broadly, shifting it from mere audience amusement to political education and societal intervention. At the same time, though, the working class remained, in his view, the "only force" for revolution.[34]

The manuscript versions of Ören's plays, with handwritten notes and corrections on them, attest to the multiple revisions they underwent in both Germany and Turkey. These he collected as "Sahne Çalışmaları" (stage work) with the intention to further revise them based on audience feedback, mirroring Brecht's own call for the interpolation, transformation, and reformation of art, a practice we see realized in Brecht's *Versuche* and his *Arbeitsjournal*. Ören's work method attests to a similar practice of adapting his works to the changing reality, to the societal conditions, and to the historic processes he found himself confronted with. After settling permanently in West Berlin in 1969, his attention shifted to Turkish workers in German society, in representations of whom Ören centers the *verfremdete* representation of reality. Foregrounding the workers' standpoint and the proletarian experience, Ören considers the social role of art and modes of representation, focusing on their ability to diminish and overcome inequalities by becoming actors of change.

Ören's understanding of literature and art, as well as his artistic practice, reveal intersections with Brecht's conceptualization of realism. For Brecht, realism was not only confined to literature, but rather was "a major political, philosophical, practical matter that must be handled and explained as such—as a matter of general human interest."[35] Moreover, "a realist artist is one who takes a productive stance toward reality," which includes the audience.[36] Therefore, rather than connoting a single determinate literary style or genre, realism is and should be, according to Brecht, understood as a *Haltung*, a "stance," which entails "a positioning towards reality."[37] Brecht further elaborates in *Messingkauf* (*Buying Brass*) that realism has a twofold task, to recognize but at the same time to see through reality, to make visible "the laws that determine how the processes of life develop."[38] It is a political aesthetic, and as such it seeks to unmask social conditions from the standpoint of the working class, considered the agent of societal change.

This conception of realism further points to the dynamic relationship between the work of art, the artist, and reality by foregrounding the fact that a work of art is influenced by and at the same time consciously influences reality.[39] Literature (and art more broadly), for both Brecht and Ören thus provides the means for social analysis and criticism with the didactic intention of intervening in reality. For the audience in the theater it is the artistic technique of *Verfremdung* that removes the familiarity of "people and processes of everyday life" and makes them "conspicuous" in order to enable "fruitful critique from a societal standpoint."[40] Its aim is "to bestow upon the spectator an interrogative, critical stance with respect to the process that is to be represented"[41] and "to show the world in such a way that it becomes manageable"[42]—not to "accept" the world, but to "master" it.[43] *Verfremdung* for Brecht is therefore "a process of historicizing, of portraying incidents and persons as historical, that is, as ephemeral" and that "of course, can happen to contemporaries" since "their attitudes can also be portrayed as time-bound."[44] The artist's approach to history is dialectical materialism, which does not reflect reality as fixed, but as a changing, continuous process produced by people and therefore transformable by them.

For Brecht, the future depends on the "Erledigung der Vergangenheit," the processing of the past.[45] The past is considered a mutable model, based on which, and to which, changes will be made in the future. In this process, it is crucial for Brecht to "show how today was fashioned out of yesterday."[46] As Marc Silberman has discussed, Brecht's plays expose "the contradictions between still-functional old behavior and new situations" that arise from changing societal structures.[47] Likewise, Ören turns to Brecht for the representation of Turkish immigration and to introduce Turkish guestworkers and their circumstances as a new chapter in German labor history.

In an *Arbeitsjournal* entry on poetry, Brecht further elaborates on the relationship of art to history by describing it as "human activity" and "social practice," as both "conditioned by history and able to shape it." Here he presents the important distinction between merely "reflecting" reality and "holding up a mirror" to it.[48] As a social and human practice, in Ören's case, literature becomes a historical archive of its time, inscribing the literary narrative itself into the history it is writing. Here the connection between artistic realism and social history comes forth most vibrantly: the mutability of the past in the present through the writing of history also means that the present itself can be altered; therefore, by writing from the point of view of the working class, a new narrative is created that helps change reality.

Cultural-Political Interventions:
Rotbuch and Die Rote Nelke

Although Ören garnered wide national acclaim with the publication of the first part of his Berlin trilogy, he was already a well-known figure in leftist circles. This was a result both of his regular publications of political poems and of his intellectual, literary, and activist involvement in the antifascist union of progressive artists Die Rote Nelke, of which he was a member from 1970 until 1973. As a member of that group he was an active participant in West Berlin's literary left, contributing to discussions taking place during the early 1970s about the politicization of literature, engaged art, and the social responsibility of the artist. While several scholars have remarked in passing upon the trilogy's political inflection and the "touching tales of class history"[49] found within its verses, we must reconsider Ören's position within the West Berlin public sphere, situating him more centrally within the subfield of leftist literary production than has typically been the case.[50] Such reconsideration necessitates rereading Ören's early writings as part of a larger politicization of German literature taking place at this time, as opposition grew to US imperialism and the Vietnam War, and the aftermath of the student protests and the extraparliamentary opposition began to be registered in contemporary literature. The intersection between reality and literature, culture and politics that preoccupied Ören, was a central concern also of publishing houses and artists' organizations. Here the intersection between his cultural-political activities within Die Rote Nelke, as well as his choice of publishing house, Rotbuch Verlag, and his literary work, provide an important, hitherto unexamined context for his work.

The trilogy's first part, *Was will Niyazi in der Naunynstraße?* became the first title in the Rotbücher series published by the only collectively managed leftist publishing house in West Berlin, Rotbuch Verlag. The series had been created after the collective's separation from Wagenbach Verlag on June 28, 1973, and was intended to provide easier access "to progressive literature for politically interested readers, and to political texts for the literary public."[51] Rotbuch split from Wagenbach because, as its editors would state in a retrospective comment, "a socialist publishing house [defines itself] not only through its program, but also through its practice, not only through its products, but also through the relations of production."[52] Rotbuch further emphasized the potential of literature, unlike theory, to "mediate between individual and societal processes."[53] Literature was perceived to "pry open ... alienation" through the representation of "societal relations and individuals who act in them as changeable," uncovering "contradictions and mechanisms of existing reality."[54] Taking this Brechtian understanding of art as inspiration, and highlighting the relationship between the artists, the workers, and the means of production, four authors—Ören, Peter Schneider, Yaak Karsunke, and F. C. Delius—made the transition to Rotbuch. This reflected their political commitment to controlling the means of literary production. These authors emphasized a broad variety of realist writing, and literature's immediate utility in the class struggle.[55]

Opposed to the monopolizing forces of the publishing industry, the Rotbuch collective perceived the publishing house as a "means to disseminate anti-capitalist and undogmatic socialist literature."[56] It further saw in literature the potential to dissolve "alienation and dulling of the senses"[57] and to expand readers' receptiveness to their own "experiences, environments, and patterns of behavior."[58] The new publishing house's emphasis on the intersection between literature and politics thus manifested itself both on the creative side, in its publishing program, and organizationally, in its structure and management, with open meetings, votes, and a governance model emphasizing debate and participation. The increasing politicization of literature throughout West Germany, especially around 1968, had also had an effect on the internal organization and management of publishing houses and management more broadly, with Rotbuch Verlag providing a particularly clear example.

In the *Festschrift* for Ören's seventy-fifth birthday, F. C. Delius, Rotbuch editor at the time, describes Ören's writing as having provided "a new literary perspective, a surprising poetically precise view on Berlin and German realities by a Turk from a previously silent majority of the first generation of guestworkers, class-struggle tinged. . . . Across everything the invisible memory bridges from Berlin to Istanbul and under the asphalt of Kreuzberg, the layers of German history."[59] While pointing out the correlation between Turkish immigration and German sociopolitical reality, and the connection between Germans and Turks and their respective histories, Delius emphasizes the literariness of this perspective, thus highlighting the intersection between aesthetics and politics.

The trilogy's first part sold approximately 12,000 copies between 1973 and 1980, which meant that it reached a larger audience than any preceding texts by his Turkish-German contemporaries.[60] By contrast with *Was Will Niyazi in der Naunynstraße?*, such texts were often published in smaller publishing houses with limited circulation.[61] Subsequently, reviews of and articles on Ören's work started to appear in local and regional West German newspapers such as the *Frankfurter Rundschau, Die Tat, Berliner Morgenpost*, and on radio stations such as WDR and NDR, broadening the scope of his reading audience and further "provok[ing] a mass-mediated dialogue in the German-language press."[62]

Faced with both national and international Cold War tensions, Helmut Peitsch notes, German writers emerged as "social critics"[63] and together with students became "spokesmen of moral and literary protest."[64] The renewed availability and rejoined discussion of writings by Marx, Freud, Marcuse, Adorno, Brecht, and Benjamin, among other figures, returned the political function of literature to the center of public discussion during the late 1960s and early 1970s.[65] In addition to revisiting these crucial aspects of German leftist intellectual history, writers also increasingly engaged with practical traditions of the workers' movement.[66] By focusing on Turkish workers, solidarity among the working class, and production conditions in Berlin that exploit labor, Ören's writings are in line with the literature of leftist artists' associations prominent at the time, not only Die Rote Nelke but also Werkkreis Literatur der Arbeitswelt. Both organizations perceived the working class to be the leading force in societal revolution and therefore held that art should serve the working-class struggle. Workers themselves could thus become subjects and objects of art, the final goal being the political mobilization of the proletariat. Literature, perceived as capable of indexing possibilities for action and conveying the (buried) truth of social relations, was to become a site of reflection, discussion, and cooperation instead of primarily a consumable commodity. Moreover, both organizations invoked proletarian-revolutionary traditions of Weimar Germany, embodied by the Bund proletarisch-revolutionärer Schriftsteller (Association of Proletarian-Revolutionary Authors) in the case of the Werkkreis and the ARBKD (Assoziation revolutionärer bildender Künstler Deutschlands, Association of Revolutionary Visual Artists) for Die Rote Nelke. The two organizations further expressed their support for trade unions and their lack of formal affiliation with established political parties.

Although my focus here is on Ören and his involvement with Die Rote Nelke, I will briefly discuss the Werkkreis as well, given its significance in the reconstruction and creation of working-class literature for and by workers after 1945. German writers—most prominently Fritz Hüser, Max von der Grün, and Hildegard Wohlgemuth of the Dortmunder Gruppe 61, a "working group for artistic engagement with the industrial working world"[67] founded in July 1961—engaged with the topic of the "working world" in a literary setting, thus reintroducing the problematic of working-class life into the West German public sphere by reviving a tradition of working-class literature that had been suppressed after the collapse of the Weimar Republic.[68] Criticizing the group's failure to include the voices of writing workers, writers such as Erasmus Schöfer, Günter Wallraff, and Peter Schütt departed from Gruppe

61 and formed the independent Werkkreis Literatur der Arbeitswelt in March 1970. They stated their intention to represent the working world in literature and to actively include workers in the writing process.[69]

The Werkkreis in particular emphasized the need to return to and revivify past cultural traditions of the worker's movement while adapting them to present circumstances. It put special emphasis on the so-called Realism Debate: "Important connecting factors are the results of the realism debates of the 1920s and 1930s, especially those formulated by Bertolt Brecht."[70] Brecht's writing was of particular importance for them on the question of the relationship between content, form, and functionality in art.[71] Beyond the Werkkreis, Brecht was not only the most read intellectual in the years of the student revolt but he also had a lasting political and aesthetic impact. The West German Brecht boycott of the 1950s now gave way to a veritable Brecht boom.[72] An increased engagement with Brecht's oeuvre occurred after the publication of his complete works in 1967.[73] Political poetry and drama were "thematically and aesthetically mainly oriented toward Brecht."[74] Moreover, in West German discussions about "literary responsibility and social impact"[75] during the early 1970s, a Brechtian type of realism was central and came to signify the relationship of the writer to "social reality," leading to an examination of the "function of realist literature in current struggles."[76]

The various workshops organized by the Werkkreis, and the publications that emerged from them, further attest to the significance of debates on realist aesthetics for the Werkkreis. More generally, in early 1970s West Germany, realism continued to anchor discussions about "literary responsibility and societal impact"[77] insofar as the patent relationship of the writer to reality made theorizing the role and function of realist writing in the context of sociopolitical conflicts a logical next step.[78]

Whereas the Werkkreis Literatur der Arbeitswelt has received significant scholarly attention, the Rote Nelke has received hardly any, despite the various interconnections, and even collaborations, between the two associations. Founded by Harald Budde in early 1968, Die Rote Nelke was conceived as representing a "commitment to the alliance between intellectuals and the working class, as well as to art as a weapon in the class struggle!"[79] While the group repeatedly rejected any party affiliation, many members expressed their support and sympathy for the DKP (German Communist Party) and the SEW (Socialist Unity Party of West Berlin).[80] However, throughout its existence, Die Rote Nelke continuously sought to emphasize its status as an independent association "open to all democratic and progressive artists."[81] In four manifestos published in February, March, July, and then September of 1968, Die Rote Nelke configured its cultural-political program, which addressed the role of art and the artist, historical precedents, political orientation and aesthetic principles. All four manifestos were later published in a special issue of *Asphalt: Zeitschrift für kritische Literatur und bildende Kunst*, the "Organ of the Roten Nelke of the Ruhrgebiet," which appeared quarterly from 1969 to 1973 and was published by Proletenpresse in Wanne-Eickel. In a special issue of *Asphalt* entitled *Die Rote Nelke: Texte, Manifeste einer Künstlergruppe* (1970), Budde's introductory piece outlines the group's aims, demands, and activities. He begins by sketching the historical context that had prompted the foundation of Die Rote Nelke, describing a time "in which forces of the extraparliamentary opposition in the FRG and West Berlin called for powerful demonstrations and effective activities against the war in Vietnam and the ruling capitalist social system."[82] Art was thus perceived as political, and existed in opposition to "antidemocratic forces . . . fascism and racism, infantilization of the public and clichés of national identity."[83] In the three later manifestos, Budde elaborates further on the Rote Nelke's aesthetic-political program and political demands. Paraphrasing Marx's thesis on Feuerbach, Die Rote Nelke's writing aimed not only to "interpret the world, but also to change it."[84] A "powerful ideological weapon," art also had to support the maintenance of democratic principles and to serve in the fight alongside trade unions.[85]

The fourth and final manifesto discusses the Weimar German tradition of the ARBKD and its relevance for Die Rote Nelke. Directly quoting from the association's manifesto, Budde points to its central premise: "The ARBKD [wants to] promote the class struggle, stylistically and thematically adjusted to the needs of the work force."[86] The group's most prominent members included Bertolt Brecht, Anna Seghers, Johannes Becher, Egon Kisch, Alfred Kurella, Georg Lukács, Erwin Piscator, and Erich Weinert. The importance of the ARBKD legacy for Die Rote Nelke was highlighted further when its cofounder, the radical communist painter und graphic designer F. E. Gehrig-Targis, who had been active in cultural politics during the Weimar Republic and took a role in the East German Academy of Arts Berlin-Weißensee after the war, joined the West German group. Following the tradition of ARBKD, between 1970 and 1972 various collectives were formed within Die Rote Nelke with differing foci ranging from music to painting and writing. Each put great emphasis on the mutual collaboration between professional and amateur artists. The Group of Working Writers is of particular importance for our consideration of Ören and his place among his contemporaries in twentieth-century German literature, since he was first a member and then, in April 1972, its chair.

The fourth issue of *Asphalt*, published in 1971, was a special issue on the Group of Writing Workers. In the editor's introduction, Harald Budde summarizes the circumstances that led to the group's formation. Following a public reading in 1970, participants emphasized that workers needed to be included in the process of writing about issues confronting their social class, including the workplace and housing. This would enable them to develop a critical awareness vis-à-vis their environment while at the same time deepening their political insights. Didacticism was coupled with agitation, where writing was seen as a means to understanding "our capitalist environment . . . and the contradictions it generates; but at the same time to show new developments."[87] This view of creative work as theoretical labor also manifested itself in the various events that were organized by this working group, ranging from readings and exhibits to discussion meetings. Events were practice-oriented, interactive, and focused on aesthetic questions echoing and actively engaging in larger cultural-political debates at the nexus of literature and the working class. In the group's action program pamphlet from August 1973 two goals are reiterated: to "represent the present artistically from the position of the working people" and to implement "art-theoretical and art-didactic" work,[88] with an emphasis on the link between theory, practice, and didacticism. This intersection between literature, the working class, and the didactic representation of reality central to the cultural-political program of Die Rote Nelke was also a core element in Rotbuch's publishing program, as previously mentioned. That Ören was active both in the Rote Nelke organization and at the publishing house is key for understanding both the origins and the ambitions of his realist aesthetics.

Members of the Group of Writing Workers also participated in public protests and demonstration against the arrest of Angela Davis, the US invasion of Vietnam, and the imprisonment of Turkish democrats by the Turkish military regime. Ören, Budde notes, exemplifies how writers can serve as role models by displaying political commitment and engagement in their writing, as well as undertaking concrete political action (strikes, leafleting, and so on). Budde introduces Ören's political poems—published in an *Asphalt* special issue—as "publicizing and making visible social conditions . . . that have a political consequence."[89]

Foregrounding the perspective of Turkish workers as well as their ability to improve upon and overcome inequalities, Ören encourages them to become agents of change. Before analyzing his learning play "Lehrstück für türkische Arbeiter," which deals with the entry of newly arrived Turkish workers into the German workplace and labor movement, in the following I discuss his Berlin trilogy and its centrality for the inscription of Turkish workers into Berlin's working-class history.

The Berlin Trilogy: Turkish Immigration and Working-Class Solidarity

From the moment the first part, *Was will Niyazi in der Naunynstraße?*, was published, reviewers, writers, and scholars pointed to Bertolt Brecht's influence and the nexus between literature and the working-class struggle.[90] Harald Budde perceived Ören's text as an "appeal to solidarity, a call to fight against the capitalist social system."[91] Writer and literary critic Carmine Chiellino classifies it as an "epic poem" and situates the trilogy in close proximity to the Brechtian "didactic poem."[92] Contributing to this perspective, my reading consults and further develops the work of Monika Frederking and Chiellino on these questions. Though both scholars point to Brechtian traces in the trilogy, and Chiellino briefly mentions the significance of Ören's "symbiotic contact . . . to recent German-language literature of the 1960s and 1970s,"[93] they do not explore institutional details of that contact, along with the aesthetic relationships, in further detail. Having reconstructed the importance of Ören's involvement with Die Rote Nelke, my own reading traces the didactic realism within his trilogy and his learning play, which I perceive as different manifestations of the literary presentation of alienated labor. Whereas the narrative poem views the perspectives of German and Turkish workers as similar, because both are exploited under capitalism (as opposed to being divided by ethnicity), in the learning play the workplace, where Turkish newcomers become workers, is central. Furthermore, Ören also modifies the characteristics of didactic realism to his many working genres, whether poetry, theater, or prose, as is exemplified in his "Lehrstück," which he wrote while he was writing the first part of the trilogy. In the "Lehrstück" he shifts the attention to the workplace (and thus emphasizing the micro-perspective) as opposed to Berlin as a city of working-class struggle and labor protest (which would emphasize the macro-perspective). However both texts focus on the shared experience of workers as well as the new impulses coming from Turkish workers.

In the trilogy, realism works as a method for the aesthetic process, as well as a set of artistic practices, marked by fragmentation, *Verfremdung*, and free verse. Furthermore, by introducing Turkish workers as new social agents and situating them in German public space, the first part of the trilogy in particular represents the new reality of production modes, exploitation, and the labor movement in Germany. It traces a genealogy of workers in Berlin's working-class neighborhood of Kreuzberg by focusing on the social panorama of Kreuzberg's inhabitants, specifically its workers, present and past. Divided into seven scenes, it introduces the inhabitants of Naunynstraße:

Niyazi Gümüskılıç, Atifet, Sabri San, Halime, Frau Elisabeth Kutzer, Klaus Feck, and Nermin, among others.[94] Even though the title character of the first part is Niyazi, there is neither a clear protagonist nor an omniscient narrator, but rather a variety of characters (and perspectives) with changing focus throughout the narrative.

Through non-linear and non-chronological structuring and the inclusion of the use of summarizing subheadings that are reminiscent of scene titles, as well as interior monologues, and analepses, Ören abstains from providing any sense of totality, completeness, or coherence with regard to the *Zeitlichkeiten* (temporalities) he represents. At the same time he allows for a multiplicity of perspectives, present and past, countering the hegemonic narratives of history that subdue difference in favor of homogeneity. This refusal of seamless description, which works to disrupt uncritical reception, is supported by his use of montage, a structuring principle also prevalent in Brecht's work.[95] In her analysis of Brecht's early plays Patrizia McBride points out that through montage, "individual elements [are] made to collide rather than coalesce in some harmonious totality."[96] Brecht also used montage to adapt and change sections of his plays: as he said parts were "montaged in or montaged out."[97] By employing montage in the trilogy— through non-linear and non-chronological structuring for example—Ören, like Brecht, draws attention to the constructed, and therefore evolving, nature of social, historical, and political processes.

In *Was will Niyazi in der Naunynstraße?* Ören's use of montage is most noticeable in the character portraits: each character is briefly introduced by a short paragraph told by a third-person narrator, which is then followed by an introduction in the first person told by the characters themselves. The passages narrated in the third person are often brief factual reports on biographical aspects of the character, such as place of birth, marital status, and occupation. These sequences stand in contrast to the passages narrated in the first person, which are a mix of retrospection and introspection, alternating between monologues, dream sequences, snippets of memory, and flashbacks. These provide the reader with insights into the characters' past, their reasons for emigrating to Berlin, but also into such matters as their economic status, for example by citing their income figures.[98] In this way, as Carmine Chiellino notes, Turkish workers "are always defined as parts of the alienated relation between labor and wage."[99] Their personal perspectives and official, external details about their lives mediate one another. At the same time we see how each character's behavior is determined by economic factors.

Niyazi gains further prominence in the second part, *Der kurze Traum aus Kağithane*, written between 1972 and 1973, where the significance of history, the worker within production modes, and the role of literature are further thematized. Here Ören engages with history in relation to literature and the working-class standpoint. Through the character of Niyazi he reveals the trilogy's overall aim: "I tried to draw attention to the importance of rewriting history from a class standpoint. This is a beginning, it has to continue; we will certainly write our own class's history."[100] Niyazi realizes the significance of the past for the future, and begins to "piece together" his own past within the historical process, in order to change the present and thus the future (*BÜ*, 118). He traces his Turkish past, ending with the 1961 constitutional changes. Throughout this personal history, he stresses that the worker is the subject of change, basing his understanding of history on dialectical materialism while also affirming Marx's and Brecht's postulation that within its inherent contradictions, the capitalist system creates the forces that would eventually destroy it (*BÜ*, 125). Moreover, in the second part, and throughout the trilogy, there is a repeated emphasis on the Marxist thesis that those who produce should have control over the modes and means of production (*BÜ*, 179).

The role of the writer and of literature, with regard to historical processes is represented by means of the relationship between Niyazi and his nameless poet friend. In letters between them and in the inclusion of the poems we find embedded an understanding of the poet as someone who juxtaposes "broken lines, fragmentary sounds and images" by telling the story, thus forming a narrative out of disconnected parts. Niyazi, in one of his letters, reiterates the necessity "to know" and "lay claim to" one's own history, a realization he comes to through the reading of poetry (*BÜ*, 179). A letter from his "poet friend" dated from 1973 confirms Ören's own approach to literature as archive and its testimonial function (*BÜ*, 182). This documentation not only has a testimonial function in the guise of a translation of temporality, but it also symbolizes a repository of individual fragments that can be reconstructed in a cohesive collective (hi)story of Berlin's working class.

In *Was will Niyazi in der Naunynstraße?* the first character introduced to the reader is Frau Kutzer, whose family history is also given. Hailing from East Prussia, Frau Kutzer's family, at that point the Brummel family, moved to Naunynstraße, Berlin, in 1848, when Franz Christian Naunyn (1799–1860) became its mayor, during a time when "capital was exploiting labor unscrupulously" (*BÜ*, 23). The point of departure is already class-based, focusing on the relationship between labor and capital, representing this family history in economic terms. Having moved there, when it was "just any street back then," the Brummel family is a constant in the history of Naunynstraße, surviving different regimes with differing ideologies (*BÜ*,

24). However, this place is marked by continuous oppression of the proletariat, highlighting the significance of the past in relation to the present.

In the aftermath of the First World War the Brummels' income decreases because the father's locksmith shop goes out of business. In 1924, with economic conditions worsening, Elisabeth Brummel, then nineteen years old, marries Gustav Kutzer. Gustav, an assembly worker at Borsig, a mechanical engineering company, is politically active and a member of the Communist Party (KPD). Whereas his wife struggles to accept her status as a member of the working class, to her husband, being a proletarian is "nothing to be ashamed of" (*BÜ*, 29). He believes that "tomorrow proletarians will take over power," and while his wife longs for material wealth and comfort, daydreaming of things they cannot afford, Gustav's political beliefs—"things she did not understand" —lend him support and a sense of fulfillment (*BÜ*, 29).

Narrating the Kutzers' past, Ören alludes to Hitler's rise to power and the dictatorship of the Third Reich. As can be expected, a key date is 1933, when husband Gustav arrives home in shock, stating: "We are being followed" (*BÜ*, 29). Thereafter, he burns his communist flyers printed with the KPD campaign slogan for the elections in 1932 and 1933: "Suicide is no solution, fight with the KPD" (*BÜ*, 30). In fear of persecution by Hitler's regime, he turns his back on politics, a circumstance that Rita Chin describes as a "silence that . . . amounts to nothing less than psychological suicide."[101] Gustav's forced silence is emblematic of the "backlash against growing political power of the working class in Germany" by the Nazi regime.[102] In addition to Gustav's political and ideological immobilization, his family's financial situation continues to deteriorate until finally they are forced to sell all their valuable belongings in the aftermath of the Second World War. In a sequence that exemplifies Ören's didactic realism particularly effectively, Frau Kutzer is shown comprehending neither her husband's ideology and political beliefs, nor the consequences of his losing them, until long after his death. Aging, alone, and impoverished, she reveals: "Now I understand him, left like a hollow tree needing something to lean on—in order not to fall over" (*BÜ*, 21–22). The contrast between Marxist and capitalist orientations is manifest in the juxtaposition of husband and wife—Gustav and Elisabeth Kutzer—as she is focused on material wealth, while Herr Kutzer foregrounds the welfare of his fellow workers, and of the working class in general, his identity being mass- and class-based.

Frau Kutzer's story is marked by the experiences of both World Wars: confrontations with death and with the victims of war, especially the loss of her loved ones. In 1924, she loses her father; in 1946, she loses her twelve-year-old son Fridolin to scarlet fever; and in 1959 her husband dies of a heart attack. The year 1959 is also crucial in another way and not randomly chosen by Ören: it symbolizes the end of workers' representation by a political party in the Federal Republic of Germany. After the Federal Constitutional Court sanctioned the dissolution of the Communist Party (KPD) in 1956, in 1959 the Social Democratic Party (SPD) ratified the Bad Godesberg program, "in which the SPD shed its traditional status of a class or workers' party for that of a mass or people's party."[103] Through the biography of the figure Gustav Kutzer, Ören subtly weaves in historic events that remind the reader of major setbacks experienced by the working class in Germany: Hitler's rise to power, persecution by the Nazi regime, the dissolution of the Communist Party after the Second World War, and the repositioning of the Social Democratic Party in 1959.

Analogies to the Nazis appear in the first part's discussion of racism and xenophobia during the early stages of labor migration, which is addressed in connection with Ali and Nermin, a Turkish couple living in Naunynstraße. Ali, now a refrigerator repair technician, left their village, Acıbayram, in 1970. As soon as he moves from the workers' dormitory to his own apartment on Naunynstraße, his wife Nermin follows him to Berlin. Two instances of Ali's experiences with discrimination are narrated. He is insulted first by his German coworkers while leaving work and then by the factory worker Klaus Feck later that same day on his way home. They call him "dirty foreigner," and blame him (for them, Ali epitomizes all guestworkers) for low wages, the increase of work hours, and their general dissatisfaction (*BÜ*, 51). Each of these instances elicits the following comment: "In their hands no machine guns, no automatics. On their heads no steel helmets, on their feet no boots, they did not wear brown uniforms and swastikas" (*BÜ*, 67). The analogy drawn between the verbal attackers and the Nazis as well as the repetition of these sentences in unaltered form emphasizes the persistence of racist ideology beyond the Third Reich. As Rita Chin notes, Ören takes "conventional German New Left linkage between capitalism and fascism in new directions" showing that, "in spite of similar work experiences and mutual economic complaints," workers are "unable to recognize their common plight."[104] Furthermore, this passage serves as a reminder of the principal impediments to the solidarization of a single, cohesive workers' movement: racism and fascism. Throughout Europe, workers' movements and their parties were shattered by fascist regimes; therefore, the fight of the workers had to take aim at both material exploitation as well as ideological oppression.

In the poem, all references to the Holocaust and the Third Reich take the form of brief statements, like the passages narrated in the third person that introduce the political contexts in which the characters live: the terror of the Nazi regime for the Kutzers, and the tumult of the student revolts in Turkey for the character Atifet. Ören does not assign any specific significance to them, nor does he emphasize one over the other. Historical and political events appear in factual enumerations that read like reports. We see this in the metafictional comments provided by the third-person narrator, who, while summarizing Frau Kutzer's family history, notes that there is "nothing else worth reporting."[105] Ören's allusions to and use of reportage, like those of Brecht, emphasize the factual over the empathic. In addition to his use of montage techniques and non-chronological structuring, he inserts bracketed sentences. These provide supplementary information on Niyazi's apartment, on Halime's earnings and expenses, and on Ali's whereabouts, thus slowing down the narrative flow and creating a sense of extemporaneity, reinforcing the distance between reader and text (*BÜ*, 34, 44, 69). By means of such montage techniques Ören, like Brecht, places equal emphasis on the alterability of the present and an understanding of history as work-in-progress.

As the title already indicates, Naunynstraße is central to the Berlin trilogy. As a physical space, it links the protagonists through their experiences as members of the working class beyond ethnic or national differentiation. Alienation becomes a common denominator for Naunynstraße's inhabitants. As Rita Chin has argued, "Ören weaves a common thread of proletarian experience. . . . And it is Naunynstraße that ultimately connects those experiences. . . . Both figuratively and historically, it binds these diverse members of the German working class together."[106]

The factual (and the fictional) Naunynstraße is a street located in the center of the district of Kreuzberg—a district that, at the time Ören was writing, was located in West Berlin bordering the East. After the Second World War, Kreuzberg was in ruins, with half of its living space and two thirds of its businesses destroyed.[107] During the early stages of labor migration to West Berlin one of the few alternatives to living in austere barracks was to move into condemned tenements slated for renovation or demolition. These were often located in traditionally working-class districts such as Kreuzberg, Schöneberg, and Wedding and were temporarily rented to migrant laborers, who could not afford to live in prosperous neighborhoods such as Zehlendorf, Wilmersdorf, Steglitz, and Charlottenburg.[108] With the construction of the Berlin Wall in 1961, Kreuzberg was transformed from a central Berlin district to an isolated area at the margins of West Berlin, bordered by the state-socialist German Democratic Republic on three sides. Because of standing plans to refurbish vast areas of Kreuzberg in the future, many houses and buildings were neither renovated nor adequately maintained.[109]

Kreuzberg's architecture, its backyards framed by the *Hinterhäuser* (rear buildings), constitutes a building design that goes back to the turn of the twentieth century, when it was the prime location for small industrial shops and factories. This is a prominent building style in workers' districts such as Tiergarten, Wedding, and Schöneberg. These buildings housed small businesses in the front parts and accommodated their workers in the *Hinterhäuser*. Buildings were structured in this way in order to meet working as well as living needs. In contrast to the buildings facing the street, the rear buildings were plain, constructed without stucco or other decorative elements. They did not have direct access to the street, lacked direct sunlight, and provided less comfort than the front building, as they were equipped only with shared lavatories and bathing facilities.[110]

Kreuzberg's backyards recur in Ören's works as both a motif and a setting. For example, in his collection *Anlatılar, 1970–1982* (Stories, 1970–1982; published in 1991), he dedicated an entire short story to these spaces, giving it the title "Arka Avlu" (Backyard, 1970). Here the narrator describes Kreuzberg from a bird's eye view: its countless roofs and chimneys, which appear stacked upon one another; its gray-black coloring; its recent accumulation of TV satellite dishes—all features that distinguish Kreuzberg from other parts of the city.[111] By emphasizing these superficial visual features, Ören evokes the overcrowdedness and poverty of the industrial inner city. But in the first part of the Berlin trilogy he offers a closer look at its inhabitants: "Only if you step into the backyards will you feel, taste, and smell what is in the air. Then you will notice . . . that here the class is living that will breach and change societal norms and reconstitute them" (*BÜ*, 83). Counterposing what is seen from a distance to that which is apprehended viscerally, by a combination of the senses, in "Arka Avlu" Ören locates the potential for change and its agents in the *Hinterhäuser* of Kreuzberg, the home of the workers. The relationship between new Turkish inhabitants of the *Hinterhäuser*, such as Niyazi, with existing German ones, such as Frau Kutzer, is made clear in the third part of the trilogy through Niyazi's interior monologue:

> Who do you think lives here? On the run-down balconies . . . planting geraniums; dragging their rheumatic feet; aren't they those elderly people going shopping? Aren't they the ones who demanded their rights against the states' rights over them, laying the foundation for today's democracy? Why are they against these rights now? . . . What do these faces tell you about the pain, fear, and resistance history wove. Aren't you the one who lives here today? Who will take over and continue, in these back yards, the moldy struggle days . . . an inherited reality changing hands . . . Yes, all of

this pushes you into a 150-year-struggle that is ever-growing and continuing to grow through production. (*BÜ*, 214)

In this passage Turkish immigrants are perceived as carrying forward the legacy of the class struggle. For Ören, Turkish guestworkers "were part of a historical process" and thus "new members of the working class in Germany"
whom he perceived as "heirs" to the German labor movement, thus pointing to their active role in the transformation and continuation of its existing
legacies.[112] Notably, this encounter is located in the Kreuzberg street, and in
its balconies and its backyards—and not in the houses of parliament or official political institutions. Ören's poetic cycle thus modifies the meaning of
the literary setting on the basis of labor and capitalist critique, by presenting
Kreuzberg not only as site of exploitation but also, in the collective life of
the neighborhood and its inhabitants, as the point of resistance and departure for collective solidarity and action.

The first part of the trilogy documents the transformation of
Naunynstraße through Turkish labor migration. It is a positive transformation, such that "without Turks, Naunynstraße, while not losing anything of
its characteristics as a street, would today, in its old days, still be in its nascent
beginnings" (*BÜ*, 34). The interaction of Turkish labor migrants with
Naunynstraße remains central throughout the trilogy. Here the physiognomy
of Naunynstraße and its buildings is likened to that of the exploited workers:
"The houses that look at you in the Naunynstraße turn their façade away and
their backside to you, like dull transport workers who do not pay attention to
the weight they carry" (*BÜ*, 82–83). The fatigue and exhaustion of its working-class inhabitants is transferred to the street, which is "dozy, sluggish," having "sleepy windows that stare at the water pumps on the curbside" (*BÜ*, 20,
82). Anthropomorphizing Naunynstraße strengthens the linkage between the
street and its inhabitants, lending body imagery to a city sector's long-standing
class association.[113] The connection between the street and its inhabitants
is further extended when the narrator personifies Naunynstraße as a mother
putting "the lost people from the foreign countries to sleep at its damp bosom"
(*BÜ*, 34). Not only is Naunynstraße a welcoming place for its new inhabitants;
it also comforts them. By conceiving of the street as mother, Ören establishes a
familial relationship between the street and its inhabitants.

Kreuzberg, and especially Naunynstraße, remain significant throughout Ören's oeuvre, reappearing in other poems and novels. In his poetry
collection *Mitten in der Odyssee* (In the Midst of the Odyssey, 1980), the
poem "Die Strassen von Kreuzberg" (The Streets of Kreuzberg) acknowledges: "The people living in these streets are those with zero capital."[114] In
Deutschland ein türkisches Märchen (Germany a Turkish Fairy Tale, 1978),

he included what he called a poem fragment entitled "Was ist los in der Naunynstraße? Fragment" (What Is Going On in Naunystrasse? Fragment), in which the plural lyrical subject—the workers—proclaim:

> This street is our street,
> even if there are no poplars growing in a row here.
> These apartments are our apartments,
> we are the architects, we are the construction workers,
> we are the owners, we are the tenants. . . .[115]

Here Ören represents the workers as a united collective, emphasized through the repeated use of "we," claiming Naunynstraße as its own—not as exclusive to Germans or to Turks, but rather as the possession of all workers.

Throughout the first part of the trilogy, Aras Ören adds the experiences of Turkish guestworkers to the proletarian history of this street and emphasizes the interaction of Turkish workers with fellow German workers. He also narrates their participation in (and continuation of) traditions in the places they immigrated to. Although the arrival of the first Turkish guestworkers passes without further detail or commentary, Ören provides detailed information on the Turkish labor migrants who subsequently join them—Niyazi, Atifet, Halime, Kazım, and Sabri, among others. All of these characters come to embody a wide variety of economic motivations for immigration.[116]

Atifet, Niyazi's close friend, came to Berlin in 1967 to work at Siemens; she is politically active and participates in demonstrations organized by the workers' union. Niyazi's neighbor Halime also came to Germany for work and because her husband is in prison in Turkey, she has to support her two children herself with occasional work at Telefunken and by working as a prostitute. Kazım lost his transportation business in Turkey and came to Berlin in 1971, where he works as a carpenter. Sabri, an unskilled laborer employed as a transport worker, came to Germany after an earthquake hit his home village. The alienation of the workers from their lives in Turkey through a necessary adaptation to the needs of the market shows the pervasiveness of the exploitation inherent to capitalism. This is most clearly seen in Halime's case, as she is forced to work two different jobs, one of which involves the commodification not only of her time and labor but also of her own body. Furthermore, the characters represent how organized protest by labor is the only possible way to change the modes of production, and thus confront and defeat capitalism. Though the forces of capital and the market mark these workers as foreigners, their collective labor struggle offers them the possibility for self-determination and to enact solidarity on the basis of class.

Pivotal to this process is the character of Niyazi, who connects characters to one another by means of his various relationships to them as friend, neighbor, and colleague.[117] Originally from Bebek, a prosperous district in Istanbul, Niyazi lives above Frau Kutzer and works as a pressman at Preussag, a steel and mining company. Since he lived in comparatively poor conditions in Bebek, he came to Berlin for better prospects: "When this thing with Germany came up, I told myself, like anyone else, me too: Germany is a little America. Go there, Niyazi, and live like the rich in Bebek" (BÜ, 37–38). Niyazi's initial goal reproduces the illusions of progress and prosperity central to capitalism, but his idea of success is still localized in Turkey. And just as Frau Kutzer dreams of being the rich woman in the Neukölln villa she cleans, Niyazi seeks a better life in Germany. The connection between these two characters is made early in the story, when both of them are briefly mentioned in juxtaposition, Niyazi going to his night shift, while Frau Kutzer is unable to fall asleep. Not only are they located next to each other in narrative sequence, but they live above and below one another in the same house, in a spatial relation that is also mirrored by their appearances in textual sequence. This presentation of the two characters highlights the interrelation of their lives, and the effects that capitalism has on both. Moreover, the Kutzers and Niyazi are interlinked through their immigrant status. While the Brummel family, later the Kutzers, moved to Berlin in the nineteenth century, the Turkish guestworkers (Niyazi, Sabri, and Halime) arrive a century later, continuing the line of labor migration. To quote Harald Weinrich, Ören thus creates "... a poetic ancestral portrait gallery, to which, without breaks, a generation of Turkish proletarians attaches itself."[118]

After his move, Niyazi begins to shed his illusions about Germany as a land of better opportunity; he admits to having realized where his place is in society—not with the wealthy whom he had aspired to join, but with the working-class of which he is already a member (BÜ, 39). The vacuousness of capitalist promises—which was central for Brecht—is rendered in the poem's narrative action: Niyazi witnesses the workers' lives, and estranged from his own life and the fruits of his labor, upon realizing that the narratives of success and prosperity that brought him to West Berlin are false, he consciously joins the masses in search of action and change.

Seven years in Berlin have changed Niyazi and made him aware of the necessity of fighting for his rights instead of quietly accepting his fate, because all "those giving their labor have the same share in the world" (BÜ, 40). He further notes: "I have learned that my right is a right too. Never again will I abdicate my right, even if it costs me my life" (BÜ, 40). He strives to enlighten other workers about their rights, and works with his comrade Horst Schmidt, a chimney repairman[119] and a regular at the Marxist night school, to recruit neighbors and friends into showing solidarity in their fight against exploitation and capitalism. Toward the end of the trilogy, Naunynstraße becomes a symbol for political change, as its inhabitants realize that they should coop-erate and help each other to improve labor conditions.[120] In a conversation with Horst Schmidt, Niyazi demands international solidarity among workers: "We live here, and here, in this street, in this neighborhood there are many, many of us who every day are being pushed against the wall anew. We have to join forces" (*BÜ*, 85–86). The "system," which denies workers the products of their work, deserves the blame for their situation, and also provides false dreams and ideals of fulfillment and self-realization that, as the trilogy shows, can only be achieved through collective labor action. Those who benefit from Niyazi's labors as he melts scrap metal in the furnace are those living in villas in South-West Berlin; those "who receive the cream are not those milking the cow" (*BÜ*, 15; 56).

Through this focus on the perspective of Kreuzberg's workers and on their ability to improve upon and overcome inequalities by becoming agents of change, and through the employment of formal techniques that disrupt passive, unquestioning absorption of the narrative material, the convergences between Brecht's and Ören's realist aesthetics become clear. The only way to overcome oppression, as suggested by Horst in the first part of the trilogy, is to join forces: "Yes, only when people show solidarity can they make themselves aware of the fact that they can be together in an organization and change something" (*BÜ*, 87). Brecht's realist aesthetics and the German labor tradi-tion are represented in the figure of Horst, whose efforts coalesce with those of Niyazi and the other immigrants; in Ören's reworking of Brecht's aesthet-ics to fit the specific problematic of 1970s West Berlin, German and Turkish workers alike renew the labor movement by moving beyond their national differences. In the end, Naunynstraße again becomes a street "in which some-thing is stirring . . . workers, Naunynstraße inhabitants, together drinking beer, having political disputes, shoulder to shoulder under the same flag" (*BÜ*, 87). The aesthetic tool with which Ören represents this historical process is a non-illusionistic, didactic Brechtian realism, which he transforms by adapting it to the historical context of Turkish migration to Germany. In his broader oeuvre Ören adapts this didactic realism to various genres, whether poetry, theater, or prose, as is evident in his "Lehrstück," to which I now turn.

Ören's "Lehrstück": Alienated Labor and Turkish Immigrants

Various other publications by Ören show that the genesis of the first part of his trilogy overlapped with the writing of the "Lehrstück." For example, a 1971 radio production, a sound collage about workers in Naunynstraße, includes characters of the trilogy.[121] Moreover, in the poetic cycle published in a special issue of *Asphalt*, the characters of Niyazi and Dieter make their first appearances.[122] While both focus on the shared experience of workers as well as on the new impulses coming from Turkish workers, the "Lehrstück" shifts the attention to the micro-perspective of the workplace as opposed to the macro-perspective of Berlin as a city of working-class struggle and labor protest.

Ören's "Lehrstück für türkische Arbeiter"[123] is a short play manuscript, seventeen pages in length that today is found among his unpublished manuscripts at the archive of the Academy of Arts. In revised and abbreviated form, it was published in German translation in Ören's novel *Manege* (1984). While dated 1970, the manuscript has handwritten notes correcting the number of Turks living in Berlin through 1974. Ören perceives the play as an "Entwurf," a sketch, and classified it as "stage work," attesting to his understanding of his work as work-in-progress. In addition to the fact that the title's designation of the play as a "Lehrstück," a learning play, is a direct reference to Brecht, Ören employs a variety of literary devices that Brecht theorized as V-effects. These were crucial to Brecht's *Lehrstücktheorie* as well as to his writings on epic theater. Ören's piece was performed for Turkish workers in May 1971 at the Technical University's cafeteria by the Işçi Tiyatrosu Berlin, the Turkish Workers' Theater Berlin.[124]

Besides the clear influences of Brecht's V-effects, Ören's own theatrical aesthetics can also be traced throughout the play. In a 1970 letter addressed to Johannes Schenk, Ören discusses in detail his views on the relationship between theater, the working class, and political action. Schenk was one of the translators of the trilogy's first part, founder of the Kreuzberger Straßentheater in 1969, and a member of the Volkstheaterkooperative Westberlin whose goal was to repeal "alienation between people."[125] In his letter Ören admits that the intellectuals utterly fail the workers by believing that they need to teach them what the revolution means, rather than realizing that the potential for revolution is already within each worker, awaiting awakening. However, he still sees the potential of street theater, and of other revolutionary forms of theater, to bring about real change. The key required for this awakening to take place is Marxism, and as such, Ören proposes to Schenk that they collaborate in developing a theater, a "testing ground" connected to the Kreuzberger Straßentheater, that "teaches the workers Marxism" based on five principles that represent the cooperation between workers and artists. These principles can be expressed as follows: first, the workers must be taught "the methods through which they can themselves solve problems"; second, it must be realized that what artists will learn from the workers "will not lead to anything other than Marxism," which is

Fig. 2.5. Işçi Tiyatrosu Berlin (TTO) ensemble performing Aras Ören's learning play at the Technical University in West Berlin in 1971. Reproduced by permission from Akademie der Künste, Berlin, Aras-Ören-Archiv.

Fig. 2.6. Işçi Tiyatrosu Berlin (TTO) ensemble performing Aras Ören's
learning play at the Technical University in West Berlin in 1971. Reproduced
by permission from Akademie der Künste, Berlin, Aras-Ören-Archiv.

inherently connected to the third principle: namely, the immanence of
"Marxism in the worker, as the doctrine to interpret the capitalist relations
of production, and to change them." Fourth, Ören proposes that artists "can
only contribute and enrich through variation," and fifth, "in the capitalist
system, the worker . . . has been distanced from his own self" with the artists
only able to show "the trap," stipulating that the worker "has to escape the
trap himself and he will also save the intellectuals." These principles reveal
not only Ören's strong belief in the capability of the workers to understand
the centrality of their role in their own emancipation but also his insistence
on reframing the artists' and intellectuals' roles as being involved with an
interactive mode of teaching rather than unilaterally leading.

The play begins with a prologue: a song sung by a chorus, in which
Ören establishes the subject(s) of the play in the first stanza: 40,000 Turks.
Further, it introduces the setting, Berlin, including its "ghettos," the places
of residence of its Turkish inhabitants. Immediately in this first stanza, their
departures from Turkey are presented as abrupt, even though Turkey per-
sists in memory, associated with "warm soil" that contrasts with their hasty
walk to the factory in the "dark of the morning" in present-day Berlin. The
second stanza of the prologue further establishes the factory as a place that

never sees spring and will never have Turkey's warmth. Right at the beginning of the play Ören sets up dichotomies between the categories of nature and industry on the one hand, interior and exterior on the other, each of which illuminates the dialectic relationship between two different lifestyles and systems of production. The second stanza of the song elaborates further on the subject and intention of the play: "We also have something to say, we have a play to play." Ören gives agency to the Turks he introduced as a mass in the first stanza through the use of direct speech and the personal pronoun "we," which he sees as including himself. By giving them a voice, he counters the dominant perception of the Turk as "silent presence"[126] and the "figure of the mute and passive Turkish worker"[127] in the German public. While in the first stanza we hear about 40,000 Turks residing in Berlin, the third stanza begins by "We, 40,000 Turks" indicating a shift from a large number described from outside in the first stanza to an inhabited collective subject who introduces itself as the said 40,000, before further elaborating on the aim in this play: "We sell our labor, like all workers. Everything begins with us and ends with us. Hear us, this is a warning: labor fights capital." In addition to the ethnic signifier, Ören represents "Turks" as class subjects, as workers. However, the position from which they speak is one of power, one that establishes them as acting subjects, and not passive objects in the labor process. The Turkish workers assert their own worth for the labor movement in the German context, at the same time staking a claim to the movement's history. This initially causes a clash with German workers, which in turn gives rise to an interaction that is represented as a dialectical relationship. Turkish workers, as in the trilogy, are represented as class subjects, as part of a collective "we," beyond ethnic confines and national divides. At the same time, there is an emphasis on the Turkish workers as catalysts for the change of labor conditions and modes of production. For Ören to choose a chorus to introduce the play's subject, topic, and point of perspective comes as no surprise, as choral speaking and songs are a central element in Brecht's theater practice; they have a didactic function, as they enable critical distance. For Brecht, choirs "enlighten the spectator about circumstances unknown to him."[128] The prologue thus establishes Turks both as members and subjects of the working class, and, second, as catalysts in the working-class struggle, by introducing them as subjects articulating long-standing demands of the German working class.

The play begins with an encounter between four Turkish workers in a factory: Hasan and Hüseyin, who are silently operating a machine, and the two newcomers Ahmet and Memet. From the onset, stage set descriptions attest to a minimal use of props and stage design. The machine that Hasan and Hüseyin are supposedly operating is not there. The emphasis is rather put on their movements, which in the stage directions are described as repetitive and "acaip," strange. The two newcomers to the factory are equipped with wooden suitcases, and are bewildered about the behavior of their fellow Turks. Talking to each other in order to identify what exactly Hasan and Hüseyin are doing, they at first (mistakenly) take these movements to be symptoms of a disease, and then decide it must be a dance. Then they ask Hasan and Hüseyin for clarification. Hasan and Hüseyin continue their repetitive mechanical movements while responding to the newcomers. Their responses are made up of short repeated sentences mirroring their piecework and thus foregrounding how the mechanical movements of labor determine behavior. This dehumanization and abstraction represents alienation by figuring a familiarity with factory processes as an acquired, machine-like posture; within this mechanistic world, the arrival of new workers becomes the arrival of replacement parts: the older workers admit the new workers mechanically, as they will also become part of the same machinery. Hasan and Hüseyin explain that this is Germany, and "here you always work," which, as it is repeated for emphasis, mimics the production mode into which they have been inscribed. This is how the new arrivals, too, are to work, without breaks—all in order to reach production quotas.

While continuing their movements, Hasan and Hüseyin sing a song to explain the situation in Germany to the newcomers. Through Brechtian *Verfremdung*, Ören makes their movements appear "conspicuous," to draw attention to the physical processes that condition their behavior and subjective orientations as they become dehumanized and alienated from their fellow men. Hasan and Hüseyin start singing with an emphasis on the uselessness of their work and listing forces that covet their money: from state to merchant, and from the barber's scissors, through the scissors' screw, to the screw's rust. On the page, the song ends in an ellipsis, pointing to the endlessness of exploitation. While the newcomers want to engage in conversation, Hasan and Hüseyin continue working, out of fear of being laid off. If they continued to talk, the "Maystır" (German: *Meister*), foreman, would tell them "Havap" ("Hau ab," or "get lost"), attesting to their replaceability. Here we see the effects of working the machines, which is apparent in their speech too, "Havap" and "Maystır" are uttered in German pronunciation but Turkish spelling and are translated only for the newcomers, since they do not understand.

The "Maystır" arrives and sends the newcomers straight to work, emphasizing that they have to work constantly or they will be let go. The newcomers go to imaginary machines and begin the work process by imitating the workers who are already present. The "Maystır" keeps repeating short sentences "olmuyor, olmuyor" (it doesn't work) and "daha çabuk" (faster), "daha seri" (more). In this classical Marxist presentation, workers stop being humans who are ends in themselves—not only because of their mechanized movements but also because the machines are taking over their minds. Accepting the modes of production and the alienation they cause is learned behavior, in the same way that resistance to it can also be learned. In the interaction between workers we see the monotony of work, and movements being portrayed as executable by anyone (no prior training or skill is necessary). The foreman's continuous and repetitive interruptions demanding that the workers work faster are accompanied by music. The stage directions point out that the foreman's utterances and Hasan's and Hüseyin's movements are in time with the music, whereas the newcomers are behind it. Thus Ören draws an analogy between the foreman and Hasan and Hüseyin that is manifested through their repetitive, machine-like behavior—a repetitive comportment whose rhythms have yet to be learned by the recent arrivals.

Ahmet and Memet are astonished, admitting that this was not what they expected to be the reality of a worker. Hüseyin's response is: "Once you become a worker . . . you understand that you can change things." They engage in a conversation, which is interspersed with the foreman's repetitive directions. Ahmet still does not understand, telling Hasan and Hüseyin that he finds them "acaip," strange.

When Hasan asks "What is a worker?" Memet, based on what he has seen until then, responds "a worker here means, faster, more" However, Hasan then clarifies: "A worker is someone who sells his labor to others, and by others we mean those who own the machines," confirming the centrality to this play of the Marxist principle of alienation from the means of production, as well as from the result of his labor. Furthermore, it reaffirms the reduction of labor to a commodity, as it needs to be sold in order to produce value. Moreover, Hüseyin explains, the foreman is in the same position as they are. Hasan continues, "You operate the machine but you are not the owner of the machine. You don't operate it in your own way, in short, you operate it at the owner's will, based on his desire for capital." Now the newcomers understand, and engage in a sequence of songs in alternation with Hasan and Hüseyin, addressing the foreman, who—like them—does not own the means of production. The final song by Hasan and Hüseyin culminates in the appeal, "Come, let's unite, you, I, they, worker, foreman, engineer, solidarity begins at the factory, let us become one force together, let us get organized on the basis of labor." The Turkish workers appeal to their German foreman for solidarity; however, he remains within his mechanical, monosyllabic, repeated utterances, pressuring them to continue to work. They briefly continue, and then engage in a dialogue regarding the product of their work. The factory produces plastic pipes; the Turkish workers are responsible for pushing buttons and pedals for certain parts of the labor process. Afterward, the products move to the warehouse, then to packaging, then to shipping. There the process is completed and they are exported. The pipes are sold, the money "going into the pockets of machine owners here," and with this money the extent of their exploitation continues to increase.

Through this dialogue, the nature of the continued accumulation of capital is laid out. In order to realize the extent and pervasiveness of their exploitation, the workers make use of Marxist tools of historical analysis. Next, Hasan announces that he will "address" how exploitation occurs by illustrating that their income is substantially less than what the owner of machines makes on the pipes; this disjuncture is identified as separating the workers from the fruit of their work, even as the extracted surplus value accumulates on the balance sheets of the factory's owner.

Hüseyin continues: "With this money he buys more machines, and continuously brings new workers; when new workers come; the man earns more money; when he earns more, he buys more machines bringing more workers. ..." And Hasan chimes in, continuing the cycle of exploitation, "when more workers come, the more he exploits; the more he exploits, the more he earns . . . he buys more machines, he brings more workers, and when more workers come the more ..." The cycle of capital accumulation presented by Hasan and Hüseyin ends, in both their accounts, the same way it begins; this is reflected in the ellipses at the ends of their statements, which reaffirm the cycle's indefiniteness. However, as we will see in the epilogue, the increasing number of workers resulting from the accumulation of capital also creates the possibility for real change to occur. Ahmet, after realizing that their efforts make the rich richer, proclaims that no matter what the consequences, he does not want to be part of this. This statement is followed immediately by the factory bell announcing a break.

An epilogue follows, in which the workers directly address the audience: "In this little play, we showed you three different situations with five people." The subject here is again the "we" of the prologue, the Turkish workers, who thus frame the action of the play, lending them further emphasis by being the voice that begins and ends the play. First, they describe Hasan and Hüseyin as individuals who, like "most of us . . . got out of the frying pan into the fire." However, even if they have "surrendered to the machine, in other words, to the will of the machines' owners," they already know that there is a solution to this matter. Then the workers shift their emphasis to Memet and Ahmet, who serve as examples of labor migrants, moving from place to place and contributing to multiplying machines as a function of progress. They are the newcomers "succumbing to this temptation" (of capitalist industry) and becoming workers. Positioned outside the labor process, at least initially, they find what they encounter strange, but in finding it strange they reach an understanding that "they are wheels within wheels," and become aware of the "dirty trick": the owners' exploitation of their labor. The third situation summarized is that of the foreman, the "mouthpiece" of the machine owners, who wears their masks and cracks the whip of their words in their name. Finally, the workers declare: "And this is our declaration, as you saw it . . . there has to be a way out of this, machine has to stay machine, human has to stay human, there has to be a way out, there has to be a way out." The answer to this follows immediately with all actors stating in unison: "We know a way out of this, we say that workers should enter the workers' party, uniting with the peasants, fight for power, and in this way lay claim to their labor."

Having reached this conclusion, the play then reveals itself as the materialization of the vision for theater Ören had described to Schenk in his letter. Using Brechtian dramaturgical tools and Marxist critique to represent and analyze different variations of their plight, the workers become aware of the relations of capitalist production and realize their potential for revolution. Furthermore, the play also connects directly to Marx and Engels' *Communist Manifesto* in two ways: first, through their claim that the increased precariousness of the workers' lives will in turn increase the solidarity among themselves as a subroutine of the capitalist accumulation process, and second, through the final chorus's echo of the perhaps most famous rallying cry of the *Manifesto*, calling on the comradeship of the proletarians as workers to unite.

Conclusion

Brecht scholar Astrid Oesmann suggests that "Brecht's writings during Germany's Weimar Republic should be seen as a coherent whole,"[129] writing against a reception history that has tended to cordon off the *Lehrstücke* or Brecht's Expressionist work from his later work. By working in the *Lehrstück* format at the same time as he composed a narrative poem in which he employs epic techniques, Ören intervened in Brecht reception, staging a counter-periodicity of Brecht's work that embraces the *Lehrstücke* alongside other techniques of Brecht's, developed at other times in the Weimar period. Moreover, Ören's engagement with Brecht cannot be traced to a single period or source, as it has multiple reference points: the Brecht reception in 1960s Turkey (non-chronological and based on Brecht's thought published in edited and collected volumes), the strong focus on Brecht's work and the Brechtian dramaturgical practices at the Theaterwoche in Erlangen, and the Brecht debates within the West German literary left in the late 1960s and 1970s.

As a member of student theater ensembles in both Turkey (the Gençlik Tiyatrosu ensemble), and Frankfurt/Main (the Neue Bühne), Ören partici-pated in student theater festivals, which provided an important forum for international exchange in the form of theoretical discussions and round-tables on working methods. With the Neue Bühne adaptation of *Die Ausnahme und die Regel*, Ören traveled to Turkey, where he participated in the international student theater festival in Istanbul in 1963, considered the first Brecht performance in Turkey on a professional stage. His connec-tion to and exchange with Öngören extends from their time together at the Gençlik Tiyatrosu through their participation in Erlangen to their research visit at the Berliner Ensemble. Moreover, Ören engaged in an active, con-tinuous, and regular conversation with Öngören through letters spanning multiple years, from 1964 to the early 1970s, in which political theater and the implementation of Brecht in Turkish theater often constituted the topic of their shared interest. From his exchange of letters with Vasıf Öngören and the publication of selections of his play Oedipus in *Tiyatro* in the early 1970s, we can further deduce that Ören closely followed developments in Turkish theater and Turkish theater discourse. After his permanent move to Germany, he engaged with Brecht through the West German literary left, where Brecht's thought, and especially his conceptualization of realist art, dominated cultural-political activities and literary engagement. In this con-text, Brecht informed not only Ören's literary poetics but also his involve-ment in cultural and political activities in Die Rote Nelke, along with his choice of the Rotbuch Verlag as his publisher—West Berlin's only collec-tively managed left-wing publishing house.

In addition to playing a pioneering role within the development of Turkish-German literature, Ören made significant contributions to debates regarding the politicization of literature in the late 1960s and early 1970s in West Germany—debates that went beyond the issue of Turkish guestworkers' presence in Germany and echoed much more widely throughout the country's literary public sphere. Literature, for Ören, was a means to document, archive, translate, and circulate the experience of Turkish immigrants, while at the same time functioning as a medium to introduce them as subjects and individ-uals in the German present, as opposed to silent, passive bystanders. Moreover, as we have seen in the Berlin trilogy and the "Lehrstück," Ören assigns to the Turkish workers a catalytic function in the German working-class struggle; it is they who can initiate the change of labor conditions in Germany by calling for solidarity. He thus envisions and represents in his writing a united prole-tariat: workers in Berlin who show solidarity, in spite of ethnic or national dif-ferences, in order to change reality.

3: Staged Pasts: Emine Sevgi Özdamar's Dramatic Aesthetic

TURKISH-GERMAN ACTRESS, dramatist, and novelist Emine Sevgi Özdamar has repeatedly cited the following sentence as her first words in German: "Mr. Besson, I have come in order to learn Brechtian theater from you."[1] Before fulfilling her dream in 1976, she came as guest worker in 1965 and had worked for two years in a factory in West Berlin. In her acceptance speech of the prestigious Kleist Prize in 2004—which she received at Brecht's former theater, the Berliner Ensemble—Özdamar looked back to the mid-1960s as the time she had "got to know Brecht, Lotte Lenya, Ernst Busch, and Kafka," when "[a] Turkish dramatist, a leftist Brechtian, took [her] to the Berliner Ensemble."[2] She did not reflect on her first two years in West Germany in terms of her economic experience in the factory, but rather as the time during which she learned German and first encountered German literature via the theater. The Turkish dramatist she mentioned is none other than Vasıf Öngören, who, beyond his crucial role within the development of Turkish political theater discussed in the previous chapters, was equally important in Özdamar's formative years in theater. In 1967 Özdamar returned to Turkey in order to attend drama school, spending three years at the well-known LCC in Istanbul. Beklan Algan, director of the 1964 *Szechwan* production discussed in the first chapter, as well as prominent director Muhsin Ertuğrul and dramatist Haldun Taner, were among her teachers there. Until her emigration from Turkey in 1976 Özdamar had performed regularly in stage productions by prominent directors, including Sermet Çağan and above all Öngören. The second and third installments of her Istanbul-Berlin trilogy *Sonne auf halbem Weg: Die Istanbul-Berlin Trilogie* (Sun Halfway: The Istanbul-Berlin Trilogy, 2006), provide an auto-fictional account of Özdamar's engagement with Brechtian theater in both divided Germany and Turkey. The second part, *Die Brücke vom Goldenen Horn* (*The Bridge of the Golden Horn*, 1998), recounts her engagement with Brecht when she was back in Turkey, including her time in drama school and her encounter with Turkish Brechtian directors and dramatists, particularly Öngören, first in West Berlin and later in Ankara and Istanbul as a member of his ensemble, the Birlik Sahnesi.[3] The final part, *Seltsame Sterne starren zur Erde* (Strange Stars Stare at the

Fig. 3.1. Emine Sevgi Özdamar with Rutkay Aziz as members of the LCC
ensemble in *Marat/Sade* (1968). Courtesy of Emine Sevgi Özdamar.

Earth, 2003), provides insight into her time at the Volksbühne in East
Berlin. Rather than placing her move from Turkey to Berlin (both East and
West) in the context of emigration, Özdamar has foregrounded theater: her
engagement and familiarity with Brecht and other German dramatists provided a connection between Turkey and divided Germany and established
continuities rather than ruptures.[4]

Pointing to the significance of Özdamar's extensive theatrical experience in various national contexts, Bettina Brandt argues for a transtheatrical approach (as opposed to a Turkish, German, or transnational focus)
to Özdamar's dramatic texts, to illustrate intersections and networks of
relationships as well as artistic practices, introducing a shift in focus from

the national to the aesthetic.[5] This transtheatrical approach highlights especially Özdamar's collaborations with directors at the Volksbühne in East Berlin and the Bochumer Schauspielhaus. Departing from Brandt's focus on intersections within Özdamar's theatrical experiences and their effect on her dramatic work, in this chapter I examine how these interlinked experiences, mediated through a continuous engagement with Brecht's theater theory and practice—in East Berlin and Bochum, but also in Istanbul and Ankara—influenced and shaped her literary aesthetic. Building on the work of B. Venkat Mani and Kader Konuk, who have analyzed Özdamar's use of theatrical elements in her non-dramatic texts, this chapter illuminates how theater itself figures both thematically and aesthetically in Özdamar's prose, particularly in *Seltsame Sterne*.[6] My analysis of *Seltsame Sterne* focuses on Özdamar's understanding of the writing process as staging, which is most clearly manifest in her incorporation of montage, music, and filmic techniques, and the juxtaposition of different times and temporalities in the narrative.

By employing literary montage as a structural principle in *Seltsame Sterne*, Özdamar, like Brecht, draws attention to the unraveling of social, historical, and political processes. Specifically, Özdamar's text stages the incompleteness and ongoing construction of the narrator's past and present, from which she must remain critically detached and to which she must contribute. Furthermore, her insistence upon the distance between observer and observed in the urban space of divided Berlin, and between reader and authorial voice in the constitution of her text, recalls Brecht's preoccupation with critical distance, perspective, and the multiplicity of enunciative registers. Through the development of an ongoing, ever-changing network of intersections between Turkish and German cultural practices in her works, Özdamar establishes connections between places and times that dissolve their a priori exclusive temporalities, and thus creates a shared and heterogeneous time.

Transtheatrical Intersections: The Volksbühne in East Berlin and the Schauspielhaus in Bochum

In 1976 Özdamar left Turkey to work with Benno Besson at the Volksbühne in East Berlin. There she worked as a dramaturg and assistant to Heiner Müller, Matthias Langhoff, and Besson himself.[7] Özdamar's time at the Volksbühne is significant because she collaborated not only with Besson but also with the directors Manfred Karge and Matthias Langhoff. Langhoff and Karge had overlapped at the Berliner Ensemble in the early 1960s, where they were close collaborators from 1961 until 1968, when they had both been engaged in efforts to resist the "musealization of the Berliner Ensemble"[8]—the same years during which Öngören attended stage rehearsals.

Besson took over artistic directorship of the Volksbühne in 1969, where he continued to champion the "ambiguity and ambivalence of Brechtian theater work."[9] Karge and Langhoff followed him there the same year, joined by Fritz Marquardt (who trained under Brecht in the early 1950s); together they worked on a radical reconceptualization of theater, the *Volksbühnenkonzept*, which was based on an advocacy of theaters as "public cultural centers," "places of communication" and "laboratories of social phantasies."[10] They understood theatrical work as based on collaboration and emphasized "collective production processes," harking back to and continuing the ensemble praxis initiated by Brecht himself at the Berliner Ensemble.

During her time at the Volksbühne Özdamar engaged intensively with its program and dramaturgy, studying, and translating Besson's production notes into Turkish, while at the same time documenting in sketches and notes the rehearsals of Marquardt's production of Heiner Müller's *Die Bauern* (The Farmers), Langhoff and Karge's production of Goethe's *Der Bürgergeneral* (*The Citizen General*), and Besson's production of Shakespeare's *Hamlet*—sketches and notes that she included in part in *Seltsame Sterne*.[11] When Besson left the Volksbühne in 1977, Özdamar

Fig. 3.2. Emine Sevgi Özdamar and Manfred Karge in Benno Besson's production of *Hamlet*. Courtesy of Emine Sevgi Özdamar.

Fig. 3.3. Emine Sevgi Özdamar, Benno Besson, and Ezio Toffolutti
during stage rehearsals for the *Caucasian Chalk Circle* (1978).
Courtesy of Emine Sevgi Özdamar.

accompanied him to Avignon, where she assisted in his Brecht productions, including *The Caucasian Chalk Circle*, an experience she relates in the final pages of *Seltsame Sterne*.[12]

From 1979 until 1984 Özdamar worked at the Bochumer Schauspielhaus, both as a member of its ensemble and as assistant director under the collaborative artistic directorship of Claus Peymann, Uwe Jens Jensen, Alfred Kirchner, and Hermann Beil.[13] By naming the ensemble the Bochumer Ensemble (BE), Peymann set it up it as a West German counterpart to the Berliner Ensemble.[14] During this time, the Schauspielhaus Bochum became the "city theater of the nation" and the prime theater for German premiere performances, its dramaturgy characterized by *Lerntheater* and elaborative program books, with an emphasis on dialogue, exchange, and communication.[15] The *Lerntheater* events, of which there were over thirty during Peymann's directorship, were conceived as platforms for conversations between audiences and directors and members of the ensemble. The directors Hermann Beil and Erich Holliger saw the *Lerntheater* events as an opportunity to educate their audiences about theater, specifically making Brecht's terms such as distance, play, and *Verfremdung* comprehensible as elements of theater working methods.[16] Confirming Brecht as one focal point, the first *Lerntheater* event was titled "Brecht in Bochum" and featured Alfred Kirchner and ensemble members discussing the staging of *Die heilige Johanna der Schlachthöfe* (*Saint Joan of the Stockyards*), which premiered in December 1979. Another *Lerntheater* event that demonstrates Bochum's engagement with the legacy of Brechtian theater practice featured a discussion about Brecht and the Berliner Ensemble with the visiting East German director and actor Ekkehard Schall in 1984. While the Volksbühne is significant for Özdamar's engagement with Brechtian theater, embodied and transformed by the work of Langhoff, Besson, Müller, and Karge, her time as member of the Bochumer Ensemble is equally important and must be seen in connection with her experiences in both East Germany and Turkey. The Bochumer Schauspielhaus reunited many of the dramaturgs, including Langhoff, Karge, and Müller, who had left the Volksbühne in East Berlin in the immediate aftermath of the Biermann expatriation. Bochum became the theater "for those trained, but later unloved at the Schiffbauerdamm in Berlin."[17] Looking back, Langhoff describes this time in Bochum as feeling like a sort of "diaspora."[18] Karge and Langhoff continued their collaborative work by developing a style that "preserved the Brechtian vocabulary of songs, projections of film clips, ... and a didactic inclination."[19] During her time there Özdamar participated in Karge and Langhoff's productions of Georg Büchner's *Woyzeck*, Anton Chekhov's *The Cherry Orchard*, and Thomas Brasch's *Lieber Georg* (Dear Georg). Özdamar commented that this was "the best time that could happen to a theater, the audience, the city, and the country. Claus Peymann, Hermann Beil, Kirchner, Achternbusch, Matthias Langhoff, Luc Bondy, Thomas Brasch, Thomas Bernhard, Heiner Müller ... It was energetic, political, intelligent, humorous, and highly artistic."[20] The atmosphere Özdamar describes is indeed mirrored in the output of the ensemble between 1979 and 1985: In addition to new productions and contemporary German plays, they staged a variety of Brecht's plays, including *Baal*, *Die heilige Johanna der Schlachthöfe*, *Mahagonny-Songspiel*, *Die Mutter* (*The Mother*), *Die Kleinbürgerhochzeit* (*A Respectable Wedding*), *Mutter Courage und ihre Kinder*, and *Herr Puntila und sein Knecht Matti* (*Mr. Puntila and his Man Matti*). At the Volksbühne in contrast, Besson, because of Brecht's heirs' tight grip on performance rights, could produce only one of Brecht's plays, *Der gute Mensch von Sezuan* (*The Good Person of Szechwan*), which he staged in three versions (in 1970, 1971, and 1975), the last production figuring in *Seltsame Sterne*.[21] For Besson, the production history of *Szechwan* bears special significance. In 1957 his production of this play was the first at the Berliner Ensemble after Brecht's death. At the same time it marked the end point of his career at the Berliner Ensemble, where it was perceived as un-Brechtian. While the Berliner Ensemble, in the hands of Helene Weigel and Elisabeth Hauptmann, "focused on the preservation and transmission of Brecht's methods, Brecht's younger collaborators" such as Besson, who was the first one to leave the Berliner Ensemble, "began to seek the freedom to experiment and develop these methods in different directions."[22] It was not until 1970 at the Volksbühne that Besson returned to *Szechwan*.[23]

Furthermore, it was at the Bochumer Schauspielhaus where in 1982 Özdamar was commissioned (by Peymann and Beil) to write her first play, *Karagöz in Alamania* (Blackeye in Germany), a "Theatercollage" that incorporated elements of plays performed during her time in Bochum.[24] Here she also wrote the dramatic monologue *Karriere einer Putzfrau* (Career of a Cleaning Woman), to which Heiner Müller contributed its subtitle: "Erinnerungen an Deutschland" (Memories of Germany). Suhrkamp editor Wolfgang Storch had approached Özdamar to contribute to a special volume on Müller, for which she submitted the monologue, dedicating it to Müller. Following this publication, Gabriele Dietze, editor for contemporary literature at the West Berlin Rotbuch Verlag, invited Özdamar to publish a book with them. Özdamar's short story collection *Mutterzunge* (Mother Tongue,

Fig. 3.4. Emine Sevgi Özdamar with Tuncel Kurtiz during stage rehearsals for *Karagöz in Alamania* (Blackeye in Germany, 1986). Courtesy of Emine Sevgi Özdamar.

1990), which marked her literary breakthrough in Germany, is the book that appeared as a result. Included in this collection, her German literary debut, are, in revised and prose form, her first two dramatic texts mentioned above, highlighting from the very beginning of her career the central role that her involvement in theater would have on her literary production.[25] Robert Cazzola, one of the jurors for the 1991 Ingeborg-Bachmann Prize competition, nominated Özdamar after reading *Mutterzunge*, marking a turning point in the German literary landscape.[26] Emine Sevgi Özdamar's winning the Ingeborg-Bachmann Prize in 1991 caused lively debate; it was considered a scandal that a non-native speaker of German—a category of authors that had been excluded until 1991 from the competition—could win such a prestigious German literary prize.[27]

In Özdamar's biography Brechtian theater practices emerge as the link and continuity between various geopolitical contexts: the Birlik Sahnesi in Ankara and Istanbul, the Volksbühne in East Berlin, and later the Bochumer Schauspielhaus in West Germany. Her encounter and engagement with Brecht's dramaturgical practices is therefore mediated, heterogeneous, and multifaceted, incorporating approaches (and rereadings) from different time periods, institutions, directors, and national contexts—including Turkey. Karge and Langhoff, who were at the Berliner Ensemble throughout the 1960s, constitute an important source of influence during the formative years of Turkish Brecht reception, and later, together with Besson and Müller, became key figures during an important decade in GDR theater. The relationship between Brechtian theater and its reception and application, both in Turkey (through directors such as Öngören), and in divided Germany, through authors and directors who took Brecht in different directions, such as Müller, Karge, Langhoff, and Besson, emerges as multilayered and non-chronological, and thus can be perceived as Brechtian itself. Not only was Brecht central to the development of experimental theater in the GDR;[28] throughout the 1960s his dramaturgical concepts and practices also assumed a similarly important role in Turkey in the creation of a political national Turkish theater, as shown in the first chapter of this book.

This interchange and engagement with Brecht's theoretical and dramatic legacy are thematized in *Seltsame Sterne* through the narrator's collaboration with Benno Besson. As is made clear in the novel, despite Besson's own close connection to Brecht when he was Brecht's student at the Berliner Ensemble, he made an artistic point of steering away from taking Brecht literally. The narrator's engagement with Besson's theater practice already begins on her journey to the Volksbühne, with her reading of Andre Müller's *Der Regisseur Benno Besson: Gespräche, Notate, Aufführungsfotos* (The Director Benno Besson: Conversations, Notes, and Performance Pictures, 1967).

Özdamar quotes the following passage from this work in *Seltsame Sterne* to underline the transformation of Brecht in the context of Besson's work: "For Besson the term 'Brecht pupil' was never tied to 'servile imitation' and 'unconditional apologia'" (*Sterne*, 30). Besson's approach to Brecht's legacy, and Özdamar's active involvement in it, are thematized further on the last page of *Seltsame Sterne*, where Besson asks Özdamar's protagonist to help him not to go back to Brecht's interpretation of the *Caucasian Chalk Circle* but to create his own. He insists that the she keep him from "return[ing] to old images," thus not only taking him away from his memories of Brecht's production, when he was an assistant, but aiding him to continuously adapt his approach to reality and its ever-changing images (*Sterne*, 247).

Staging the Past: Montage, Temporality, Recovery

Seltsame Sterne portrays the female narrator's life in her late twenties in East and West Berlin during the years 1976 to 1977 and is divided into two parts, characterized by a fragmentary structure. The first part includes quotations from Brecht and Weill songs, Besson's archive notes, and news headlines, while the second part incorporates dialogues, play excerpts, diary entries, original sketches, and notes from Özdamar's time at the Volksbühne. Özdamar intentionally blurs the boundaries between author and narrator, as well as between generic forms—diary, fiction, and autobiography. Throughout both parts she also repeatedly quotes her own work, establishing connections between her literary texts, which, as Liesbeth Minnaard has shown, "refer to and even pre- and re-tell each other." This "web of oeuvre-immanent intertextualities," according to Minnaard, creates a sense of "fictional continuity" albeit "in a rather discontinuous form."[29] In addition to the intertextual connections among her literary writings, Özdamar also establishes linkages between her published interviews and her literary oeuvre. Her interviews, as I show, provide another discourse, where she stages something that is in dialogue with her fictional work. In this sense, Özdamar, like Ören, emphasizes the interrelatedness of all her writing, practicing and promoting an understanding of her literary writing as work-in-progress that resists totality and attests to the openness of the work of art. Just as for Brecht the stage consists of "a montage of mobile elements,"[30] Özdamar's interviews and literary texts comprise mobile elements that reappear in new contexts.

Özdamar's representation of divided Berlin and the events of the German Autumn in *Seltsame Sterne* presents a novel perspective and creates, as various scholars have argued, a new subject of German memory discourse:

the migrant.[31] Reviewers have also pointed to the relationship between Özdamar's literary oeuvre and historiography by reading *Seltsame Sterne* as "memory book"[32] and "a piece of German-German contemporary history."[33] While the novel's engagement with and representation of the past, or rather multiple pasts, is a central aspect of my analysis, I will introduce a change in focus from migration to theater and concentrate on the narrative staging of the past, rather than engaging with interventions into specifically German memory discourses and historiography. Özdamar herself has pointed to the significance of the past for her writing, and has commented extensively on the intersections between biography and fiction, history and literature, and theater and prose in interviews following the publication of *Seltsame Sterne.*

In these conversations, theater emerges as the pivotal aspect around which everything else revolved: from her regular border crossings between East and West, her poetic choices, to her experience of East and West Berlin as a whole. Because of her Turkish citizenship, Özdamar, like Ören and Öngören, had the rare privilege of moving between both parts of Berlin, a frequent topic in her interviews, especially in the aftermath of the publication of *Seltsame Sterne.* One example is her interview with the newspaper *Berliner Zeitung*, where Özdamar said of her impressions of both East and West Berlin "I had this theater gaze."[34] She perceived her frequent border crossings as occurring between two separate stage sets: "I actually commuted between two stages. In the West was the shared flat, in the East the Volksbühne."[35] A year later in an interview with *Die Welt*, she again compared the process of crossing the border to theater: "I normalized the Wall. I experienced what was happening at the border crossing as theater."[36] As narrated in *Seltsame Sterne*, she did not perceive her ability to cross the border as overcoming an obstacle but rather as a path to theater, equating her movement between both parts of Berlin to an on-stage scene change.

While *Die Brücke vom Goldenen Horn* also incorporates news clippings, albeit less frequently, *Seltsame Sterne* is the only novel in which Özdamar included diary entries. For Özdamar this was "dramaturgically important for a country [the GDR] that does not exist anymore."[37] This quotation further attests to the novel's theatricality, which in addition to centering thematically on theater, the Voksbühne in particular, is structurally conceived of in dramatic terms—as for example through its scenic development.

Özdamar and by extension her narrator perceive the Cold War border as theater and in temporal rather than in geopolitical terms. According to Özdamar "The Wall wasn't a stone Wall, it was a time Wall."[38] While experiencing travel between both parts of Berlin as moving between two different stage sets, Özdamar also viewed it as a change in temporality: "I constantly changed into a different time."[39] She further conceived of her movement between East and West Berlin, but also between Turkey and divided Germany, as "Zeitsprünge," leaps in time.[40] Places are thus understood in terms of time and temporality—not through national, geopolitical, and ethno-cultural markers of difference.

Temporality is also significant in terms of Özdamar's intertextual references to music and literature—a pivotal element of her montage practice. Özdamar explained that through her inclusion of poem excerpts by early twentieth-century German-Jewish poet Else Lasker-Schüler in *Seltsame Sterne* she "experienced a different time," a "time before the catastrophes."[41] Literary and musical references thus enable an encounter with different temporalities, while carrying multiple spatiotemporal connotations. This receives special emphasis in *Seltsame Sterne* because of her incorporation of excerpts of Brecht's songs and poems. The multiple media that converge in the novel support the connection between and simultaneity of various temporalities, past and present, Turkish and German, precisely through the rupture with their traditional modes. The text then suggests that the separation of different temporalities (German, Turkish, Istanbul, East and West Berlin) is artificially created to keep them separate. The recurring transnational, transtheatrical, and trans-historical engagement with Brecht thus allows for otherwise impossible connections, proximities, and simultaneities to emerge.

According to Özdamar, writing about the past enables her to "preserve something different, to stage the old world one more time, as if [she] could see it with different layers on stage in order to make it accessible anew and never forget, as a staging."[42] The impetus to preserve the past is linked to the use of dramatic techniques, which reveals the narration of the past as a creative act. In comparing her writing style to the process of staging, Özdamar emphasizes that writing is not so much about a factual preservation of something as it occurred, not an act of reproduction, but an opportunity for rediscovery and a means for a new encounter. And although she admits that her own experiences are the basis for her writing, she explains, "when one starts writing. . .one does not reproduce the past, but rather goes on another journey."[43]

Her approach to the past and its literary preservation is mirrored in her montage practices that bring together seemingly disparate elements— temporalities, places, cultures, but also genres—to create a sense of simultaneity through their recomposition. In each novel, as Özdamar told the *Frankfurter Allgemeine Zeitung*, she covers a certain "time period, in which a story is lived to its end. Like in a fairy tale: Once upon a time there was a 68 movement. Once upon a time there was a Wall. I liked to write about these times. It is also necessary. If you miss this, only statistics remain."[44] We find this thought in various other interviews in slight variation. A year earlier, after the publication of *Seltsame Sterne*, Özdamar highlighted the relationship between literature and the past as follows: "The stories that I tell have all almost become fairy tales: Once upon a time in Turkey, there was a 68 movement. The third book involves a story taking on fairy-tale traits: Once upon a time there was a Wall. If you miss writing in this phase, only statistics remain."[45] This contrasting of writing with statistics thus recurs in multiple interviews and includes, as this last interview excerpt illustrates, the Turkish past. The process of the past turning into a fairy tale is countered through writing, which may rehistoricize that past and thus bring it back into the present, resulting in a convergence of multiple places and temporalities in her literary work. By developing a multifaceted narration in which personal statements are in dialogue with her literary work, Özdamar writes in a mode of history that falls in between dehumanized past in the form of statistics and an idealized, romantic vision in the form of the fairy tale. Her writing can thus be seen as an intervention into the ethics and epistemology of history.

Özdamar, through the narrator in *Seltsame Sterne*, comments on the significance of the past for the present, as mediated through the theater: "In the theater, the dead arise . . . the dead want to continue living, in order to intervene in future (hi)stories of the world."[46] The dead include both characters in the plays as well as their authors. Again, we find this fictional utterance in a similar formulation in an interview: "I am happy after each book, because I found all these people again."[47] Like Brecht, Özdamar thus reutilizes past material in the remaking of the present and future. Moreover, her evocation of theater as space to revive the dead bears a striking resemblance to Heiner Müller's understanding of theater's function as "Totenbeschwörung," necromancy—as a dialogue with the dead that has to continue "until they reveal how much future was buried with them."[48]

Language, Theater, Politics

The narrator's Turkish background and status as immigrant in Özdamar's literary texts have been a key focus in Özdamar scholarship. For example, Monika Shafi reads the narrator in *Die Brücke* as an "unaffected observer of the German scene" but as a "political activist in Istanbul."[49] Moray McGowan presents the narrator in *Seltsame Sterne* as a "quasi-ethnographic participant observer" and "fresh-eyed newcomer."[50] Laura Bradley interprets the narrator's fascination with Brecht and her perspective on the GDR as that of an "outsider."[51] Rather than reading the narrator's experience in terms of migratory experience and therefore her perception of divided Berlin in juxtaposition to her Turkish past, I propose to shift the focus to Özdamar's continued engagement with theater and theatrical activity, which are manifest in her montage practice and the use of music.

The narrator's (continued) engagement with Brechtian theater in *Seltsame Sterne* is marked by active participation and involvement. Her engagement was triggered by a Turkish dramatist and it developed further in drama school and theater ensembles in Turkey, prior to her time at the Volksbühne. Throughout *Seltsame Sterne* the narrator studies Brecht's writings and practice of theater, translates archival notes at the Volksbühne, and composes her own sketches and notes on three particular productions during rehearsals and performances, thus highlighting the staging of theater as a work-in-progress, to which she contributes.[52] The narrator's preoccupation with "theater aesthetics" is furthermore an important topic within the narrative. For instance, on the basis of the collages, notes, and sketches she created, she is admitted to the Université Paris VIII Vincennes to write a doctoral thesis on "theater aesthetics" focusing on the Volksbühne. An excerpt of the original outline of the proposal, including director Frank Castorf's suggestions to Özdamar and his and the narrator's notes, is included in the text, and underlines the significance of the *Volksbühnenbewegung* of the Weimar period for contemporary practices. Incorporated as a fragment, comprising only the first page, and left without comment within the narrative, the conceptualization of the project focuses on an understanding of present practices as a "recourse to the artistic, militant-operative tradition of the Volksbühne movement" through the work of Besson, Langhoff, and Marquardt (*Sterne*, 241). The fact that the narrator works on the translation of Besson's archive notes about his *Szechwan* production (as well as taking notes at other performances) in order to send them to her Turkish theater friends further emphasizes the work-in-progress notion. For it is the Turkish Brechtians, in this case Öngören and his collaborators, who will transform these notes into a play.[53]

In chapter 1 I traced the significance of Brecht for the emergence of a national Turkish political theater tradition. Özdamar, a participant in the Turkish interpretation and implementation of Brecht, has herself repeatedly called attention to the significance of Brecht in the Turkish context: "I belong to the 68ers. This movement also existed in Turkey and is unthinkable without Brecht, whom we adored."[54] Her first encounter with Brecht is narrated in *Die Brücke vom Goldenen Horn*. Her hostel warden Öngören, a central figure in the narrator's politicization, introduced her to authors such as Rosa Luxemburg, Maxim Gorky, Fyodor Dostoyevsky, and Friedrich Engels and took her to the theater, including the Berliner Ensemble and the

Berlin-based Turkish workers' party. During this stay in West Berlin she purchases the two Brecht records (by Ernst Busch and Lotte Lenya) that figure so centrally in *Seltsame Sterne* and that will accompany her to Turkey and back to divided Germany, thus bridging various temporalities and places. *Die Brücke vom Goldenen Horn* also documents the narrator's collaboration with Öngören in Turkey, referring to his successful play How Can Asiye be saved? (staged by his Birlik Sahne in Ankara and Istanbul) as the "politische[s] Hurenstück"[55] (political whore play) in which the narrator, like Özdamar herself, performed. The genesis of this play also was marked by movement and transitions between East and West Berlin and Turkey—Öngören began to write it while in Germany and completed it in Turkey. *Die Brücke vom Goldenen Horn* also recounts the closing of Öngören's theater and the arrest of members of his ensemble during the *Asiye* performance (*Brücke*, 303). Beyond the experiences with Öngören, the novel gives further insight into the narrator's time at drama school in Istanbul, introducing her teachers, the "Körperist" (body man) und "Kopfist" (head man), the latter the Brechtian teacher who urges the students, including the narrator, to analyze history (*Brücke*, 205, 209). At drama school Brechtian historical analysis is contrasted with method acting,[56] an opposition that possibly mirrored that between Taner and Algan, the latter having studied method acting in New York. However throughout the text theaters, directors, and plays remain unnamed, appearing indirectly or merely as deictic references.

In addition to these indirect references to the Turkish reception of Brecht, his poems and songs recur as intertexts in Özdamar's literary texts as well as her interviews. The following lines from "Nannas Lied" (Nanna's Song, 1936) are especially striking: "Thank the Lord the whole thing's quickly over, all the loving and the sorrow, my dear. Where are the teardrops you wept last evening? Where are the snows of yesteryear?"[57] Brecht's words were a source of comfort and "promised a utopia,"[58] as Özdamar explains, and, as is expressed in the preceding lines of "Nannas Lied," also a hope for better times. The utopia promised by Brecht's words in "Nanna's Lied" to Özdamar while in Istanbul became a reality in Berlin: "What Brecht's song promised me in Istanbul, really happened in Berlin."[59]

The German language, via literature and theater, afforded a kind of refuge from the militarist regime in Turkey. The 1970s in Turkey were characterized by political unrest and terror. Accusing the Süleyman Demirel regime of failing to solve the country's economic and social problems, the Turkish military intervened once again in 1971. This time the military did not dissolve the government and parties as it had in 1960, but it nullified basic democratic rights and overruled fundamental freedom de facto. Thousands of democrats and socialists were imprisoned, and the Turkish

Workers' Party (TIP), democratic and socialist organizations, oppositional newspapers, magazines, and publishing houses were banned. The repression of any group that was considered leftist, especially the workers' party and its union, and the oppression of political opposition to the military regime in general constituted the backdrop for all legal amendments.[60] Özdamar extensively describes this tumultuous period in the final pages of *Die Brücke vom Goldenen Horn*: "For people, the streets were forbidden. ... They banned unions and assemblies. The police arrested and tortured. ... The police searched houses for leftist books" (*Brücke*, 311). In the face of political oppression, prosecution, and intimidation, as evidenced by these preceding lines, Özdamar's narrator leaves for Berlin.

The language of Brecht was also the incentive for Özdamar's immigration to Germany, as she claims in an interview:

> I had the feeling that my Turkish words had become sick. They say that you lose your mother tongue in a foreign country. But you can also lose your mother tongue in your own country. ... That's why I wanted to go to Germany and work with a Brecht pupil. Because Brecht has a language. Perhaps, I hoped that my sick Turkish words would thereby recover.[61]

Early in *Seltsame Sterne*, Özdamar's narrator similarly anthropomorphizes her Turkish words as "krank," sick, as in the interview excerpt: "I am unhappy in my language. For years, we have been saying only sentences like: They will hang them. Where were the heads? No one knows where their graves are. They did not release the corpse! The words are sick. My words need a sanatorium" (*Sterne*, 23). In need of a "sanatorium" for the Turkish language, the narrator, like Özdamar, emigrated to Germany and involved herself with German theater: with Brecht's legacy, to be precise. As Özdamar said in an interview "I wanted to know what Brecht left with his students."[62]

Özdamar relates both her own and the narrator's inability to express themselves in their mother tongue directly to the dictatorship in Turkey— its censorship, violence, and political oppression. We already see this in *Die Brücke vom Goldenen Horn*, where the narrator states, "I could not speak anymore, every word in my mouth hurt" (*Brücke*, 327). As Yasemin Yildiz has convincingly argued, for Özdamar "German is the language in which a traumatic story can be told, rather than being a traumatized or traumatizing language." Yildiz further demonstrates how "the translational exchange between the two tongues creates a constellation in which German offers the means to remember and rework a Turkish trauma—a trauma brought on by state violence, but brought to language in migration."[63] My reading of Özdamar extends Yildiz's focus by looking at how music, in addition to and beyond language, offers a means to recover from the Turkish past, while simultaneously functioning to process the German present and link it to the past. Music, for Özdamar, like language, is perceived in theatrical terms, establishing continuities between the narrator's Turkish past and her German present, between Istanbul and divided Berlin.

For Özdamar's narrator, Istanbul as a result of political turmoil and the impossibility of continuing work at the theater, has become the city of "darkness," while East Berlin is experienced as "pretty," with a "soft heart" (*Sterne*, 124, 138). But above all the East stands for "theater sentences in the work notes" to Besson's *Szechwan* production, yet another indication of the importance of theater for Özdamar's representation and imagination of East Berlin (*Sterne*, 68). At the same time, theater connects Istanbul to East Berlin: "Drama school Istanbul and East Berlin. Same costumes, same gestures. The two schools are 2000 kilometers apart from each other" (*Sterne*, 193). Although she regularly crosses the border, she admits: "In Berlin I never thought of the Wall" (*Sterne*, 244). The narrator's involvement with theater, where she had "become happy," allows her to realize her goals in a way that was denied to her in Istanbul. But as her friend Gabi notes: "Yes, but your happiness is not the happiness of others. You are normalizing the Wall. For you living here means an expansion of your possibilities to work and live. Others perceive their possibilities as restricted" (*Sterne*, 182). Her East German friends feel in East Berlin the same limitation she felt in Istanbul, which for the narrator, in contrast, has become the place where her theater career can develop most fully.

Özdamar's montage of news clippings and diary entries, disjointed from the narrative text, disrupts the narrative flow, leaves political events, occurrences, and ensuing debates uncommented, and emphasizes the narrator's presumed detachment from the East German political reality and constraints experienced and felt by those around her. On the rare occasions in *Seltsame Sterne* when she addresses the political concerns voiced by those surrounding her, she finds herself outside the conversation, without access to what is being said: "When Müller, Maron, and Gabi speak, I feel like I am in a foreign language course" (*Sterne*, 202). B. Venkat Mani has interpreted the narrator's detachment as "interested, but not excited; disengaged and studiedly detached but not aloof."[64] Claudia Breger on the other hand has argued that through montage Özdamar "provides the reader with opportunities to repeatedly reevaluate complex, overdetermined constellations."[65] Taking Breger's observation as a point of departure, I perceive the narrator's detachment as a dramatic strategy. The narrator's detachment emerges from the novel's montage structure: diary entries, news headlines, and notes are incorporated but without the intervention of explanatory narrative sequences in between to achieve coherence and totality. However, as I will illustrate, Özdamar represents the narrator and her experiences of and interactions with her surroundings through montage, juxtaposing political theoretical discourse and theatrical practice.

The narrator's detachment from political discourse and theoretical discussions is already present in *Die Brücke vom Goldenen Horn* and therefore not specific to her experience in Germany as newcomer or migrant.[66] Various instances in *Die Brücke vom Goldenen Horn* present the narrator as similarly detached in the context of theoretical-political conversation, where in cubist fashion she glues words together to make sense of what she hears those around her say. On other occasions the narrator feels like an actress who has forgotten her text or like a spectator outside the conversation (*Brücke*, 231, 233). As in the passage in *Seltsame Sterne* quoted earlier, in *Die Brücke vom Goldenen Horn* Özdamar already uses the analogy to a "foreign language course" to indicate the abstractness of political theory and discourse. Here the narrator compares the language of various Turkish newspapers to "Fremdsprachen," foreign languages (*Brücke*, 296). Although all the newspapers are published in Turkish, their political content, orientation, and ideological differences made them appear as if written in "three foreign languages": leftist, fascist, and religious (*Brücke*, 296). The foreignness of language emanates from its use and function in theoretical and political discourses and not as a result of the binary juxtaposition between foreign and native. Political discourse, as perceived by the narrator in both *Die Brücke vom Goldenen Horn* and *Seltsame Sterne*, is presented as foreign and as opposite to practice. The categories of foreign and national, local and global are subverted in her writings, as the montage of temporalities, places, images, and music creates a multiplicity of convergences in Özdamar's representation of divided Berlin and its connection to Turkey.

In various interviews, as well as in *Seltsame Sterne*, Özdamar has attributed the narrator's, and her own, reason for emigration to the theater to the incentive to leave for Berlin to work with Besson, as the quote at the beginning of this chapter indicates. However, her reason for leaving is also based on the impossibility of continuing her work in the theater in Turkey.[67] The closing of Öngören's theater becomes a reason to leave, because in Turkey "words could not be staged anymore."[68] Theater is presented as a necessity; it was not only the impetus to leave, but might also be the motivation for a possible return to Turkey, as the narrator admits in *Seltsame Sterne*: "If I could work at the theater in Istanbul, I would go back" (*Sterne*, 124). For Özdamar, theater is a "staging of words" that enunciates a discursive space for political action—an endeavor that political turmoil and oppression had rendered impossible in Turkey, but which was still possible at the

Volksbühne through Besson's theater work. Yet Özdamar seeks to employ Brecht's dramatic language, a language of the theater that (in her view) is practically oriented, concerned with action, rather than preoccupied with obscure, theoretical disputation. She explains "I was not political in the traditional sense. The theater was my political place. Not theory."[69] Brecht's language as conceived by Özdamar and as manifest in her prose encompasses his dramaturgy, theory, poems, songs, and plays.

Her experience of the German language is rooted in theater, because Özdamar's "first encounter with German was via the theater."[70] Not only did drama help her to achieve access to German language and literature; it also enabled her to express herself in the foreign language, as she admits, "I am certain that these dramatists [Kleist, Büchner, Brecht] did a lot to lure my words into the open."[71] In addition to allowing her mother tongue to "recuperate," her immersion in German drama thus served as a point of entry to the German language and a catalyst for own writing.

German theater also provides Özdamar with a connection to the life she had to leave behind. In numerous interviews she explains how her involvement with theater in Germany and with German dramatic literature allowed her to keep a connection to Turkey: "German theater, its plays, seemed to me like an extension of my country."[72] Later Özdamar elaborated: "But I never felt like an emigrant ... because Büchner and Brecht are also staged in Turkey."[73] German drama thus generates a sense of continuity, constancy, and above all familiarity between Turkey and divided Germany. Through drama, Özdamar finds a means in East Berlin to maintain, revive, and continue a part of her life that she had been forced to abandon in Turkey. In *Seltsame Sterne* this continuation is realized through Brecht: His *Mann ist Mann* (*Man Equals Man*) at Öngören's theater is the last play the narrator performed before emigrating, and upon arriving in Berlin, her first destination is the Volksbühne in order to learn Brechtian theater.[74] Theater thus links the narrator's various experiences in Turkey and East Germany in the second and third part of her trilogy. Theater frames the narrative of the *Die Brücke vom Goldenen Horn*. It marks the beginning of the novel where the narrator states "theater is my life," and concludes the novel with her decision to leave for Berlin to work with Besson (*Brücke*, 12). *Die Brücke vom Goldenen Horn* thematically connects to *Seltsame Sterne* through its focus on the theater and the narrator's wish to learn Brechtian theater from Besson.

Theater, in addition to being an important setting within *Seltsame Sterne*, also figures as a metaphor for the city of Berlin itself, and on a metalevel functions as the narrator's gateway to the German past and language as well as her means to connect her various experiences (past, present, Turkish,

East and West German). Theater becomes a lens through which surroundings are experienced, and thus is the aesthetic manifestation of Özdamar's theater gaze, pointed out in the aforementioned interview. Sonja Klocke has drawn our attention to how in the novel East and West Berlin function like a revolving stage, in order to "interchangeably produce images" of either city section.[75] The revolving stage, a "theatrical device for scene changes, or shifts, by which three or more settings are constructed on a turntable around a central pivot and revolved before the audience,"[76] was a prominent device in Brecht's *Mother Courage* production. It allowed for quick scene changes, and it was also "episierend," epicizing, because while Courage moves forward throughout the play, her movement is presented as circular.[77] For Brecht, the stage construction developed out of the plot of the play. In this way both halves of Berlin, despite being represented by different stage sets, work together to function as a whole, linking disparate times and places in their staging.[78] As the narrator commutes daily between East and West Berlin, once she enters the East, she acknowledges, "West Berlin is again a thousand years behind me" (*Sterne*, 169). When she moves from one part of the city to the other, echoing Özdamar's earlier interview remarks, the setting she leaves behind disappears and remains static—like the stage set that disappears with the movement of the revolving stage. In *Cosmopolitical Claims*, B. Venkat Mani refers to this kind of temporary oblivion as effecting an "instant amnesia."[79] Upon her return, the narrator continues where she left off, highlighting the stagedness of the distance she felt between the two halves of the city. It is therefore always the narrator who—whether by walking or by remembering—gives life to settings in East or West Berlin or Istanbul. She only conceives of either city section's existence when she is physically there, within it: "Every time I came here, I forgot the other part of the city, as if a large sea divided these two parts from one another" (*Sterne*, 18). Istanbul, on the other hand, is projected onto both parts of divided Berlin through the act of remembrance. In terms of the mise-en-scène, one can imagine a screen on stage reproducing images of her past in Istanbul. The use of filmic projections is linked to theater, figuring most prominently in the narrator's perception of the cities, and thus establishes a threefold connection that drives the narrative and unpacks Özdamar's connections to Istanbul, divided Berlin, and the past.

Through the inscription of Turkish memories onto both parts of Berlin, Özdamar creates non-chronological and non-linear links between Istanbul and divided Berlin. Despite the patent differences that emerge as the cities are narrated in her text, the geographic, ideological, and physical boundaries within and between them appear porous and fluid. Özdamar's writing thus not only crosses national boundaries but also investigates them and contests their limitations through staging.

In an interview with Dave Horrocks and Eva Kolinsky, Özdamar describes her early experiences in Cold War Germany as follows:

> Whether you want to or not, you find yourself in two places at once. On the one hand you have the experience of your everyday existence in the new land, which is long and drawn out but has gaps in it; on the other hand you have sudden memories of the land you came from. But the whole thing runs like a simultaneous film in which images and yearnings merge without any gaps. When the two come together in this way, it makes for a beautiful encounter.[80]

Özdamar sets up a contrast between her German present and her Turkish past. She compares her sudden memories of her home country to a movie that runs simultaneously with her present. Her Turkish memories appear as flashes simultaneous with her present experiences in Germany, which are characterized by a sense of incompleteness—by "gaps" still to be filled. Her present in divided Berlin is in progress, whereas her past in Turkey is concluded. There seems to be no dominant storyline, but a continuous merging through montage. Özdamar, like Brecht, affirms the past's significance in the making of a new present.

Her Turkish past's structural resemblance to a film—a series of continuously running images—receives special emphasis in *Seltsame Sterne*. Here, memories of Istanbul are frequently superimposed upon the narrator's experiences of Berlin. Specifically, these passages take the form of analepses, introducing snapshots (and soundscapes) of her past in Turkey. As a result, the three cities—her past in Istanbul and her present in East and West Berlin—merge with each other, sutured together by acts of remembrance, which enable her to experience all three places simultaneously.

Music, Time, Space

In addition to metaphors emanating from the theater (already present in *Die Brücke vom Goldenen Horn*), from prompters, stage props, scene changes, and forgotten scripts, to pedestrians viewed as spectators, all used to characterize the narrator's experience of her surroundings, sounds and music play a significant role within the novel in her perception and representation of divided Berlin and their connection to Istanbul: "The voices of Berlin: The alarm clock. Birds' twittering, motors, children, streetcar. The voices of Istanbul: water sellers, candy sellers, grain sellers, white canes on the pavement, the suddenly soaring pigeons, seagulls' cries, honking ships at the Bosporus, the chirping of the crickets, cats on the roofs, etc." (*Sterne*, 147). Though it does not refer to specific parts of either city, the description of the various voices belonging to them allows the reader to visualize the images belonging to these evocations of sound collages. Juxtaposed within the text, placed in quick succession, these soundscapes are emblematic of both cities.

The centrality of music in Özdamar's works should not come as surprise, given Brecht's own relationship with music, and music's significance in his oeuvre. As Kim H. Kowalke notes, "Only one of his nearly fifty completed dramatic works lacks music. Over 600 of his more than 1,500 poems refer to musical genres in title or structure."[81] Against the "attempts to hypnotize"[82] inherent in other forms of theater, Brecht always insisted on music's complete independence and defined its interpretive function as "comment[ing] in its own manner on the themes dealt with."[83] In 1956, shortly before his death, Brecht reiterated that within theater, poetry, music, and image offer a threefold treatment of the topic, thus forming a "collective of independent arts."[84] Both the intermediality and the coexistence of genres in his works are emphasized through the inclusion of music.

In *Seltsame Sterne*, songs by Brecht, Eisler, Weill, and Biermann are central to the experience and representation of each city and their relationship to each other. Significant in Özdamar's trilogy is "Das Lied von der Moldau" (The Song of the Moldau), which is part of Brecht's *Schweyk im Zweiten Weltkrieg* (*Schweyk in the Second World War*, 1943), a "resistance play" he wrote while in exile[85] and for which Hanns Eisler composed the musical setting. Coming at the end of the play, the song is, to quote Mark Roche, an "assertion of the passage of time, the destruction of the powerful, and the renewal of society."[86] Early in *Seltsame Sterne* Özdamar's narrator sings the following lines from this song: "The great shall not stay great, the darkness is lifting. The night has twelve hours, but at last comes the day" (*Sterne*, 27).[87] After the Turkish military searches the narrator's home in Istanbul, this song promises hope and optimism, and eventually a change in power structures.

In Brecht's play, the character of Anna Kopecka sings "Das Lied von der Moldau" after the SS searched and demolished her bar "Zum Kelch" in Prague. By situating this song in *Seltsame Sterne* right after the military search, Özdamar creates an analogy between the Turkish military regime and the German fascist dictatorship in Brecht's *Schweyk im Zweiten Weltkrieg*. As German fascism was eventually defeated, the hope is that the oppressive Turkish military regime will be as well. In an interview, Eisler calls the "Song of the Moldau" a *Lichtstrahl*, a ray of light, which "suggests a way out, the solution." He then continues "And what does this song say? That after only twelve hours, the day breaks—nothing but the simple laws of nature. Impossible to give more hope in this moment. This is cold comfort, but also a necessary minimum. They say: Our life is changing, as days and times change—no more and no less."[88] Repeatedly emphasizing the comforting nature of Brecht's works, Özdamar incorporates "Das Lied von der Moldau" in *Seltsame Sterne* precisely because of its ability to provide hope and consolation as pointed out by Eisler. The resistance against fascism links Özdamar's experiences with Brecht's: "And Brecht's experience with fascism became my experience in Turkey as well."[89] It is worth pointing out that Özdamar in fascist Turkey takes recourse to Brecht's use of music. Throughout his exile during the 1930s and 1940s the "mobilization of antifascist forces through the means of music, theater, and literature" was a significant incentive for Brecht, and together with Eisler he collaborated on a collection of songs, *Bertolt Brecht-Hanns Eisler: Lieder, Gedichte, Chöre* which was published in 1934 by one of the most important exile publishing houses. The collection was intended to encourage emigrants and antifascists in the resistance to sing.[90] In addition to occupying a central role in her prose and the narrator's experience of Turkish fascism, Özdamar, in an interview, shared that she, like her narrator, sang these songs to her Turkish friends.[91]

Another song relevant to *Seltsame Sterne* is "O Falladah, die du hangest!" (*O Falladah, There You Are Hanging*). The narrator hears it for the first time when her roommate, Peter, who has become her "Stadtführer" (city guide) sings it in East Berlin while they are walking down Frankfurter Allee together; and later in the novel she sings it to her lover, Graham (*Sterne*, 78). This song, based on a Brecht poem, was set to music by Eisler in 1932. The date of composition is not clear, although Brecht hand-dated the poem to 1919 and set it in the context of postwar famine and revolution.[92]

Frankfurter Allee does not seem to be a random choice by Özdamar, for it is also the setting of the poem. When Brecht wrote the poem, it was a central transit axis, but also a site of poverty, crime, and prostitution in Berlin. He knew the area well from his visits to his friend and colleague Alfred Döblin, who had lived there since 1919. After the Second World War, it was one of the most completely destroyed areas of Berlin and was chosen by the East German government as a starting point for reconstruction. Karl-Marx-Allee, which is an extension of Frankfurter Allee, was the location of the Karl-Marx-Buchhandlung, a socialist bookstore. There Brecht participated in the first *Schriftstellerbasar* (writers' convention) in 1953 where publishing houses showcased new publications with the writers present for book signings. In the novel, Özdamar's narrator regularly passes this bookstore on her way to the Volksbühne. She thus retraces Brecht's steps in Berlin by visiting sites that were significant for him: the Volksbühne, the Karl-Marx-Buchhandlung, the Berliner Ensemble, and his grave at the Dorotheenstädtischer Friedhof. Through the use of songs Özdamar unveils the multiple pasts that exist in their plurality within the present as a multi-layered formation.

Besides visiting the places Brecht frequented in the past, the narrator attends the theater regularly to watch his and other plays. After her arrival in Berlin, one of the first plays she watches in East Berlin is Brecht's didactic play *Die Mutter* (*The Mother*, 1931), for which Eisler again composed the music. While watching the play, the narrator frantically takes notes. Excerpts from the song "Wie die Krähe" (Like the Crow) sung by the chorus made up of revolutionary workers, are incorporated as intertext.[93] We encounter the same text passage in *Die Brücke* at the factory in West Berlin, thus establishing a connection between the West German past and the East German present of the narrative (*Brücke*, 91). Furthermore, the incorporation of excerpts from the chorus contributes to a Brechtian articulation of the past in the present. According to Brecht, choruses "are intended to invite the spectator to form his/her own opinion, call for his/her emancipation toward a represented world and representation itself"[94] which seems to be mirrored in the distance and detachment evident in Özdamar's narrator throughout the novel. The recurrence of song excerpts mirrors Brecht's own practice of repurposing and reworking material. It is a battle song, a *Kampflied*, located right at the beginning of Brecht's play. For Eisler, the battle song had to serve the purpose of "galvanization for the struggle and political education."[95] Therefore its characteristics were determined as follows: "great comprehensibility, easy legibility, and resolute precise position," at the same time underlining that the form is dependent on the content of each musical piece.[96] On the function of music in *Die Mutter*, Brecht concurs: "Far more deliberately than in any other play of the epic theater, the music in *Die Mutter* was designed to induce in the spectator [a] critical approach. . . . In a remarkable manner it [Eisler's music] makes possible a certain simplification of the toughest problems, whose solution is a life and death matter for the working class."[97]

While the narrator in *Seltsame Sterne* does not really engage with the song excerpt she is noting down, her repeated involvement with political songs and theater throughout the novel begs us to reconsider her perceived silence and detachment vis-à-vis German political reality. Brecht's collaborative songs with Eisler already constituted a constant companion for the narrator in Turkey, where they matched and reflected the narrator's commitment to and involvement in left-wing politics. While the instances of the narrator's reception of Brecht/Eisler songs remain uncommented upon, they implicitly reveal her political orientation, especially because they are linked to theater. In addition to Brecht's elaboration on the use of music in *Die Mutter*, in his original staging directions he requested that texts and visual materials be projected onto a screen—a technique Özdamar also emulates in *Seltsame Sterne* through the snapshot-like incorporation of Istanbul memories and the interpolation of newspaper clippings and other documentary materials.[98] Brecht conceived of visual and filmic material as an "optischer Chor," optic chorus, underscoring that their function was similar to that of music on the stage, as another independent representation of the topic.[99] In *Seltsame Sterne* Özdamar uses both as independent but interlinked stage practices in her staging of the Turkish past, in relation to the narrated German present, which at the time of publication is past, historicizing the events in a Brechtian fashion.

In her shared apartment in Wedding in West Berlin, "an old workers' district, where communists fought behind the barricades," the narrator and her roommates regularly listen to (unspecified) records by Brecht (*Sterne*, 48). Other songs that surface in Wedding are the "The International," sung by their neighbor, the "old communist Alfredo," and Kurt Weill's "Berlin im Licht" (Berlin in Lights) sung by Manfred, the narrator's roommate (*Sterne*, 164). "Berlin im Licht" was jointly written with Brecht for the four-day festival *Berlin im Licht* held in October 1928, "which celebrated both the ultramodern shop-window lighting and neon advertisements of the city center ... and the city's illuminated monuments and commercial buildings."[100] It is worth noting that the historical landmarks and buildings illuminated in the 1920s may not have existed in the aftermath of the Second World War. In contrast to the Brecht/Eisler songs, this Weill song celebrates Berlin's glamour and similarity to cities such as Paris and London. In addition to the songs with which Özdamar's narrator was already familiar, her new experiences in divided Berlin come with new songs, suggesting another temporality, Berlin's past (prior to its division), in this case Berlin during the Weimar period (a Berlin before Hitler that will never come back).

Brecht's songs and plays establish a continuity and constant in the narrator's life as they accompany her from Istanbul to East and West Berlin. In addition to the Brecht songs, the narrator's musical encounters include Wolf Biermann, a protégé of Eisler's. Biermann's music, without specific detail, is only mentioned in the context of his expulsion from the GDR in November 1976. It causes great agitation among the narrator's friends and colleagues, mediated through diary entries, once again left uncommented. Biermann's expatriation, in fact, marked a turning point for many theater practitioners in the East, when various directors and dramatists, including Müller and Langhoff, signed a petition asking the GDR government to reconsider their decision.[101] Besson, whose involvement in Heiner Müller's work had brought him into conflict with GDR cultural policy, decided to leave East Germany shortly after the Biermann affair, accompanied by Özdamar.[102] The GDR Kulturministerium and Brecht's heirs were increasingly imped- ing his work at the theater; this is captured by a brief diary entry in *Seltsame Sterne* (*Sterne*, 233). While the narrator leaves this part uncommented, nar- rative distance should not be equated with indifference, particularly in light of the significance of theater as the primary political arena. Furthermore, Biermann, who had been discovered by Eisler at the Berliner Ensemble in the late 1950s, "sought to recuperate Brecht from the heritage industry that promoted him" and "projected an image of Brecht that clashed with the SED-approved icon" by using material from Brecht's work to comment criti- cally on the GDR.[103] Biermann represents, along with Langhoff, Besson, and Müller, another seminal figure who transformed Brecht's work.

In addition to songs with clear roots in the history of the German work- ing class and protest songs, Mozart and Schubert are mentioned in passing: "Schubert saddens, Mozart does not" (*Sterne*, 197). Introduced to Schubert's music by the influential political figure and dissident East German writer Rudolf Bahro, who is listening to his music as they talk, the narrator decides to buy a record by the composer (*Sterne*, 91; 92). While Schubert is play- ing in the background, Bahro criticizes the GDR's governing elite. In this instance what affects the narrator and elicits an emotional response is the music, rather than the topic of conversation.

While Brecht helps her to process Turkish oppression, Mozart serves as a source of comfort when she is nostalgic for Istanbul: "Oh, beautiful years, to be on stage in Berlin, Josef, oh, forest in Istanbul, oh, the dead, the killed. I did not go backwards, I fled forward, all is good. The loneliness is useful, even if sometimes in the afternoon it is difficult, when I come home. Then I listen to Mozart, and I feel better" (*Sterne*, 104). Here the narrator ideal- izes Mozart as providing an emotional refuge. She does not name specific compositions, instead merely mentioning the names of these two particular composers and the emotional response they elicit. And although she does not explain why these two composers have different effects on her, classical music, like the Brecht songs, also serves as a constant in her experience of divided Berlin and its relationship to Turkey.

In the novel music also functions as a metaphor for her perception of Berlin. East and West Berlin seem to be mutually incommensurate to her: "I could not think both parts together. . . . To envision both parts as a whole was as difficult as visualizing Freddy Quinn and Mozart on one record" (*Sterne*, 18). Although she juxtaposes the divided parts with each other by contrasting *Schlager* (pop songs) and classical music, Istanbul serves as the link to and between both parts. Furthermore, music figures as the common denominator for all three cities. This is further manifest in the representation of East and West Berlin as separate stage sets, part of a revolving stage, including projections of Istanbul onto both parts. The instances where the narrator sings or listens to music pass without comment, and she mentions the music simply as part of an enumeration of events, thus setting up music as part of the montage (through which a multiplicity of genres, media, places, and temporalities are set in proximity). Music enables the narrator to connect all three cities on the aural level. Her mapping of divided Berlin and its connection to Istanbul is thus not only physically but also aurally constituted. In the Brechtian sense, music serves as an independent medium to present and comment on the theme on its own, but in conjunction with the narrative it provides another means of connecting various temporalities.

Conclusion

By highlighting the interconnectedness of Özdamar's engagement with and in the theater, particularly Brecht's legacy in various geopolitical contexts, in East Berlin, Bochum, Istanbul, and Ankara, in this chapter I examined her transtheatrical experiences as a source of influence for her prose. The Istanbul-Berlin trilogy chronicles this engagement particularly through its second and third parts, the latter being the main focus of this chapter. The narrator's encounter and engagement with Brecht is represented as spanning more than two decades and is marked by continuous movement between divided Germany and Turkey, aesthetically manifesting itself in the constant linking of the three larger geopolitical entities, East and West Germany and Turkey. By focusing on the continuities in Özdamar's and the narrator's theatrical experiences, my analysis introduced a shift from a focus on labor migration as historic context for her work to theater.

My analysis further illustrated how Özdamar's fictional work stands in dialogue with her interviews, which adds another dimension to her dramatic aesthetic of using montage practices and blurring genre boundaries. Her works are therefore related to each other through intertexual references, including her interviews, with the factual embedded in the fictional and vice versa. Montage is the literary device through which an interconnectedness and at the same time openness of her texts are realized, and topics, themes, facts, and stories are put in new contexts, allowing for a continued development and (re)reading of her work. Theater emerges as the common denominator, thematically and structurally, in fiction and interviews, for past and present. Through its relationship to interview comments, theater is presented as her political medium and form. Özdamar's works thus emerge as a political act in which writing the past not only serves as a means to preserve, but also as a way to bring back the past for present consideration.

Özdamar's theatrical approach is based on her continued engagement with Brecht, which encompasses his work on theater in both theory and practice, with a particular focus on music. Despite the narrator's movement between cities and countries, the narrative constellations Özdamar stages highlight continuities and similarities emanating from theatrical practice, not immigration. Furthermore, the narrator's clearly represented detachment becomes an active political position in the face of political songs and theater, but also in relation to figures she engages with who were culturally and politically significant in challenging the status quo. Whereas Besson, Langhoff, Müller, Karge, and Biermann are considered critical of the GDR regime, with their artistic and theatrical work impeded by the government, Özdamar's narrator's detached position allows her to both engage with politics through theater and to preserve a reconstructed memory of those events through her narration.

On the one hand, Özdamar's narrator appears to be oblivious to the division of Berlin by the Wall. She contrasts East and West with each other, as seen in the juxtaposition of pop and classical music, and she prefers the East over the West as the location of theater. But what finally links these two cities is her memories of Istanbul as they are summoned during her experience of both Berlins. By presenting the city's division as artificial or superficial, both Berlins' evocation of her Istanbul memories places them on common ground with respect to one another. Furthermore, theater establishes continuities between Istanbul and East Berlin, while also highlighting similarities that emanate from her work in theater.

As we have seen, Özdamar's literary topography of Berlin constitutes the city as a site with transnational affiliations and associations, in which the city's places emerge as dynamic, transformative, and multilayered in signification. In Özdamar's text, the topography of divided Berlin is being appropriated and made habitable for all the narrator's attachments. This transnational topography of divided Berlin is not only legible but also audible, and highlights snapshots of her Istanbul past and Brechtian traces of her present. Music, in addition to language, enables the narrator to overcome her traumatic past and permits access to her German present, linking Istanbul to Berlin, East and West, on a spatial, political, and temporal level, disavowing hegemonically established separations between the three cities in the context of the Cold War.

Conclusion

THE FOCUS OF THIS BOOK HAS BEEN literary encounters between Turkish and German writers and theater intellectuals. The discussion began in the 1950s with the Erlangen student theater festival, which preceded the labor recruitment contract between Turkey and Germany in 1961 that marked the beginning of large-scale Turkish (labor) immigration to West Germany. In this book I have uncovered the significant influence of Turkish cultural-political debates and literary practices on German cultural traditions in the decades since the Second World War, showing how international collaboration and exchange focusing on Brecht proved central for negotiations of the relationship between aesthetics and politics in the German and Turkish public spheres. The Turkish Brecht reception, as the first chapter illuminated, drew from a variety of intersecting discourses and practices, on the national and international level, that thought beyond Cold War divisions, and consulted Brechtian theory and practice as it took shape in both East and West German institutions. Turkish dramatists and directors, I argued there, emphasized the necessity of adapting Brechtian concepts to address national concerns as well as political and historical events, and of placing them in dialogue with Turkish aesthetic traditions and the Turkish literary left.

Even as I explored the significance of the Turkish archive for Turkish-German and German studies, my analysis also revealed its continued relevance for studying the work that prominent Turkish-German writers Aras Ören and Emine Sevgi Özdamar wrote after their emigration to Germany. Furthermore, my analysis highlighted the cultural effects of Turkish immigration and the inscription of Turkish subjects into German discourses of working-class culture and literary politics beyond ethnicity and nationality in divided Germany. Ören's involvement in leftist artist circles foregrounded the collaboration between intellectuals and the working class. With Brecht's work at their very center, these debates focused on the intersection between aesthetics and politics. Ören introduced Turkish workers into German discourses on labor protest and working-class solidarity, presenting them as catalysts for change, providing a counter-perspective to predominant presentations of Turks as mute others in the German public. His preoccupation with Brecht, as I have illustrated, predated his move to West Berlin in

1969 and was rooted in his theater career. This career included Ören's work with the Gençlik Tiyatrosu ensemble, his participation in the Erlangen and Istanbul theater festivals, and his activities as a member of the Neue Bühne Frankfurt, all important venues. Ören's engagement with Brecht began in the context of his theater work in Turkey and continued after his move to West Berlin in a variety of formats, such as the multi-genre Berlin trilogy, but also in his unpublished learning play. He presents the Turkish role within the German labor activism movement in relation to contemporary debates on racism. Specifically, Ören foregrounds the necessity of solidarity in the fight against the exploitation of labor, despite ethnic and national differences, returning to a focus on class.

Prior to her literary breakthrough in Germany with *Mutterzunge* (1990), Emine Sevgi Özdamar moved in Turkish literary circles that included prominent figures such as Nedim Gürsel, Mustafa Irgat, Can Yücel, and Memet Fuat. Her book on Ece Ayhan, *"Kendi Kendinin Terzisi Bir Kambur": Ece Ayhan'lı Anılar, 1974 Zürih Günlüğü, Ece Ayhan'ın Mektupları* ("The Hunchback as His Own Tailor": Memories of Ece Ayhan, 1974 Zurich Diary, Ece Ayhan's Letters, 2007), the only work she wrote in Turkish, discusses this period. In it, letters and diary entries attest to the reciprocal influence Ece Ayhan, prominent poet of the *Ikinci Yeni* (Second New) poetry movement, and Özdamar exerted on each other's work. In this period, as I showed in the last chapter, Özdamar's interaction and professional relationship with Turkish Brechtian directors Öngören and Taner and Algan was of vital importance, and these collaborative relationships loomed large in her Istanbul-Berlin trilogy. As with Ören, Özdamar's encounter with Brecht occurred through working with Turkish dramatists and directors, first in West Berlin and then in Turkey. She acted in a number of stage adaptations of Brecht's work by Öngören's ensemble, the Birlik Sahnesi; this ensemble's approach to Brecht had been shaped by a variety of contexts—temporal, political, and geographical. Later, her interest in Brecht continued when she worked in East and West German theaters, highlighting links between her theatrical experience in divided Germany and Turkey, and the continuities between the Volksbühne and the Schauspielhaus Bochum. As was the case with the Erlanger Theaterwoche's importance for Ören and the Turkish Brecht reception, in Özdamar's theatrical career we see various intersections between East and West. While Özdamar is also a playwright, my analysis suggests the influence of her theater experience on her prose. Theater figured not only aesthetically but also thematically, with the presence of the Volksbühne East Berlin, and its program, in her narrative. The narrator's work in the theater archive and her assistantship for Benno Besson involved her in seminal theater projects at a time when Volksbühne directors were facing increasing pressure from GDR cultural institutions. Her interviews, read in dialogue with her fictional work, illuminated her understanding of the significance of a theater aesthetic, further addressing the relationship between fact and fiction, history and the present, and of temporality to space.

There are significant intersections between Ören and Özdamar, embodied not only in their collaborations with Vasıf Öngören, but also in their poetic choices. These include a common focus on montage and forging relationships between various texts within their oeuvre, as well as literature's role with regard to the past (and its significance for the present). This is made apparent in the openness of their literary work as a whole, which insists on the importance of continual reinterpretations for the production of meaning. Moreover, by situating the Turkish Brecht reception as the context through which to read their work, this book shifts our attention away from thinking about Turkish writers in Germany purely through the lens of labor migration, instead construing their work as a continued exchange in the realm of theater.

By looking at the transformations of Turkey's political and cultural landscapes during these writers' last decade there, in this book I have reconstructed how debates that had begun in Turkey and that centered on the social responsibility of the artist and the politics of aesthetics, came to divided Berlin with these Turkish writers such as Ören and Özdamar—and how, once there, they came to transform ongoing German debates on similar themes.

While in this book I focused on hitherto unexamined aspects of Turkish-German cultural exchange with an emphasis on Brecht, further work on encounters that occurred in the mid-1970s and early 1980s lies ahead. For though this time period is often seen in the context of labor recruitment, it witnessed the development of a very active Turkish art scene, particularly in West Berlin. Two of the seminal Brechtian plays discussed in the first chapter made it into theater programming in West Berlin: Haldun Taner's *The Ballad of Ali Keshan* (directed by prominent actor, film director, and playwright Tuncel Kurtiz in 1980) and Vasıf Öngören's *How can Asiye be saved?* (directed by well-known director Çetin Ipekkaya in 1985) were performed by the Türkisches Ensemble at the Schaubühne am Halleschen Ufer and the Tiytrom respectively.

Turkish-German cultural production in its early stages took place in a variety of genres and media, including music, visual arts, theater, and film. In the 1970s and 1980s various West Berlin-based cultural institutions, especially the Kunstamt Kreuzberg,[1] Künstlerhaus Bethanien, the Deutsch-Türkische Gesellschaft e.V.,[2] and the Türkischer Akademiker- und

Künstlerverein, organized a number of recurring cultural events (often in collaboration with each other), financially supported by the Berlin Senate: ausländischer berliner, Fest auf dem Mariannenplatz, and Türkische Kulturwochen. Alongside performances by theater ensembles such as Berlin Oyuncular, Arbeitertheater Türkeizentrum,[3] Öngören's Kollektiv Theater, and the Türkisches Ensemble, there were musical performances by the Turkish workers' choir of West Berlin and the Orientrock band Kobra, film screenings of Yılmaz Güney's films, and panel discussions on Turkish literature with Haldun Taner and Vasıf Öngören.

The highly successful exhibit "Mehmet kam aus Anatolien" (Mehmet came from Anatolia) was a collaboration between the Türkischer Akademiker- und Künstlerverein and the Kunstamt Kreuzberg in the context of the twenty-fifth Berliner Festwochen in 1975. The exhibit focused on various aspects of Turkish life (and experiences) in Germany, ranging from living and working conditions to childcare and leisure activities. Moreover, Turkish economic and political realities prior to emigration were documented in text and photos. It also displayed works by Turkish artists residing in West Berlin: the sculptor Mehmet Aksoy, the painter Hanefi Yeter, and the ceramist Mehmet Çağlayan. The exhibit attracted 26,000 guests and went on tour in other West German cities, among them Bonn, Munich, Frankfurt am Main, and Bochum. The following year, 1976, saw another collaboration in the form of the concert, "Die betrübte Freiheit" (Gloomy Freedom) which took place in the West Berlin Philharmonie in April, bringing together the Hanns-Eisler-Chor and the Turkish workers' choir West Berlin, but also Chilean protest singer-song-writers. The repertoire included Brecht/Eisler songs as well poems by Nazım Hikmet and Pablo Neruda set to music. The last song on the program featured all participants in unison singing Brecht/Eisler "Solidaritätslied" (Brecht and Eisler's Solidarity song from 1931). This emphasis on multinational collaboration and solidarity was also realized with the program brochure, where the poems and songs were printed in Spanish, German, and Turkish.

The Türkischer Akademiker- und Künstlerverein also organized a Nazım Hikmet festival in 1977 in honor of his seventy-fifth birthday, with a variety of events and performances, including dramatist and actor Genco Erkal, musicians Ruhi Su and Sümeyra, as well as the Hanns-Eisler-Chor and Tahsin Incirci's Turkish workers' choir. One of the main goals was to make Hikmet's work known in West Germany; in East Germany he was already part of the school curriculum. The events of the festival drew sustained coverage in major newspapers from both East and West: among others, the *Tagespiegel*, the *Frankfurter Rundschau*, the *Berliner Morgenpost*, *Die Welt*, *Der Abend*, and *Die Wahrheit* reported on the various festival components.

Part of the festival was an international Nazım Hikmet symposium taking place at the Academy of Arts in West Berlin. The symposium featured prominent literary translators and critics such as Annemarie Bostroem, Stephan Hermlin, Chyngyz Aitmatov, Paul Wiens, and Asım Bezirci.

The promotion of Turkish culture beyond folklorization, orientalization, and essentialization, was a common denominator in all these events. With regard to the postwar period, Turkish-German studies scholarship has focused predominantly on the later (post-unification) period. Within this scholarship, the mediums of film and literature have long played a central role, with the status of postmigrant theater increasing over time; however, almost no attention is given to the cultural activities of the 1970s and 1980s. Because the above-mentioned festivals and organizations promoted music, fine arts, and above all theater, with artists from Turkey as well as Turkish intellectuals in exile in West Berlin, our (re)assessment of the early stages of Turkish-German cultural production must expand to include the Turkish archive. Moreover, that all these developments took place within a funding structure and public-relations environment that promoted Turkish culture but also highlighted Turkish-German collaboration and encounters allows us to uncover continuities and ruptures with regard to current forms and practices. How, for example, do early theatrical experiments relate to today's postmigrant theater? How did musical encounters in the 1970s change in the following decades, until hip hop's success in the 1990s? What is the significance of past practices for Shermin Langhoff's first-hand experience with Turkish workers and exiles in the early 1980s, for her work as the current director of the Gorki Theater and initiator of the postmigrant theater movement, today? An engagement with past practices and their relationship to the present would allow us to reconsider Turkish-German encounters of the past, while also enabling us to reread their cultural-political legacies.

Notes

Introduction

[1] "Dialog der Literatur- und Theaterwissenschaftler," in *Brecht-Dialog 1968: Politik auf dem Theater; Dokumentation 9. bis 16. Februar 1968*, ed. Werner Hecht (Berlin: Henschel, 1968), 101.

[2] In addition to fifteen Brecht productions, participants, including directors, actors and stage designers, as well as publishers, translators, and literary and theater critics, from thirty countries, such as Argentina, Brazil, Bulgaria, Cuba, France, Great Britain, Egypt, Syria, Lebanon, India, Iraq, Italy, Japan, Sri Lanka, and the United States, came together in a series of colloquia and workshops to discuss specificities of Brecht reception in their countries. Werner Hecht, ed., *Brecht-Dialog 1968*, 6. Unless otherwise noted all translations are my own.

[3] Werner Hecht, "Vorbemerkung," in "Brecht auf den Bühnen der Welt: Materialien zum Brecht-Dialog 1968 (1); Berichte aus den Ländern," supplement to *Theater der Zeit* 22 (1968): 3.

[4] Another point of intersection was the contributors' near-universal complaint about the difficulty of obtaining reliable translations of Brecht's plays and writings on theater—or of producing such translations themselves (into Arabic in Lebanon for example).

[5] "Probleme der internationalen Brecht-Rezeption," in *Brecht-Dialog 78: Kunst und Politik, 10.–15. Februar 1978; Dokumentation,* ed. Werner Hecht, Karl-Claus Hahn, and Elifius Paffrath (Berlin: Henschel, 1979), 65.

[6] Ibid., 53.

[7] Ibid., 52.

[8] For a list of all attendees, see Hecht, Hahn, and Paffrath, *Brecht-Dialog 78: Dokumentation*, 298.

[9] Werner Hecht, "Brecht—Werk und Wirkung," in *Brecht 80: Brecht in Afrika, Asien und Lateinamerika: Dokumentation*, ed. Werner Hecht, Karl-Claus Hahn, and Elifius Paffrath (Berlin: Henschelverlag Kunst & Gesellschaft, 1980), 7.

[10] Ibid.

[11] Ibid., 11.

[12] Ibid.

[13] "Probleme der internationalen Brecht-Rezeption," 59. On the reception of Brecht in Egypt, see Magdi Youssef, "The Reception of Bertholt (sic!) Brecht in Egypt," *Proceedings of the Congress of the International Comparative Literature Association* 7 (1973): 657–61.

[14] Marc Silberman, "A Postmodernized Brecht?," *Theater Journal* 45, no. 1 (1993): 3.

[15] In addition to these international discussions organized by GDR cultural institutions, Germanists based in the United States founded the International Brecht Society in 1968 in New York City, whose goal was to "encourage the international study of all aspects of Bertolt Brecht's life and work, . . . the inter-disciplinary study of the interrelationship of the modern arts and society at large," and to foster ". . . international exchange of scholarly and experimental work across aesthetic and political boundaries" (Marc Silberman, "A Brief History of the International Brecht Society," accessed March 15, 2017; http://www.brechtsociety.org/ibs_history#history). Besides holding symposia and conferences, the International Brecht Society has published a yearbook since 1971 in order to "document the progression of the international Brecht reception." *Brecht-Jahrbuch* (1974), ed. John Fuegi, Reinhold Grimm, and Jost Hermand (Frankfurt am Main: Suhrkamp Verlag, 1975), 2.

[16] Here, as in the Brecht-Dialog in 1968, intersections between Brecht's methods and traditional theatrical traditions, and adaptations of Brecht to local forms, were addressed: intersections between Brecht's epic theater and the Ping Tan genre in China, the incorporation of tribal dances and indigenous folk music instruments in the Philippines, the use of folk elements and the drama-poem dula-tula in Thailand, similarities between Brecht's dramaturgy and Nigerian indigenous traditions, and folk traditions in India. Huang Zuolin, "A Brief Account of Brechtian Reception in China," in *Brecht in Asia and Africa: The Brecht Yearbook XIV*, ed. John Fuegi et al. (Hong Kong: University of Hong Kong, 1989), 2; Carl Weber, "Brecht is at Home in Asia," in Fuegi et al., *Brecht in Asia and Africa*, 41; Maria Luisa F. Torres, "Brecht in the Philippines: Anticipating Freedom in Theatre," in Fuegi et al., *Brecht in Asia and Africa,* 138; Sandra L. Richards, "Wasn't Brecht an African Writer? Parallels with Contemporary Nigerian Drama," in Fuegi et al., *Brecht in Asia and Africa*, 168–81.

[17] On the shift from the age of three worlds to global culture, see Michael Denning, *Culture in the Age of Three Worlds* (London: Verso, 2000). On the relationship of the West German New Left and the Third World, see Quinn Slobodian, *Foreign Front: Third World Politics in Sixties West Germany* (Durham, NC: Duke University Press, 2012).

[18] Established in 1946, the Studiobühne Erlangen was West Germany's most active and well-known student theater ensemble in the postwar period; the student theater festival began three years later, in order to "show Germany's democratic face to the outside world." Marlies Hübner, "Studententheater im Beziehungsgeflecht politischer gesellschaftlicher und kultureller Auseinandersetzung, mit einem Ausblick

auf die Theaterszene der sechziger und siebziger Jahre" (PhD diss., Friedrich-Alexander-University Erlangen, 1987), 42.

[19] Upon his return to West Germany, Statkus was summoned to appear at the interior ministry in Bonn. His visit to the GDR did not have further consequences, as he reassured political officials that he was traveling in his capacity as president of the European Student Theater Union, an organization founded at the Erlangen festival the previous year, and not in his capacity as director of the festival.

[20] Hübner, "Studententheater im Beziehungsgeflecht," 59.

[21] Hübner, *Internationales Studententheater in Erlangen, 1946—1968* (Erlangen: Universitäts-Buchdruckerei Junge & Sohn, 1995), 55.

[22] Quoted in Lea Sophie Schiel, *Theater im politischen Kampf: Motivation und Konsequenz der Auflösung der internationalen Theaterwoche der Studentenbühnen in Erlangen, 1968* (Berlin: Gesellschaft für Theatergeschichte, 2016), 51.

[23] As Schiel notes, the festival's opening to Eastern Europe had occurred with the invitation of the acting academy of Ljubljana in 1952, with more ensembles from the former CSSR, Poland, and Romania, as well as the GDR (East Berlin and Rostock) to follow. See Schiel, *Theater im politischen Kampf*, 51.

[24] Poland and East Germany are the prime examples here. Hübner, "Studententheater im Beziehungsgeflecht," 352.

[25] The festival in Erlangen was not an isolated case. In 1968 the Turkish ministry of interior canceled the Istanbul Festival, the "International Peace Festival" held since 1955. This festival had seen its state funds cut in 1965, based on accusations of supporting communism, particularly through its emphasis on Internationalism. The Turkish state was primarily opposed to participation from "Ostblockstudenten," students from the Eastern bloc. Yet the student theater ensemble from Stuttgart (West Germany), and members from Nancy (France) and Nigeria were also refused entry (they had not received notification of the festival's cancellation in time). Yüksel Pazarkaya, "Das aufgelöste Festival," *Stuttgarter Zeitung*, August 20, 1968.

[26] Hübner, "Studententheater im Beziehungsgeflecht," 353. In 1966 the Ankara university student ensemble could not participate because of the government's refusal to issue exit permits (ibid., 432).

[27] Ibid., 59–60.

[28] John Rouse, *Brecht and the West German Theatre: The Practice and Politics of Interpretation* (Ann Arbor: UMI Research, 1989), 88.

[29] For instance, according to theater critic Henning Rischbieter, despite the boycott in the aftermath of the erection of the Wall in 1961, with a "Brecht abstinence" in leading German-speaking theaters in Vienna, Zurich, Cologne, Düsseldorf, Hamburg, and Berlin, the number of Brecht performances in the West actually remained constant. Henning Rischbieter, "Was wird bei uns gespielt? Eine Analyse der Aufführungsstatistik der letzten 6 Spielzeiten," *Theater heute* (Feb. 1963): 25.

[30] Schiel, *Theater im politischen Kampf*, 33.

[31] The first Brecht production by the Studiobühne Erlangen was *Die Massnahme* (*The Measures Taken*) in 1955, which at that time was banned in the Federal Republic, and thus its performance perceived as an "affront" to the West German public, where Brecht's return to East Berlin had not been forgiven. The ensemble tried to work around the performance ban through staging it as a "scenic reading" (Hübner, "Studententheater im Beziehungsgeflecht," 202). After Brecht's death in 1956 the Studiobühne honored him by performing a reading. Two years later in 1958 it staged *Furcht and Elend im Dritten Reich* (*Fear and Misery of the Third Reich*), which was very well received and praised for its contemporaneous relevance. See "Lehr- und Warnstück vor der Diktatur," *Erlanger Tageblatt*, February 27, 1958.

[32] Hübner, *Internationales Studententheater*, 112.

[33] Hübner, "Studententheater im Beziehungsgeflecht," 241.

[34] Jan Knopf, *Brecht-Handbuch in fünf Bänden*, vol. 1, *Stücke* (Stuttgart: Metzler, 2001), 98.

[35] Quoted in Schiel, *Theater im politischen Kampf*, 33.

[36] Dieter Herrmann, "Erlanger Impressionen, 1961," *Berliner Zeitung*, July 29, 1961.

[37] Schiel, *Theater im politischen Kampf*, 54.

[38] For instance, at the 1961 Erlangen festival, which had Brecht's work as its major theme, Istanbul's Gençlik Tiyatrosu ensemble performed *Kafes arkasında* (Behind the Lattice, 1929), a comedy by Müsahipzade Celâl—the most successful Ottoman playwright of the early twentieth century.

[39] Yüksel Pazarkaya, "Literatur ist Literatur," in *Eine nicht nur deutsche Literatur: Zur Standortbestimmung der "Ausländerliteratur,"* ed. Irmgard Ackermann and Harald Weinrich (Munich: Piper, 1986), 63.

[40] Aras Ören, "Von der Würde des Künstlers gegenüber dem missionarisch-bürokratischen Egoismus," in Ackermann and Weinrich, *Eine nicht nur deutsche Literatur,"* 90–93.

[41] Emine Sevgi Özdamar, "Dank," *Jahrbuch: Bayerische Akademie der schönen Künste* 13, no. 1 (1999): 883.

[42] Leslie A. Adelson, *The Turkish Turn in Contemporary German Literature: Toward a New Critical Grammar of Migration* (New York: Palgrave Macmillan, 2005), 26.

[43] On the German literary interaction with the Middle East, see Nina Berman, *German Literature on the Middle East: Discourses and Practices, 1000–1989* (Ann Arbor: University of Michigan Press, 2011).

[44] Adelson, *The Turkish Turn*, 21.

[45] B. Venkat Mani, *Cosmopolitical Claims: Turkish-German Literatures from Nadolny to Pamuk* (Iowa City: University of Iowa Press, 2007), 5. In addition to Adelson and Mani, Azade Seyhan has striven to resituate Turkish-German literature

in the context of German literature. In her comparative study *Writing outside the Nation* Seyhan focuses on "contemporary tales of migration, exile, and displacement" that "recuperate losses incurred in migration, dislocation, and translation." Azade Seyhan, *Writing outside the Nation* (Princeton, NJ: Princeton University Press, 2001), 5, 4. My work, on the other hand, is focused on interactions between Turkish and German writers and cultural practices, preceding migration and continuing through migration. The (hi)stories central to this book are not marked by loss but rather by an ongoing engagement with Brecht.

46 B. Venkat Mani, *Cosmopolitical Claims*, 7.

47 David Gramling, "What Is Turkish-German Studies up Against? Occidentalism and Thigmotactics," *Colloquia Germanica* 44, no. 4 (2014), 389. In particular, Gramling cited Sabahattin Ali's *Kürk Mantolu Madonna* (*The Madonna in the Fur Coat*, 1943), Orhan Pamuk's *Kar* (*Snow*, 2002), and Ahmet Haşım's *Frankfurt Seyhatnamesi* (Frankfurt Travelogue, 1933).

48 Gramling, "What Is Turkish-German Studies up Against?," 389.

49 Adelson, *The Turkish Turn,* 245.

50 David Gramling, "What Is Turkish-German Studies up Against?," 387.

51 Deniz Göktürk's efforts to introduce German audiences to contemporary Turkish authors during the 1990s warrant special mention. In addition to inviting Turkish authors to Berlin, she is the German translator of numerous Turkish-language texts, including the literary works of Aras Ören and Bilge Karasu. See Deniz Göktürk, "Imagining Europe as a Realm of Transfiguration," *Critical Multilingualism Studies* 2, no. 1 (2014): 129–47.

52 Mert Bahadir Reisoğlu, "Interlacing Archives: History and Memory in Emine Sevgi Özdamar's *Die Brücke vom Goldenen Horn*," *Colloquia Germanica* 44, no. 4 (2014): 422–37; Karin Yeşilada, *Poesie der Dritten Sprache* (Tübingen: Stauffenburg Verlag, 2012); Randall Halle, "The Europeanization of Turkish/German Cinema: Complex Connectivity and Imaginative Communities," *Jahrbuch Türkisch-deutsche Studien* (2015): 15–38; Deniz Göktürk, "Interrupting Unity: The Berlin Wall's Second Life on Screen—A Transnational Perspective," in *Debating German Cultural Identity since 1989*, ed. Anne Fuchs, Kathleen James-Chakraborty, and Linda Shortt (Rochester, NY: Camden House, 2011), 82–99. Berna Güneli, "Remixing Film Histories: Fatih Akın and the Creation of a Transnational Film History," *Colloquia Germanica* 44, no. 4 (2014): 450–66.

53 See Slobodian for a discussion of the introduction of the foreigners' law as "an attempt by the federal government to designate non-Germans in the Federal Republic as economic actors—a labor force to be recruited and dismissed at will—and disenfranchise them as political actors" (*Foreign Front*, 50).

54 Leslie A. Adelson, "Against Between: A Manifesto," in *Unpacking Europe: Towards a Critical Reading*, ed. Salah Hassan and Iftikhar Dadi (Rotterdam: NAi, 2001), 246.

[55] On the status of Turks as non-citizens in Germany, see Damani Partridge, *Hypersexuality and Headscarves: Race, Sex, and Citizenship in the New Germany* (Bloomington: Indiana University Press, 2012).

[56] Ruth Mandel, *Cosmopolitan Anxieties: Turkish Challenges to Citizenship and Belonging in Germany* (Durham, NC: Duke University Press, 2008), 3.

[57] Yasemin Yildiz, "Turkish Girls, Allah's Daughters, and the Contemporary German Subject: Itinerary of a Figure," *German Life and Letters* 62, no. 3 (2009): 466.

[58] Ibid., 475.

[59] Fatima El-Tayeb, *Undeutsch: Die Konstruktion des Anderen in der postmigrantischen Gesellschaft* (Bielefeld: transcript, 2016), 157.

[60] Ibid., 162.

[61] Ibid., 9, 164, 146. On the narrative construction of Turks as "perpetual guest workers, arrested in a state of cultural and social liminality" see also Levent Soysal, who illustrates how the presentation of Turks as inherently foreign and embodiments of "radical otherness" in public, popular, and scholarly discourses renders "their participation invisible, and presents their situation as anomie." Levent Soysal, "Labor to Culture: Writing Turkish Migration to Europe," *South Atlantic Quarterly* 102, no. 2–3 (2003): 491–508, here 493.

[62] Fatima El-Tayeb, *Undeutsch*, 36.

[63] Ibid., 153.

[64] In this connection, Adelson's reading of Ören's literary representation of Turkish migration at the relational nexus of capital and labor, advanced in *Turkish Turn*, represents a notable exception. In the third chapter, entitled "Capital and Labor," she analyses "pivotal encounters between Turkish migration and capitalist reconstruction in postwar Germany" in literary texts by Aras Ören, Emine Sevgi Özdamar, and Zafer Şenocak (28). Through a "contrapuntal reading" (144) of Ören's novella *Bitte nix Polizei* (Please, No Police, 1981), Adelson argues against the reduction of its protagonist Ali Itir to a "human victim of social circumstance" (142), instead reading him as "literary figure of ethnic labor" with the "capacity to index the cultural capital of migration" (144).

Chapter One

[1] Letter from Brecht to Hanns Eisler, dated March 1941, Bertolt Brecht Archive, call number BBA2707.

[2] On the impact of German-Jewish exiles on Turkey's humanist reform see Kader Konuk, *East West Mimesis: Auerbach in Turkey* (Stanford, CA: Stanford University Press, 2010). On Ernst Reuter, see Barış Ülker, "Urbanization and Modern Governmental Reason: Ernst Reuter's Exile in Turkey," *Jahrbuch Türkisch-deutsche Studien* (2015): 79–96.

[3] Anne Dietrich, *Deutschsein in Istanbul* (Opladen: Leske + Budrich, 1998), 257.

[4] See, for example, Werner Hecht, Karl-Claus Hahnm and Elifius Paffrath, eds., *Brecht 78: Brecht-Dialog Kunst und Politik, 10.—15. Februar 1978; Dokumentation* (Berlin: Henschelverlag Kunst und Gesellschaft, 1979); Adel Karasholi, *Brecht in arabischer Sicht* (Berlin: Brecht-Zentrum der DDR, 1982); Fuegi et al., *Brecht in Asia and Africa: The Brecht Yearbook XIV*; Lorene B. Ellis, *Brecht's Reception in Brazil* (New York: Peter Lang, 1995); and Loren Kruger, *Post-Imperial Brecht: Politics and Performance, East and South* (Cambridge: Cambridge University Press, 2007).

[5] Examples include Özdemir Nutku, *Türkiye'de Brecht* (Istanbul: Tiyatro Yayınları, 1976); Zehra Ipşiroğlu, *Tiyatroda Devrim* (Istanbul: Çağdaş Yayınları, 1988); Sargut Sölcün's chapter on Brecht in his monograph *Tarih Bilinci ve Edebiyat Bilimi* (Ankara: Dayanışma Yayınları, 1982), as well as special issues of the following journals: *Oyun* 9 (1964), *Varlık* 911 (1983), and "Brecht Dosyası," special issue, *Alman Dil ve Edebiyat Dergisi* 18 (2006). In addition to these publications in Turkish, Albert Nekimken's published doctoral dissertation on Brecht is notable, as it is the first—and only—comprehensive study of Brechtian dramatists, adaptations of Brecht, and Brecht reception in Turkey between 1955 and 1977. See Albert Nekimken, *Brecht in Turkey, 1955–1977: The Impact of Bertold [sic] Brecht on Society and the Development of Revolutionary Theatre in Turkey* (Istanbul: Isis, 1998).

[6] The special issue of *Notate* in 1984 titled "Brecht in der Dritten Welt" included a brief contribution on the reception of Brecht in Turkey. See Yılmaz Onay, "Im Brennpunkt des Kampfes: Zur Brecht-Rezeption in der Türkei," *Notate* 4 (1984): 3–4. The Brecht scholar Reinhold Grimm went to Ankara in 1979 for a lecture series, and documented his trip, including his encounters with Taner, Erkal, and Berksoy, in the form of an "essayistischer Reisebericht." See Reinhold Grimm, "Falladah in Ankara, 1979: Begegnungen mit (und zwischen) Brecht und den Türken," *Monatshefte* 75, no. 1 (1983): 6–24.

[7] Metin And, *Başlangıcından 1983'e Türk Tiyatro Tarihi* (Istanbul: Iletişim Yayınları, 2004), 172; also see Talat S. Halman, "The Evolution of Turkish Drama," in Halman, *Modern Turkish Drama: An Anthology of Plays in Translation*, ed. Halman (Minneapolis: Bibliotheca Islamica, 1976), 37.

[8] Oya Başak, "60 Yıllık Çabanın Özeti," in *Muhsin Ertuğrul'a Saygı*, ed. Metin And (Istanbul: Çeltüt Basımevi, 1969), 11.

[9] Ibid., 28.

[10] And, *Başlangıcından 1983'e*, 172.

[11] Igor Lipovsky, *The Socialist Movement in Turkey* (Leiden, Netherlands: Brill, 1992), 1; Özgür Ulus, *The Army and the Radical Left in Turkey* (London: I. B. Tauris, 2011), 4; Feroz Ahmad, *The Turkish Experiment in Democracy* (London: C. Hurst for the Royal Institute of International Affairs, 1977), 186.

[12] Ulus, *Army and Radical Left*, 4.

[13] Lipovsky, *Socialist Movement*, 1.

[14] Ibid., 5; see also Ahmad, *Turkish Experiment*, 186.

[15] Ayhan Yalçın, *Türkiye Cumhuriyeti Anayasaları* (Istanbul: Geçit Kitabevi, 1982), 78.

[16] Ibid.

[17] Ibid.

[18] Ibid.

[19] Ibid., 80–81.

[20] The Institute for Theater Studies at the University of Ankara was founded in 1958 but did not obtain a professorship until 1964. I will return to the details later in this chapter.

[21] Talat S. Halman, "Turkish Literature in the 1960s," in Halman, *Rapture and Revolution: Essays on Turkish Literature by Talat S. Halman* (Syracuse: Syracuse University Press, 2007), 90.

[22] Murat Şevki Çoban, "Genco Erkal: Politik Tiyatronun Yeniden Gündeme Geldiğini Hissediyorum," Agora Kitaplığı, accessed 24 September 2016, http://agorakitapligi.com/genco-erkal-politik-tiyatronun-yeniden-gundeme-geldigini-hissediyorum.

[23] Cf. Gülayşe Erkoç, "1960–1970 Dönemi Tiyatro Hareketleri," *Tiyatro Araştırmaları Dergisi* 13 (2002): 22.

[24] Eren Buğlalılar, *Theatre and Struggle: A Sociological Analysis of the Political Theatre in Turkey between 1960–1971* (MS Thesis, METU, Ankara, 2012), 55; and Uygur Kocabaşoğlu, "Cumhuriyet Dergiciliğine Bir Bakış," in *Türkiye'de Dergiler—Ansiklopediler (1849–1984)*, ed. Deniz Insel (Istanbul: Gelişim Yayınları, 1984), 4.

[25] Jacob M. Landau, *Radical Politics in Modern Turkey* (Leiden, Netherlands: Brill, 1974), 50.

[26] Ibid., 65.

[27] Ibid., 67.

[28] Cevat Çapan, "Cumhuriyet Dönemi Tiyatro Dergileri," in Insel, *Türkiye'de Dergiler*, 131.

[29] Suhrkamp published the single volume *Bertolt Brecht, Schriften zum Theater: Über eine nicht-aristotelische Dramatik* in 1957 and the multi-volume *Schriften zum Theater* from 1963 to 1964.

[30] Çapan, "Cumhuriyet Dönemi," 133.

[31] See for example *Istanbul Şehir Tiyatroların Dergisi*'s special issue on Brecht published in March 1964 when *Der gute Mensch von Sezuan* (*The Good Person of Szechwan*) was performed, or *Dormen Tiyatrosu Aylık Tiyatro Dergisi*'s twelfth issue for the ensemble's 1964 performance of *Herr Puntila und sein Knecht Matti* (*Mr. Puntila and His Man Matti*), and Ankara Sanat Tiyatrosu's extended program brochure for their 1979 *Die Rundköpfe und die Spitzköpfe* (*Round Heads and Pointed Heads*) performance.

[32] For a discussion of intersections between Brecht's epic theater and Turkish folk theatrical traditions, see Özdemir Nutku, "Orta Oyununda Yabancılaştırma Kavramı,"

Tiyatro Araştırmaları Dergisi 1 (1970): 33–47; Metin And, *50 Yılın Türk Tiyatrosu* (Istanbul: Iş Bankası Kültür Yayınları, 1973), 458, 463; and Yüksel Pazarkaya, *Rosen im Frost: Einblicke in die türkische Kultur* (Zurich: Unionsverlag, 1998), 203–24.

[33] "Şehir Tiyatrosunda Hadise Çıkaranlar," *Gece Postası*, March 23, 1964; and HA, "Şehir Tiyatrosunda Dün Gece Gençler Bir Temsile Mâni Oldular," *Hürriyet*, March 23, 1964.

[34] Lipovsky, *Socialist Movement*, 174.

[35] Ahmad, *Turkish Experiment*, 379; Lipovsky, *Socialist Movement*, 185.

[36] Ahmad, *Turkish Experiment*, 379 and "Şehir Tiyatrosunda Hadise"

[37] HA, "Şehir Tiyatrosunda."

[38] "Yurttan Akisler," *Akis*, March 28, 1964.

[39] "Sezuanin Iyi Insani ve Istanbuldaki Tepkiler," *Ses*, April 4, 1964.

[40] "Tiyatro Olayi Sanıklarının Duruşmasına Dün Başlandı," *Cumhuriyet*, March 27, 1964.

[41] These articles were abolished in 1991.

[42] A.A., "Tiyatro Basanlar Nefret Uyandırdı," *Ulus*, March 25, 1964; and Özdemir Nutku, *Darülbedayi'nin Elli Yılı* (Ankara: Ankara Üniversitesi Basımevi, 1969), 83.

[43] "Yurttan Akisler."

[44] "Türkiyede Ilk Brecht Carrar Ana'nın Silâhları," *Oyun* 7 (1964): 5.

[45] A. A., "Tiyatro Basanlar."

[46] "Yurttan Akisler."

[47] Hayati Asılyazıcı, "Bertolt Brecht Olayı," *Oyun* 9 (1964): 11.

[48] Çetin Özek, "Mutsuz Sezuan," *Oyun* 9 (1964): 8.

[49] "Yurttan Akisler."

[50] Mine Söğüt, *Adalet Cimcoz: Bir Yaşamöyküsü Denemesi* (Istanbul: Yapı Kredi Yayınları, 2000), 171–72.

[51] "Sezuan'ın Iyi Insanı Tepki Uyandırdı," *Ses*, March 28, 1964.

[52] Nekimken, *Brecht*, 145 and 465; Nutku, *Darülbedayi'nin*, 85; and Oya Kaynar, "Muhsin Ertuğrul: The Leader of the Turkish Theatre" (PhD diss., University of Minnesota, 1968), 172.

[53] Nutku, *Darülbedayi'nin*, 81

[54] Talat S. Halman, "The Evolution of Turkish Drama," in Halman, *Modern Turkish Drama: An Anthology of Plays in Translation* (Minneapolis: Bibliotheca Islamica, 1976), 37; Kaynar, *Muhsin Ertuğrul*, 158.

[55] Kaynar, *Muhsin Ertuğrul*, 165.

[56] Ankara Üniversitesi Dil ve Tarih-Coğrafya Fakültesi, "Tiyatro Bölümü," accessed September 23, 2016, http://www.dtcf.ankara.edu.tr/tiyatro-bolumu.

[57] This theater department ran a student theater ensemble, the DTCF Topluluğu, which participated in the Erlangen student theater festival, to which I will turn later in this chapter.

[58] Nutku, *Darülbedayi'nin*, 86; "M. Ertuğrul Olayını Özel Tiyatrolar Da Protesto Etti," *Cumhuriyet*, March 19, 1966.

[59] Dostlar Tiyatrosu, "Tiyatro," accessed September 22, 2016, http://dostlartiyatrosu.com/tiyatro.html.

[60] Bertolt Brecht, "Über experimentelles Theater," in *Werke: Große kommentierte Berliner und Frankfurter Ausgabe,* ed. Werner Hecht, Jan Knopf, and Werner Mittenzwei, 24 vols., vol. 22/1, *Schriften 2: Teil 1* (Berlin: Aufbau Verlag, 1988), 557.

[61] Bertolt Brecht, "Schluss," in *Werke*, vol. 23, *Schriften 3*, 374.

[62] On the the significance of Brecht's dramaturgy and theater practice for Erkal and the Dostlar Tiyatrosu ensemble, see Ela Gezen, "Brecht on the Turkish Stage: Adaptation, Experimentation, and Theatre Aesthetics in Genco Erkal's *Dostlar Tiyatrosu,*" *German Life and Letters* 69, no. 2 (2016): 269–84.

[63] "Gelecek Yüzyılların Yazarı," *Milliyet*, Feb. 10, accessed March 18, 2017, http://www.milliyet.com.tr/1998/02/10/sanat/san2.html.

[64] *Nürnberger Zeitung*, 11 October 1964, printed in Haldun Taner, *The Ballad of Ali Keshan*, trans. Nüvit Özdoğru (Ankara: International Theatre Institute, 1970), xviii.

[65] Haldun Taner, *Keşanlı Ali Destanı*, 26th ed. (Ankara: Bilgi Yayınevi, 2013), 22.

[66] Quoted in Haldun Taner, *The Ballad of Ali of Keshan*, trans. Nüvit Özdoğru (Ankara: International Theatre Institute, 1970), xvi.

[67] Özdemir Nutku, "Keşanlı Ali Destanı," *Türk Dili* 155 (1964): 864.

[68] Nekimken, *Brecht*, 100.

[69] "Die Geschichte des Ali aus Kesan," *Bonner Stadtanzeiger*, October 5, 1964.

[70] Ayşegül Yüksel, *Haldun Taner Tiyatrosu* (Ankara: Bilgi Yayınevi, 1986), 81.

[71] Nekimken, *Brecht in Turkey*, 1.

[72] Zehra Ipşiroğlu, *Tiyatroda Yeni Arayışlar* (Istanbul: Düzlem Yayınları, 1992), 229.

[73] Halman, "Turkish Drama," 25. For a discussion of the various influences and their possible correlations see, Halman, "Turkish Drama," 25, and Pazarkaya, *Rosen*, 191.

[74] Max Walter Schulz, "Gespräch mit Haldun Taner," *Sinn und Form* 23, no. 3 (1971): 693–98.

[75] Ayhan Sümer, "Haldun Taner'le," *Varlık* 620 (1964): 13.

[76] Metin And, "The Turkish Folk Theater," *Asian Folklore Studies* 38, no. 2 (1979): 166; and Halman, "Turkish Drama," 25.

[77] Sümer, "Haldun Taner'le," 13.

[78] Schulz, "Gespräch mit Taner," 695.

[79] In line with the editors of the updated and revised *Brecht on Theater*, I will leave *Verfremdung* untranslated in order to refrain from using terms such as alienation, distanciation, and defamiliarization, which have been "theoretically misleading," as the editors discuss in detail. Similarly, I will follow their use of the English neologism V-effects for *Verfremdungseffekte*. "General Introduction," in *Brecht on Theatre*, edited by Marc Silberman, Steve Giles, and Tom Kuhn (London: Bloomsbury, 2015), 5.

[80] Pazarkaya, *Rosen*, 218.

[81] Ibid.

[82] For the critical reception of Taner's *Ballad* see Nekimken, *Brecht in Turkey*, 109–16.

[83] Erol M. Boran, "Eine Geschichte des türkisch-deutschen Theaters und Kabaretts" (PhD diss., Ohio State University, 2004), 112.

[84] "Vasıf Öngören'le Konuşma," *Tiyatro* 1 (1970): 29.

[85] Albert Nekimken, "The Impact of Bertolt Brecht on Society and the Development of Political Theater in Turkey" (PhD diss., University of California Riverside, 1978), 268.

[86] Erbil Göktaş, *Vasıf Öngören'in Tiyatro Dünyası* (Istanbul: Mitos-Boyut, 2004), 9.

[87] Ören accompanied Öngören for a short period, returning to Turkey for his military service from 1963 to 1965. Later Öngören and Ören remained in close contact by mail throughout the 1960s.

[88] "Yılın Sanatçıları Ile Söyleşi: Vasıf Öngören," *Tiyatro* 41 (1977): 36–38.

[89] Georg Stenzaly, "Ausländertheater in der Bundesrepublik und Berlin-West am Beispiel der türkischen Theatergruppen," *Zeitschrift für Literaturwissenschaft und Linguistik* 56 (1984): 133.

[90] Ankara Birliği, "Çıkarken," *Ankara Birliği Dergisi* 1 (1970): 4.

[91] Ibid.

[92] Ankara Birliği, "'Ankara Birliği' Sahnesi Kuruluş Bilgisi," *Ankara Birliği Dergisi* 1 (1970): 13.

[93] Ibid.

[94] Vasıf Öngören, "Ulusal Tiyatro Devrimci Tiyatrodur," *Ankara Birliği Dergisi* 1 (1970): 14.

[95] "Vasıf Öngören'le Konuşma," 29.

[96] Vasıf Öngören, interview by Zeynep Oral, *Milliyet Sanat Dergisi* 224 (March 25, 1977), 3.

[97] Ibid.

[98] Ibid.

[99] "Vasıf Öngören'le 'Devrimci Tiyatro' Sorunları Üzeirne Bir Konuşma," *Militan* 6 (1975): 49–50.

[100] "Yılın Sanatçıları Ile Söyleşi: Vasıf Öngören," 37.

[101] Ibid.

[102] Kemal Tözer, "Yeni Bir Tiyatro, Yeni Bir Deneme," *Cumhuriyet* November 5, 1975.

[103] Ibid.

[104] Hasan Izzettin Dinamo, "Faşizmin Korku ve Sefaleti," *Cumhuriyet* April 6, 1976.

[105] Tözer, "Yeni Bir Tiyatro."

[106] "Yılın Sanatçıları Ile Söyleşi," 37.

[107] Göktaş, *Vasıf Öngören'in*, 78.

[108] Öngören initially asked Aras Ören to translate the play, but used his own translation in the end.

[109] Göktaş, *Vasıf Öngören'in*, 55.

[110] Nutku, *Türkiye'de Brecht*, 76.

[111] In addition to Öngören's own plays, the Kollektiv Theater staged the work of Bertolt Brecht and Nazım Hikmet. Plays in their repertoire, such as Öngören's stage adaptation of Hikmet's *Human Landscapes from My Country* (staged in 1980) and Öngören's Kitchen of the Rich (staged in 1981), were performed in Turkish and German and accompanied by bilingual program brochures to reach both Turkish and German audiences.

[112] His use of "Säulenheiliger" is in reference to the festival journal *Spotlight*, which presented prominent participants or central figures as "Säulenheilige" of the day (Hübner "Studententheater im Beziehungsgeflecht," 321).

[113] Wolfgang von Rimscha, "Internationale Theaterwochen der Studentenbühnen," in *Erlanger Stadtlexikon*, ed. Christoph Friederich (Nuremberg: Tümmels, 2002), 388.

[114] Schiel, *Theater im politischen Kampf*, 40; Hübner, "Studententheater im Beziehungsgeflecht," 346–47.

[115] Schiel, *Theater*, 13; 38–39.

[116] The festival was not held in 1956, 1958, and 1967.

[117] During Peymann's time as director of the *Bochumer Schauspielhaus*, Özdamar was a member of the ensemble and assistant to the director. I will discuss her theatrical career in more depth in chapter 3.

[118] Quoted in Schiel, *Theater*, 20.

[119] Ibid., 54; and Hübner, "Studententheater im Beziehungsgeflecht," 57.

[120] Schiel, *Theater* 34.

[121] Hübner, "Studententheater im Beziehungsgeflecht," 415.

[122] Ibid.

[123] The Gençlik Tiyatrosu ensemble also participated in 1955, 1960, 1961, 1963, 1964, and 1966.

[124] "Yılın Sanatçıları Ile Söyleşi," 36.

[125] Yüksel Pazarkaya, "Erlangen Tiyatro Şenliği," *Oyun* 14 (1964): 16.

[126] Ibid.

[127] Nalan Sinay, *Yaşamı, Sanat Anlayışı ve Yapıtlarıyla Sermet Çağan* (Istanbul: Mitos-Boyut, 2012), 31.

[128] Ibid., 32.

[129] Ibid., 70.

[130] Ibid., 71.

[131] It was closed down after the March 12 coup in 1971.

[132] Fakir Baykurt was the most popular among the exiled writers whose work focused on the guestworkers' experiences in Germany.

[133] Sinay, *Yaşamı*, 33.

[134] TÖS, *TÖS Dosyası* (Ankara: Töre-Devlet Yayınevi, 1973), 63.

[135] TÖS, *Ilk Iki Yılda Türkiye Öğretmenler Sendikası (TÖS): 1965–1967* (Ankara: Balkanoğlu, 1967), 54–55.

[136] Theater critic and dramatist Özdemir Nutku was also affiliated with the union and involved in TÖS Theater by giving seminars.

[137] Schiel, *Theater im politischen Kampf*, 39.

[138] Yüksel Pazarkaya, "Erlangen Şenliği 'Savaş Oyunu' ve Bir Kaç Nokta," *Oyun* 28 (1966): 21.

[139] The acronym DTFC stands for *Ankara Üniversitesi Dil ve Tarihi-Coğrafya Fakültesi* (Ankara University's School of Language, History, and Geography).

[140] "Kısa Kısa," *Milliyet*, August 7, 1965, 6.

[141] "Erlangen Tiyatro Festivalinde Türkiye'nin Kazandığı Başarı," *Milliyet*, August 11, 1965, 6.

[142] For a complete list of editors, see Schiel, *Theater im politischen Kampf*, 146–48.

[143] See Yüksel Pazarkaya, "Kritik Istambul," *Spotlight* 11, no. 7 (July 30, 1965): 4–5.

[144] Hübner, "Studententheater im Beziehungsgeflecht," 322–23.

[145] mi, "Kritik Ankara Kriegsspiel," *Spotlight* 11, no. 8 (July 31, 1965): 3.

[146] Darko Suvin, "Mit und ohne Skandal," *Die Weltwoche*, July 8, 1965.

[147] Özdemir Nutku, "Ayak-Bacak Fabrikası," in *Sermet Çağan Bütün Oyunları* by Sermet Çağan (Istanbul: Mitos-Boyut, 1993), 21.

[148] Ibid., 22.

[149] Sermet Çağan and Özdemir Nutku, *Kriegsspiel: Ein szenischer Bericht*, trans. Max Fisch (Weinheim: Deutscher Theaterverlag, 1969), 29.

[150] "Uluslararası Kültür Şenliği Başlıyor," *Milliyet* August 8, 1965, 6.

[151] "Organizasyon Yönünden. . .," *Milliyet* August 19, 1964, 6.

[152] "Tiyatro Festivaline Hazırlık," *Milliyet* November 6, 1957, 3.

[153] Pazarkaya, "Erlangen Şenliği 'Savaş Oyunu,'" 19–24.

[154] Nutku, *Türkiyede Brecht*, 10.

[155] Emine Sevgi Özdamar, *"Kendi kendinin Terzisi Bir Kambur": Ece Ayhan'lı Anılar, 1974 Zürih Günlüğü, Ece Ayhan'ın Mektupları* (Istanbul: Yapı Kredi Yayınevi, 2007), 25. On Çağan's stage adaptation of *Senora Carrar's Rifles*, see Özdemir Nutku, "Carrar Ananın Silahları," in *Türkiye'de Brecht*, 63–73.

Chapter Two

[1] Aras Ören, *Was will Niyazi in der Naunynstraße? Ein Poem*, trans. H. Achmed Schmiede and Johannes Schenk (Berlin: Rotbuch Verlag, 1973) constitutes the first part, *Der kurze Traum aus Kağıthane*, trans. H. Achmed Schmiede (Berlin: Rotbuch Verlag, 1974) the second, and *Die Fremde ist auch ein Haus,* trans. Gisela Kraft (Berlin: Rotbuch Verlag, 1980) the third part of the Berlin trilogy. The three parts were originally written in Turkish, as was the case with all of Ören's works, and they were published sequentially in German translation.

[2] Aras Ören, "Vorstellungskraft und Zeit," in *Privatexil: Ein Programm? Drei Vorlesungen*, trans. Cem Dalaman (Tübingen: Konkursbuchwelt, 1999), 20.

[3] "Telefon-Interview von Karl-Heinz Jakobs mit Aras Ören: Deutsche Einheit ist eine Einbahnstraße," *Neues Deutschland*, 15 March 1991, 15. On their performance in Ankara, see Özdemir Nuktu, "Ankara'da Bir Brecht," in *Türkiye'de Brecht*, 55–59.

[4] In addition to Sermet Çağan, prominent actors and directors such as Tuncel Kurtiz, Haldun Dormen, Erol Keskin, Ege Ernart, Suna Keskin, Bilge Şen, and Müjdat Gezen were members of the Gen-Ar Tiyatrosu ensemble.

[5] In 1966 Ören went on a tour of Turkey with Çağan's TÖS Theater as an actor in the second play, *Suçsuzlar: Sacco ve Vanzetti*, which was based on Howard Fast's *The Passion of Sacco and Vanzetti: A New England Legend* (1953).

[6] Aras Ören, "Kör Oidipus," *Tiyatro* 11 (1972): 36–50.

[7] In a letter from Öngören (in Berlin) to Ören (in Istanbul) in March 1964 Öngören requests more information on the journal that Ören had brought to his attention. Academy of Arts, Aras-Ören-Archive.

[8] For example, Bertolt Brecht, "Epik Tiyatro," trans. Kamural Şipal, *Ataç* 17, no. 2 (1963): 18–22; Bertolt Brecht, *Tiyatro İçin Küçük Araç*, trans. Teoman Aktürel (Istanbul: Can Yayınları, 1962); and Bertolt Brecht, *Galile*, trans. Adalet Cimcoz (Istanbul: Izlem Yayınları, 1963).

[9] Nekimken, *Brecht in Turkey*, 8.

[10] Bertolt Brecht, "Dialektik und Verfremdung," in *Werke*, vol. 22/1, *Schriften 2: Teil 1*, 402.

[11] Aras Ören. "Eine Metropole ist kein Völkerkundemuseum," in *Privatexil: Ein Programm?*, 53.

[12] Ören, "Vorstellungskraft," 6.

[13] Aras Ören, "Selbstbild mit Stadt," in *Privatexil: Ein Programm?Drei Vorlesungen*, 30.

[14] Aras Ören, "Eine Metropole ist kein Völkerkundemuseum," 43.

[15] Ören, "Selbstbild," 20.

[16] Ibid. Like Ören, Emine Sevgi Özdamar, as I will show in the next chapter, represents Berlin as incomplete and full of gaps, assigning immigrants a crucial function in the revival of West Berlin.

[17] Robert Bosch Stiftung, "Adelbert-von-Chamisso-Prize of the Robert Bosch Stiftung," accessed 24 September, 2016, http://www.boschstiftung.de/content/language2/html/4595.asp.

[18] Aras Ören, "Dankesrede zur Preisverleihung," in *Chamissos Enkel: Literatur von Ausländern in Deutschland*, ed. Heinz Friedrich (Munich: Deutscher Taschenbuch Verlag, 1986), 27.

[19] Mani, *Cosmopolitical Claims*, 5.

[20] Ören, "Von der Würde des Künstlers," 90–93.

[21] Ören, "Völkerkundemuseum," 52.

[22] Ören, "Selbstbild," 27.

[23] Ören, "Deutschland wie gut geht es dir mit den anderen?" in *Dichter predigen in Schleswig Holstein*, ed. Hans Joachim Schädich (Stuttgart: Radius, 1991), 20.

[24] Interview with Aras Ören, Academy of Arts, Aras-Ören-Archive, call number 31.3817.

[25] Radio Interview with Aras Ören by SWF December 8, 1974, Academy of Arts, Aras-Ören-Archive, call number 31.3823.

[26] Ören, "Völkerkundemuseum," 48.

[27] Radio Interview with Aras Ören by Südwest Funk, December 8, 1974.

[28] Ören, "Völkerkundemuseum," 46.

[29] Radio Interview with Aras Ören by the WDR, January 9, 1972, Academy of Arts, Aras-Ören-Archive, call number 31.3823.

[30] Ören, "Völkerkundemuseum," 50.

[31] Rita Chin, "Imagining a German Multiculturalism," *Radical History Review* 83 (2002): 60.

[32] B. Venkat Mani, "Phantom of the 'Gastarbeiterliteratur': Aras Ören's Berlin Savignyplatz," in *Migration und Interkulturalität in neueren literarischen Texten*, ed. Aglaia Bloumi (Munich: Iudicium, 2002), 118.

[33] Preface to "Kör Oidipus" (1966), booklet, Academy of Arts, Aras-Ören-Archive.

[34] Letter from Aras Ören to Johannes Schenk, November 23, 1970, Academy of Arts, Aras-Ören-Archive.

[35] Bertolt Brecht, "Against Georg Lukács," in *Aesthetics and Politics,* trans. Ronald Taylor (London: Verso, 1980), 76.

[36] Bertolt Brecht, "26.11.48," in *Arbeitsjournal,* ed. Werner Hecht, vol. 2, *1942–1955* (Frankfurt am Main: Suhrkamp, 1973), 863.

[37] David Barnett, *Brecht in Practice* (London: Bloomsbury, 2015), 104.

[38] Bertolt Brecht, "Miscellaneous Texts: B124," in *Brecht on Performance,* ed. Tom Kuhn, Steve Giles, and Marc Silberman, trans. Charlotte Ryland et al. (London: Bloomsbury, 2015), 98.

[39] Bertolt Brecht, "Notizen über realistische Schreibweise," in Brecht, *Werke,* vol. 22/1, *Schriften 2: Teil 1,* 626.

[40] Bertolt Brecht, "Die Strassenszene: Grundmodell einer Szene des epischen Theaters," in *Werke,* vol. 22/1, *Schriften 2: Teil 1,* 377.

[41] Bertolt Brecht, "Kurze Beschreibung einer neuen Technik der Schauspielkunst, die einen Verfremdungseffekt hervorbringt," in *Werke,* vol. 22/2, *Schriften 2: Teil 2,* 641.

[42] Bertolt Brecht, "Short Description of a New Technique of Acting That Produces a *Verfremdung* Effect," in *Brecht on Theater*, 188.

[43] Bertolt Brecht, "On Experimental Theater," in *Brecht on Theater*, 144.

[44] Ibid., 143.

[45] Bertolt Brecht, "Kulturpolitik und Akademie der Künste," In *Werke,* vol. 23, *Schriften 3,* 259.

[46] Bertolt Brecht, "Über die epische Schauspielkunst: Der Wechsel," in *Werke,* vol. 22/2, *Schriften 2: Teil 2,* 670.

[47] Silberman, "A Postmodernized Brecht?," 8.

[48] Bertolt Brecht, "24.8.40," in *Arbeitsjournal,* vol. 1, *1938–1942,* 158.

[49] Adelson, *Turkish Turn,* 141.

[50] In her monograph *The Guest Worker Question in Postwar Germany* (Cambridge: Cambridge University Press, 2007), Rita Chin discusses the cultural criticism of labor recruitment by leftist artists and intellectuals, examining public discussions about guestworkers. With specific regard to Ören, she suggests that "Ören shared many of the ideas and artistic programs that we now associate with the New Left and the extraparliamentary opposition movement of the late 1960s and early 1970s" (70). Her analysis does not consider his involvement with the Rote Nelke

specifically, and is instead based on a close reading of the first part of the Berlin trilogy, during which reading she points to ethnic tensions between Ören's working-class characters and concludes that he "both reaffirms and complicates the conventional critiques of the West German New Left" (77).

51 Rotbuch Verlag *Herbstprogramm* (1973), Academy of Arts, Aras-Ören-Archive.

52 Rotbuch Verlag, "Vom Wagenbach- zum Rotbuchkollektiv," in *Das kleine Rotbuch: Almanach 1973* (Berlin: Rotbuch: 1973), 56.

53 Rotbuch Verlag, *Das kleine Rotbuch: Almanach 1973*, 42.

54 Ibid.

55 Wolfram Schütte, "Artisten in der Zirkuskuppel und als Bodenturner? Nach einem Besuch bei Wagenbach und im Rotbuch-Kollektiv," *Frankfurter Rundschau*, March 2, 1974, feuilleton, 2.

56 Ibid.

57 Rotbuch Verlag, *Herbstprogramm.*

58 Ibid.

59 F. C. Delius, "Der Erzvater, als er Anfang dreißig war," in *Ceci n'est pas une Festschrift: Aras Ören zum 75. Geburtstag*, ed. Egbert Baqué (Berlin: Egbert Baqué Contemporary Art, 2014), 8.

60 Monika Frederking, *Schreiben gegen Vorurteile: Literatur türkischer Migranten in der Bundesrepublik Deutschland* (Berlin: Express, 1985), 31–32.

61 Ibid.

62 Chin, *The Guest Worker Question in Postwar Germany*, 78.

63 Helmut Peitsch, *Nachkriegsliteratur, 1945–1989* (Göttingen: V&R unipress, 2009), 33.

64 Paul Michael Lützeler, "Von der Intelligenz zur Arbeiterschaft: Zur Darstellung sozialer Wandlungsverhältnisse in den Romanen und Reportagen der Studentenbewegung," in *Deutsche Literatur in der Bundesrepublik seit 1965*, ed. Paul Michael Lützeler and Egon Schwarz (Königstein: Athenäum, 1980), 117. An earlier example of the sociopolitical influence and impact of writers in the postwar period is the *Gruppe 47*. Founded by Hans Werner Richter, it was a literary circle associated with prominent West German and Austrian writers such as Robert Walser, Ingeborg Bachmann, Hans Magnus Enzensberger, Heinrich Böll, and Günter Grass. Retrospectively, Richter summarizes the central aims as follows: first, the "formation of democratic elites" in literature and journalism; second, a "practically applied method of democracy" with the goal of widespread impact; and third, the achievement of both goals without any sort of collective thought and program. Hans Werner Richter, "Fünfzehn Jahre," in *Almanach der Gruppe 47: 1947–1962*, ed. Hans Werner Richter (Reinbek: Rowohlt, 1962), 11.

65 Keith Bullivant, "Literatur und Politik," in *Gegenwartsliteratur seit 1968*, ed. Klaus Briegleb and Sigrid Weigel (Munich: dtv, 1992), 279.

[66] Peitsch, *Nachkriegsliteratur*, 262; Ursula Reinhold, *Literatur und Klassenkampf: Entwicklungsprobleme der demokratischen und sozialistischen Literatur in der BRD (1965–1974)* (Berlin: Dietz Verlag, 1976), 189; Hermann Schlösser, "Literaturgeschichte und Theorie in der Literatur," in *Gegenwartsliteratur seit 1968*, ed. Klaus Briegleb and Sigrid Weigel (Munich: dtv, 1992), 386.

[67] Peter Kühne, *Arbeiterklasse und Literatur: Dortmunder Gruppe 61; Werkkreis Literatur der Arbeitswelt* (Frankfurt am Main: Fischer Taschenbuch Verlag, 1972), 55.

[68] See Alexander von Borman, "Arbeiterliteratur in der Bundesrepublik seit 1965," in Lützeler and Schwarz, *Deutsche Literatur in der Bundesrepublik seit 1965*, 99–114.

[69] In East Germany the cultural program *Bitterfelder Weg*, initiated at the first Bitterfelder Conference in 1959, aimed to involve writers in work and workers in writing. (In fact, some members of the *Gruppe 61*, such as Max von der Grün, had contacts with writers associated with the *Bitterfelder Weg*, including Willi Bredel and Erwin Strittmatter). Seeking to develop a socialist consciousness in the literary sphere that was shaped not only by abstract knowledge but also by lived experience, the *Bitterfelder Weg* urged workers to become involved in the writing process, and encouraged writers to study working conditions by participating in the socialist construction and then write about it. It thus evinced continuities with the *Arbeiterkorrespondentenbewegung* founded by the KPD in 1924 to train and involve workers as correspondents in the communist press. Literary works associated with the cultural program of the *Bitterfelder Weg* are Brigitte Reimann's *Ankunft im Alltag* (Arrival in Everyday Life, 1961), Erik Neutsch's *Spur der Steine* (Traces of Stones, 1964), Erwin Strittmatter's *Ole Bienkopp* (1963), Karl-Heinz Jakobs's *Beschreibungen eines Sommers* (Descriptions of a Summer, 1961), and Christa Wolf's *Der geteilte Himmel* (Divided Heaven, 1963). On the *Bitterfelder Weg* and its relation to *Gruppe 61*, see Peitsch, *Nachkriegsliteratur*, 254–65.

[70] Werkkreis Literatur der Arbeitswelt, *Partei ergreifen: Für die Einheit der Werktätigen mit einer antikapitalistischen Literatur und Kunst* (Berlin: Verlag der Arbeitswelt, 1974), 1.

[71] As for example, Werkkreis Literatur der Arbeitswelt, *Realistisch schreiben: Der Werkkreis in der Entwicklung einer antikapitalistischen Literatur in der Bundesrepublik* (Erkenschwick: Werkkreis-Textdienst, 1972), and Werkkreis Literatur der Arbeitswelt, "Partei ergreifen" (1974).

[72] Michael Schneider, "Bertolt Brecht—ein abgebrochener Riese: Zur ästhetischen Emanzipation von einem Klassiker," *Literaturmagazin* 10 (1979): 27.

[73] Schlösser, "Literaturgeschichte," 386.

[74] Schneider, "Bertolt Brecht," 28.

[75] Ursula Reinhold, *Tendenzen und Autoren: Zur Literatur der siebziger Jahre in der BRD* (Berlin: Dietz, 1982), 13.

[76] Reinhold, *Literatur und Klassenkampf*, 201.

[77] Reinhold, *Tendenzen und Autoren*, 13.

[78] Reinhold, *Literatur und Klassenkampf*, 201.

[79] Harald Budde, "Kunst als Waffe im Klassenkampf," *Asphalt* 3 (1970): n.p.

[80] By the mid-1970s the Rote Nelke turned away from the SEW, KPD, and other "linksdogmatische Organisationen," because of these organizations' continued efforts to undercut its political independence. See Harald Budde, "Der Umgang mit proletarisch-revolutionären Traditionen am Beispiel der Assoziation Bildender Künstler Deutschlands (ASSO)," *Deutschland Archiv* 17 (1984): 1068–76.

[81] Die Rote Nelke, "Parteilichkeit ohne Parteipolitik: Die Rote Nelke—Westberlin." *Sozialistische Zeitschrift für Kunst und Gesellschaft* (1974): 61.

[82] Budde "Kunst als Waffe."

[83] Budde "Manifest Nr. 1," *Asphalt* 3 (1970): n.p.

[84] Budde "Manifest Nr. 3," *Asphalt* 3 (1970): n.p.

[85] Budde "Manifest Nr. 2," *Asphalt* 3 (1970): n.p.

[86] Quoted in Budde "Manifest Nr.4," *Asphalt* 3 (1970): n.p.

[87] Budde, "Von der Notwendigkeit des Schreibens," *Asphalt* 4 (1971): 1–2.

[88] *August 1973: Aktionsprogramm der Künstlervereinigung Die Rote Nelke Westberlin e.V.,* 2, Academy of Arts, Aras-Ören-Archive.

[89] Budde, "Vorwort," *Asphalt* 6 (1971): 4.

[90] See Frederking, *Schreiben gegen Vorurteile*, and Carmine Chiellino, *Am Ufer der Fremde: Literatur und Arbeitsemigration, 1870–1991* (Stuttgart: Metzler, 1995).

[91] Harald Budde, "Niyazi in der Naunynstrasse, oder: Das Leben in der Trümmerlandschaft," *Die Tat*, January 12, 1974.

[92] Chiellino, *Am Ufer*, 314.

[93] Ibid., 313.

[94] My analysis is based on the Turkish original. Issues of translation or multilingualism are not the primary concern of this monograph and do not play a key conceptual role in my analysis, which instead focuses on literary adaptation and appropriation, and on the understanding of the aesthetics of politics in the mature Cold War period. On the presence of multilingual contexts in Turkish-German literature see Yasemin Yildiz, *Beyond the Mother Tongue: The Postmonolingual Condition* (New York: Fordham University Press, 2012); on monolingualization processes in the German literary context and translational monolingualism see David Gramling, *The Invention of Monolingualism* (New York: Bloomsbury, 2016); finally, on the Turkish-German translational relationship see Kristin Dickinson's dissertation, "Translation and the Experience of Modernity: A History of German Turkish Connectivity" (PhD diss., University of California Berkeley, 2015).

[95] A brief note on my emphasis on the use of montage as a signal element of the works under discussion: Brecht did not invent montage, nor was he its exclusive

practitioner in the 1920s and 1930s. Moreover, his was hardly the only theater aesthetic engaged with by the Turkish theater intellectuals under discussion. In addition to Brecht's increased popularity on Turkish stages throughout the 1960s, plays by Eugene Ionesco, Edward Albee, Jean Anouilh, Samuel Beckett, John Osborne, and Harold Pinter were first staged by theater ensembles such as Arena Tiyatrosu, AST, Dostlar Tiyatrosu, and Kent Oyuncuları, to name a few (Erkoç, "1960–1970 Dönemi Tiyatro Hareketleri," 27). Nevertheless, given Turkish theater intellectuals' understanding of montage as a practice frequently used by Brecht that became crucial for their own work (alongside some of his genre constructs)—an understanding I share—in my exploration of their adaptive transformation of his technique, I grant montage elements a privileged status as a connecting element between Brecht's work and those of the authors I discuss.

[96] Patrizia McBride, "De-moralizing Politics: Brecht's Early Aesthetics," *Deutsche Vierteljahrsschrift* 82, no. 1 (2008): 104.

[97] Bertolt Brecht, quoted in Reiner Steinweg, *Das Lehrstück* (Stuttgart: Metzler, 1972), 32.

[98] Chiellino, *Am Ufer*, 317.

[99] Ibid.

[100] Aras Ören, *Berlin Üçlemesi: Poem* (Istanbul: Remzi Kitabevi, 1980), 167. Henceforth cited as *BÜ*.

[101] Chin, *Guest Worker Question*, 67.

[102] Andrei S. Markovits and Philip S. Gorski, *The German Left: Red, Green and Beyond* (New York: Oxford University Press, 1993), 3.

[103] Ibid., 34.

[104] Chin, *Guest Worker Question*, 76–77.

[105] In the Turkish original, the writer uses the verb "kayıt etmek" (*BÜ*, 25), which translates into "to record," extenuated in the German translation as "erwähnen" (Ören, *Was will Niyazi*, 14).

[106] Chin, "Multiculturalism," 57.

[107] Cf. Heinrich Kaak, *Kreuzberg* (Berlin: Colloquium, 1988).

[108] Cf. Hartmut Häussermann and Andreas Kapphahn, *Berlin: Von der geteilten zur gespaltenen Stadt? Sozialräumlicher Wandel seit 1990* (Opladen: Leske + Budrich, 2000).

[109] Barbara Lang, *Mythos Kreuzberg: Ethnographie eines Stadtteils (1961–1995)* (Frankfurt am Main: Campus, 1998), 230.

[110] Ruth Mandel, "A Place of Their Own: Contesting Spaces and Defining Places in Berlin's Migrant Community," in *Making Muslim Space in North America and Europe*, ed. Barbara Metcalf (Berkeley: University of California Press, 1996), 149.

[111] Aras Ören, "Arka Avlu," in *Anlatılar, 1970–1982* (Berlin: Babel, 1991), 14.

[112] Ören, "Eine Metropole ist kein Völkerkundemuseum," 50.

[113] Frederking, *Schreiben gegen Vorurteile*, 66.

[114] Aras Ören, "Die Straßen von Kreuzberg," in *Mitten in der Odyssee: Gedichte*, trans. Gisela Kraft (Frankfurt am Main: Fischer, 1980), 15.

[115] Aras Ören, "Was ist los in der Naunynstraße?," in *Deutschland, ein türkisches Märchen: Gedichte*, trans. Gisela Kraft (Frankfurt am Main: Fischer, 1982), 97.

[116] Frederking, *Schreiben gegen Vorurteile*, 76.

[117] Ibid., 62.

[118] Harald Weinrich, "Deutschland—ein türkisches Märchen: Zu Hause in der Fremde—Gastarbeiterliteratur," in *Deutsche Literatur, 1983: Ein Jahresüberblick*, ed. Volker Hage and Adolf Fink (Stuttgart: Reclam, 1984), 233.

[119] In the German version, "baca tamircisi" (*BÜ*, 83) [chimney repairman] is mistakenly translated as "Töpfer" (Ören, *Was will Niyazi*, 64).

[120] Frederking, *Schreiben gegen Vorurteile*, 65.

[121] "Mikro a go go" Hessischer Rundfunk 3. Programm, October 3, 1971, Academy of Arts, Aras-Ören-Archive, call number 31.3822.

[122] Ören's contribution consists of nineteen poems in this special issue. Aras Ören, "Texte," *Asphalt* 6 (1971): 5–19. See Ela Gezen, "Aras Ören and the (West)German Literary Left," *Literature Compass* 13, no. 5 (2016): 324–31.

[123] The title in Turkish is *Ahmet'le Memet-Hasan'la Hüseyin—Ustabaşı ve Makinalara Dair* (literally translates into Ahmet and Memet-Hasan and Hüseyin—about the foreman and the machines). Academy of Arts, Aras-Ören-Archive, n.p.

[124] Without having either footage or reviews of this performance, it is impossible to address to what extent Ören adhered to or deviated from performance practices relevant to Brecht's own conception(s) of the learning play. Moreover, since Brecht's learning plays' target groups varied, there was neither a uniform technique nor a formal arrangement to which Ören's intervention could be compared. According to literary scholar Klaus-Dieter Krabiel, Brecht's fragment "Zur Theorie des Lehrstücks" (On the Theory of the Learning Play ,1937) is the only text that could be considered a "sketch of a theory of a play genre" (289). Here Brecht stated that "for the performance of the learning play instructions of epic theater are in effect. The study of V-effects is imperative" ("Zur Theorie des Lehrstücks," in *Werke*, vol. 22/1, *Schriften 2: Teil I*, 351–52). A year later, in a note titled "Über Fortschritte" (On Progress), Brecht mentions in passing the significance of *Einfühlung* for the learning play, but leaves unresolved the relationship between *Einfühlung* and V-effects regarding the learning play's performance practices (Klaus-Dieter Krabiel, *Brechts Lehrstücke: Entstehung und Entwicklung eines Spieltypus* [Stuttgart: Metzler, 1993], 290). According to David Bathrick, the main differentiation between epic theater and the learning play, despite the centrality of *Verfremdung* for both, is that the learning play "breaks up the traditional text-stage-audience relationship" through improvisation. Bathrick, *The Powers of Speech: The Politics of Culture in the GDR* (Lincoln: University of Nebraska

Press, 1995), 118. Similarly, Roswitha Mueller points to the learning play's structural innovation in the "abolition of the division between performance and audience." Mueller, "Learning for a New Society: The *Lehrstück*," in *The Cambridge Companion to Brecht*, ed. Peter Thompson and Glendyr Sacks (Cambridge: Cambridge University Press, 2006), 105. Bathrick, like Kriebus, foregrounds the learning play's "polyvalence" and its "noncalculable experimental character," arguing that its "point is to isolate and explore given factors of a reality as a means of concretizing and questioning them *within the experience of the actor-viewer*" (Bathrick, *Powers of Speech*, 118, 131).

As a reader of the Turkish theater journal *Tiyatro*, Ören was probably familiar with Brecht's *Der Jasager und der Neinsager* (*The Yes-sayer and the No-sayer*) and *Das Badener Lehrstück vom Einverständnis* (*The Baden-Baden Lesson on Consent*), published in the journal in Turkish translation in 1970 and 1971 respectively. He may also have been aware of the highly popular and hotly debated Schaubühne production of *The Mother* in the learning-play format in 1970 (on this performance and its reception, see Laura Bradley, *Brecht and Political Theatre: The Mother on Stage* [Oxford: Oxford University Press, 2006], 93–134). In the early 1970s, when Ören wrote his learning play, political theater was undergoing processes of redefinition in both German states (Bradley, *Brecht and Political Theatre*, 133). The interest in learning plays increased in the mid-1970s with the foundation of learning-play collectives, and the organization of seminars, colloquia, and performance weeks within and outside the educational setting (Krabiel, *Brechts Lehrstücke*, 313).

[125] Kreuzberger Straßentheater, "Nachbemerkung vom Kreuzberger Straßentheater," in *Straßentheater*, ed. Agnes Hüfner (Frankfurt am Main: Suhrkamp, 1970), 241; and Ulla Hahn, *Literatur in der Aktion: Zur Entwicklung operativer Literaturformen in der Bundesrepublik* (Wiesbaden: Akademische Verlagsgesellschaft Athenaion, 1978), 104.

[126] Arlene Teraoka, "The Other Speaks Back," *Cultural Critique* 7 (1987): 80.

[127] Deniz Göktürk, "Turkish Delight–German Fright: Migrant Identities in Transnational Cinema," in *Mediated Identities*, ed. Deniz Derman, Karen Ross, and Nevena Dakovic (Istanbul: Bilgi University Press, 2001), 147.

[128] Bertolt Brecht, "Vergnügungstheater oder Lehrtheater," in *Werke*, vol. 22/1, *Schriften 2: Teil 1*, 110.

[129] Astrid Oesmann, *Staging History: Brecht's Social Concepts of Ideology* (New York: SUNY Press, 2005), 1.

Chapter Three

[1] See Annabel Wahba, "Ost-Berlin roch wie Istanbul," *Der Tagesspiegel*, April 18, 2005; "Wörter ohne Kindheit," *Börsenblatt*, 23 September, 2008; Edo Reents, "Willkommen in der Sprache," *Süddeutsche Zeitung*, 26 February, 1999.

[2] Emine Sevgi Özdamar, "Rede zur Verleihung des Kleist-Preises," November 21, 2004.

[3] Özdamar's semiautobiographical novels, *Das Leben ist eine Karawanserei, hat zwei Türen, aus einer kam ich rein, aus der anderen ging ich raus* (*Life is a Caravanserai: Has Two Doors, I Came in One, I Went Out the Other*; Cologne: Kiepenheuer & Witsch, 1992), *Die Brücke vom Goldenen Horn* (Cologne: Kiepenheuer & Witsch, 1998), and *Seltsame Sterne starren zur Erde: Wedding-Pankow, 1976/77* (Cologne: Kiepenheuer & Witsch, 2003) constitute a trilogy: *Sonne auf halbem Weg: Die Istanbul-Berlin Trilogie* (Cologne: Kiepenheuer & Witsch, 2006).

[4] Claudia Schülke, "Sesshafte Nomadin." *Börsenblatt*, October 16, 2003; also see Bettina Göcmener, "In der Fremde wird die Heimat magisch," *Berliner Morgenpost*, November 27, 2002.

[5] Bettina Brandt, "Emine Sevgi Özdamar als Theatermacherin: Eine Vorstudie zu 'Karagöz in Alamania,'" in *Text und Kritik*, ed. Yasemin Dayıoğlu-Yücel (Munich: edition text+kritik, 2016), 27.

[6] B. Venkat Mani examines her incorporation of "various elements of several theatrical traditions ... non-Western and Western," such as the Turkish aesthetic traditions of *Meddah* (public storyteller and mimic) and *Karagöz* (the main figure in Turkish shadow theater) in Özdamar's earlier book, *Die Brücke vom Goldenen Horn*. B. Venkat Mani, "The Good Woman of Istanbul: Emine Sevgi Özdamar's *Die Brücke vom Goldenen Horn*," *Gegenwartsliteratur: German Studies Yearbook* 2 (2003): 35. Kader Konuk investigates Özdamar's "staged speech" (inszeniertes Sprechen), focusing on Özdamar's staging of accented German in *Die Brücke* in "Identitätssuche ist ein [sic!] private archäologische Graberei: Emine Sevgi Özdamars inszeniertes Sprechen," in *Aufbrüche: Kulturelle Produktionen von Migrantinnen, Schwarzen und jüdischen Frauen in Deutschland*, ed. Cathy S. Gelbin, Kader Konuk, and Peggy Piesche (Königstein im Taunus: Ulrike Helmer, 1999), 67. See also Sonja Klocke's, remarks on Özdamar's "aesthetics of performance" within her discussion of Özdamar's orientalization of the GDR and German memory discourse, in her "Orientalisierung der DDR? Spuren von DDR-Literatur und antifaschistischer Tradition in Emine Sevgi Özdamar's *Seltsame Sterne starren zur Erde*," in *Nach-Bilder der Wende*, ed. Inge Stephan and Alexandra Tacke (Cologne: Böhlau-Verlag, 2008), 142. For an analysis of Özdamar's *Seltsame Sterne starren zur Erde* in the framework of an aesthetic of narrative performance, see Claudia Breger, *An Aesthetics of Narrative Performance: Transnational Theater, Literature, and Film in Contemporary Germany* (Columbus: Ohio State University Press, 2012).

[7] Özdamar appeared as an actress in numerous roles at the Kammerspiele Munich, the Schauspielhaus Frankfurt, the Oper Frankfurt, and Théâtre de la Ville and Théâtre Amandiere in Paris, and throughout her career in theater she worked with directors Franz Xaver Kroetz, Karl Kneidl, Claus Peymann, and Einar Schleef, in addition to Müller, Karge, Langhoff, and Besson.

[8] Henning Rischbieter, ed., *Durch den eisernen Vorhang: Theater im geteilten Deutschland, 1945 bis 1990* (Berlin: Propyläen Verlag, 1999), 115.

[9] Antje Dietze, *Ambivalenzen des Übergangs: Die Volksbühne am Rosa-Luxemburg-Platz in Berlin in den neunziger Jahren* (Göttingen: Vandenhoeck & Ruprecht, 2015), 76.

[10] Petra Stuber, *Spielräume und Grenzen: Studien zum DDR-Theater* (Berlin: Links, 2000), 223–40.

[11] For a detailed reception and production history of these plays, particularly in light of their regime criticism and state censorship, see Laura Bradley, *Cooperation and Conflict: GDR Theatre Censorship, 1961–1989* (Oxford: Oxford University Press, 2010); and Moray McGowan, "'Sie kucken beide an Milchtopf': Goethe's Bürgergeneral in Double Refraction," in *Language—Text—Bildung: Essays in Honor of Beate Dreike*, ed. Andreas Stuhlmann and Patrick Suder (Frankfurt am Main: Peter Lang, 2005), 79–88.

[12] Özdamar, *Seltsame Sterne*, 226. Henceforth cited as *Sterne*.

[13] Cf. Brandt, "Özdamar."

[14] Roland Koberg, *Claus Peymann: Aller Tage Abenteuer; Biografie* (Berlin: Henschel, 1999), 227.

[15] Rischbieter, *Eiserner Vorhang*, 208; and Manfred Brauneck, *Die Welt als Bühne: Geschichte des europäischen Theaters*, vol. 5 (Stuttgart: Metzler, 2007), 344.

[16] Evelyn Deutsch-Schreiner, *Theaterdramaturgien von der Aufklärung bis zur Gegenwart* (Cologne: Böhlau Verlag, 2016), 273.

[17] Koberg, *Claus Peymann*, 235.

[18] Ibid., 236.

[19] Ralf Remshardt, "Conquering the South Pole and Other Places in Germany: Manfred Karge's Plays," in *Essays on Twentieth-century German Drama and Theater: An American Reception, 1977–1999*, ed. Hellmut Hal Rennert (New York: Peter Lang, 2004), 313.

[20] Emine Sevgi Özdamar, "Spaß beiseite," *Theater der Zeit* 62 (2007): 52.

[21] Brauneck, *Welt als Bühne*, 432.

[22] Laura Bradley, "Introduction," in *Edinburgh German Yearbook 5, Brecht and the GDR: Politics, Culture, Posterity*, ed. Laura Bradley and Karen Leeder (Rochester, NY: Camden House, 2011), 8.

[23] Christa Neubert-Herwig, ed., *Benno Besson: Theaterspielen in acht Ländern; Texte, Dokumente, Gespräche* (Berlin: Alexander Verlag, 1998), 11.

[24] Brandt, "Özdamar," 33. On this play and its performance, see Lizzie Stewart, "Countermemory and the (Turkish-)German Theatrical Archive: Reading the Documentary Remains of Eminer Sevgi Özdamar's *Karagöz in Alamania* (1986)," *Transit* 8, no. 2 (2013) and "Ümmü in Alamania? Female Voice and Song in the Premiere Production of Emine Sevgi Özdamar's *Karagöz in Alamania* (1986)," *Oxford*

German Studies 45, no. 3 (2016): 252–74. Among the first scholars to critically engage with Özdamar's plays is theater and performance scholar Katrin Sieg. She reads Özdamar's *Keloglan in Alamania* (1991) within the performative framework of ethnic drag, which uncovers "continuities, permutations and contradictions of racial feelings in West German culture," discussing the play's "political potential of travesty." Katrin Sieg, *Ethnic Drag: Performing Race, Nation, and Sexuality in West Germany* (Ann Arbor: University of Michigan Press, 2009), 2; 223.

[25] Yasemin Dayıoğlu-Yücel and Emine Sevgi Özdamar, "'Das mutigste Mädchen, das diese steile Straße hochläuft': Gespräch mit Emine Sevgi Özdamar über ihre Begegnungen mit Schriftstellern (August 2015)," in *Text und Kritik*, ed. Yasemin Dayıoğlu-Yücel (Munich: edition text+kritik, 2016), 87.

[26] Ibid., 87–88.

[27] For further information see Karen Jankowsky, "German Literature Contested: The 1991 Ingeborg-Bachmann-Prize Debate, 'Cultural Diversity,' and Emine Sevgi Özdamar," *German Quarterly* 70, no. 3 (1997): 261–76.

[28] Bathrick, *The Powers of Speech*, 131.

[29] Liesbeth Minnaard, *New Germans, New Dutch: Literary Interventions* (Amsterdam: Amsterdam University Press, 2008), 72.

[30] Bertolt Brecht, "Über den Bühnenbau der nichtaristotelischen Dramatik," in *Werke*, vol. 22/1, *Schriften 2: Teil 1*, 233.

[31] Leslie A. Adelson, "Back to the Future: Turkish Remembrances of the GDR and other Phantom Pasts," in *The Cultural After-Life of East Germany: New Transnational Perspectives*, ed. Leslie Adelson (Washington, DC: American Institute for Contemporary German Cultural Studies, 2002), 93–109; Susanne Rinner, *The German Student Movement and the Literary Imagination: Transnational Memories of Protest and Dissent* (New York: Berghahn, 2013); Kader Konuk, "Taking on German and Turkish History: Emine Sevgi Özdamar's *Seltsame Sterne*," *Gegenwartsliteratur: German Studies Yearbook* 6 (2007): 232–56; Laura Bradley, "Recovering the Past and Capturing the Present: Özdamar's *Seltsame Sterne starren zur Erde*," in *New German Literature: Life-Writing and Dialogues with the Arts*, ed. Julian Preece, Frank Finlay, and Ruth J. Owen (Bern: Peter Lang, 2007). 283–95; Margaret Littler, "Cultural Memory and Identity Formation in the Berlin Republic," in *Contemporary German Fiction*, ed. Stuart Taberner (Cambridge: Cambridge University Press, 2007), 177–95; and Beverly Weber, *Violence and Gender in the "New" Europe: Islam in German Culture* (New York: Palgrave Macmillan, 2013).

[32] "Emine Sevgi Özdamar: Hermann Beil spricht den Kleist-Preis zu," *Frankfurter Allgemeine Zeitung*, July 5, 2004.

[33] Daniel Bax, "Deutschland, ein Wörtermärchen," *die taz*, November 20, 2004.

[34] Cornelia Geissler, "Die 40. Tür im Märchen," *Berliner Zeitung*, March 5, 2003.

[35] Ibid.

[36] Bettina Göcmener, "Die Immigration beginnt erst jetzt," *Die Welt*, November 20, 2004.

[37] Wahba, "Ost-Berlin."

[38] Emine Sevgi Özdamar, interview by Rotbuch Verlag, 6.

[39] Wahba, "Ost-Berlin."

[40] Özdamar, interview by Rotbuch Verlag, 5.

[41] Daniel Bax, "Deutschland." For an analysis of Else Lasker Schüler in Özdamar's *Seltsame Sterne*, see Konuk, "Taking on German and Turkish History," 232–56.

[42] Özdamar, interview by Rotbuch Verlag, 7.

[43] Sabine Schmidt, "Die Türkei im Banne Brechts," *Rheinische Post*, April 22, 1998.

[44] Nils Minkmar, "Wir wohnen in einer weiten Hölle," *Frankfurter Allgemeine Zeitung*, November 21, 2004.

[45] Geissler, "40. Tür im Märchen."

[46] Özdamar, *Seltsame Sterne*, 170. Özdamar writes: "in die kommenden Geschichten der Welt," where "Geschichten" could refer to both history and story.

[47] Annika Joeres, "Schwarzäugig in Alemania," *die taz*, August 9, 2006.

[48] Wolfgang Heise and Heiner Müller, "Vorwärts zurück zu Shakespeare in einer auch von Brechts Theater mit veränderten Welt: Gespräch zwischen Wolfgang Heise und Heiner Müller," *Theater der Zeit* 2 (1988): 25. I would like to thank the anonymous reader for bringing this to my attention.

[49] Monika Shafi, "Talkin' 'bout My Generation: Memories of 1968 in Recent German Novels," *German Life and Letters* 59, no.2 (2006): 214, 202.

[50] McGowan, "Milchtopf," 85.

[51] Bradley, "Recovering," 287, 289, 290.

[52] Mani, *Cosmopolitical Claims*, 114.

[53] Wahba, "Ost-Berlin"; and Özdamar, *Seltsame Sterne*, 73.

[54] Cited in Erol M. Boran, "Eine Geschichte des türkisch-deutschen Theaters," 138.

[55] Özdamar, *Die Brücke*, 299. Henceforth cited as *Brücke*.

[56] Margaret Littler, "Machinic Agency and the Powers of the False in Emine Sevgi Özdamar's *Die Brücke vom Goldenen Horn* (1998)," *Oxford German Studies* 45, no. 3 (2016): 300.

[57] Bertolt Brecht, "Round Heads and Pointed Heads," trans. Tom Kuhn, in *Bertolt Brecht: Collected Plays*, ed. Tom Kuhn and John Willet (London: Methuen, 2001), 22.

[58] Minkmar, "Hölle."

[59] Özdamar, "Dank," 882.

[60] Feroz Ahmad, *The Making of Modern Turkey* (London: Routledge, 1993), 148.

[61] Wahba, "Ost-Berlin."

[62] Sabine Schwabe and Mithu M. Sanyal, "Ein Mund mit zwei Zungen," *Düsseldorfer Stattzeitung,* February 2, 1993.

[63] Yildiz, *Beyond the Mother Tongue,* 168.

[64] Mani, *Cosmopolitical Claims,* 103.

[65] Breger, *An Aesthetics of Narrative Performance,* 121.

[66] For a detailed discussion of the relationship between theory and praxis in *Die Brücke,* see Mani, "Good Woman," 94.

[67] Sigrid Löffler, "Laudatio auf Emine Sevgi Özdamar," 873–77; and Emine Sevgi Özdamar, "Dankrede," in *Der Hof im Spiegel* (Cologne: Kiepenheuer & Witsch, 2001), 127–28.

[68] Bax, "Deutschland."

[69] Wahba, "Ost-Berlin."

[70] David Horrocks and Eva Kolinsky, "Living and Writing in Germany: Emine Sevgi Özdamar in Conversation with David Horrocks and Eva Kolinsky," in *Turkish Culture in German Society Today,* ed. David Horrocks and Eva Kolinsky (Providence, RI: Berghahn Books, 1996), 47.

[71] Ibid., 48.

[72] Göcmener, "In der Fremde."

[73] Schülke, "Sesshafte Nomadin," 33.

[74] In various interviews Özdamar mentions the same plays; see for example Geissler, "40. Tür im Märchen."

[75] Sonja Klocke, "Orientalisierung," 142.

[76] "Revolving stage," Encyclopedia Britannica Online, accessed March 19, 2017, http://www.britannica.com/EBchecked/topic/500684/revolving-stage.

[77] Jan Knopf, *Brecht-Handbuch: Theater; Eine Ästhetik der Widersprüche* (Stuttgart: Metzler, 1980), 398. On the use of the revolving stage in *Mother Courage,* see Freddie Rokem, "The Meanings of the Circle in Brecht's Theatre," in *Bertolt Brecht: Centenary Essays,* ed. Steve Giles and Rodney Livingstone (Amsterdam: Rodopi, 1998), 109–20.

[78] Cf. Klocke, "Orientalisierung," 144.

[79] Mani, *Cosmopolitical Claims,* 106.

[80] Horrocks and Kolinsky, "Living and Writing," 53–54.

[81] Kim H. Kowalke, "Brecht and Music: Theory and Practice," in Thomson and Sacks, *The Cambridge Companion to Brecht,* 242.

[82] Bertolt Brecht, "Anmerkungen zur Oper *Aufstieg und Fall der Stadt Mahagonny,*" in *Werke,* vol. 24, *Schriften 4: Texte zu Stücken,* 79.

[83] Bertolt Brecht, "Short Organon" in *Brecht on Theatre,* ed. Marc Silberman, Steve Giles, and Tom Kuhn, trans. Jack Davis et al. (London: Bloomsbury Methuen Drama, 2015), 253.

[84] Bertolt Brecht, "Kollektiv selbstständiger Künste," in *Werke*, vol. 23, *Schriften 3: Schriften 1942–1956*, 413.

[85] Albrecht Betz, *Hanns Eisler: Political Musician* (Cambridge: Cambridge University Press, 1982), 230.

[86] Mark W. Roche, "Comic Reduction and Comic Negation in Brecht," in *Bertolt Brecht: Centenary Essays*, ed. Steve Giles and Rodney Livingstone (Amsterdam: Rodopi, 1998), 130.

[87] Translation taken from John Willett and Ralph Manheim, eds., *Bertolt Brecht: Collected Plays* (London: Methuen, 1976), 116. Özdamar similarly addresses the significance of "Das Lied von der Moldau" in various interviews; see for example "Wörter ohne Kindheit," *Börsenblatt,* September 23, 2008, 22

[88] Hanns Eisler, "Schweyk und der deutsche Militarismus," in *Materialien zu einer Dialektik der Musik* (Leipzig: Philipp Reclam jun., 1973), 297.

[89] Wahba, "Ost-Berlin."

[90] Joachim Lucchesi and Ronald K. Shull, "'Die Musik wird da viel ausmachen...': Eine Einführung," in *Musik bei Brecht*, edited by Joachim Lucchesi and Ronald K. Shull (Berlin: Henschelverlag Kunst & Gesellschaft, 1988), 36.

[91] Wahba, "Ost-Berlin."

[92] Michael Bienert, *Mit Brecht durch Berlin: Ein literarischer Reiseführer* (Frankfurt am Main: Insel, 1998), 215–33.

[93] Werner Mittenzwei and Fritz Hofmann, eds., *Bertolt Brecht: Stücke I* (Berlin: Aufbau-Verlag, 1973), 44.

[94] Bertolt Brecht, "Zu: 'Die Mutter,'" in *Werke*, vol. 24, *Schriften 4: Texte zu Stücken*, 159.

[95] Hanns Eisler, "Unsere Kampfmusik," in Eisler, *Materialien zu einer Dialektik der Musik*, 81.

[96] Ibid.

[97] Bertolt Brecht, "On the Use of Music in an Epic Theater," in *Brecht on Theater: The Development of an Aesthetic*, ed. and trans. John Willett (London: Shenval, 1964), 88.

[98] Mittenzwei and Hofmann, *Bertolt Brecht: Stücke I*, 355.

[99] Bertolt Brecht, "Aus dem ABC des epischen Theaters," in *Werke*, vol. 21, *Schriften 1: Schriften, 1914–1933*, 211.

[100] Jürgen Schebera, *Kurt Weill: An Illustrated Life*, trans. Caroline Murphy (New Haven, CT: Yale University Press, 1995), 125.

[101] Bradley, *Cooperation and Conflict*, 123.

[102] "Ein Gespräch mit Manfred Karge," *Theater der Zeit* 46 (1991): 27; and Rischbieter, *Eiserner Vorhang*, 113.

103 Bradley, "Introduction," 12–13; see also David Robb, "The Legacy of Brecht in East German Political Song," in Bradley and Leeder, *Edinburgh German Yearbook 5: Brecht and the GDR*, 183–200.

Conclusion

1 The Kunstamt Kreuzberg was committed to and active in municipal work with one fourth of its program focusing on "an engagement with the cultures of foreigners living in the district" (quoted in Manfred Brauneck, *Ausländertheater in der Bundesrepublik Deutschland und in West-Berlin: 1. Arbeitsbericht zum Forschungsbericht "Populäre Theaterkultur"* [Hamburg: Hamburg University, 1983], 70). It financially supported the Turkish theater group Kreuzberg Halk Sahnesi (founded in 1978) directed by Bülent Talay.

2 The Deutsch-Türkische Gesellschaft, established in 1980, aimed to foster "mutual understanding between the Turkish and German populations" while promoting the "integration of the foreign population by maintaining their cultural identity." Integration was understood as realization of political and social equality while increasing the willingness of Germans to actively participate in this process. In addition to organizing cultural events, its objectives included taking position on current issues of *Ausländerpolitik*, establishing a library, organizing workshops, and supporting related projects. Its cochairs were social democratic member of parliament Rainer Klebba and Industrial Metal Union (IG Metall) official Necati Gürbaca. Among the thirty founding members were Krista Tebbe, director of the Kunstamt Kreuzberg. In addition to Aras Ören and Vasıf Öngören, composer and musician Tahsin Incirci, translator and poet Gültekin Emre, and painter Hanefi Yeter were all members. Michael Böhm, "Verein guter Nachbarn," *Der Abend*, April 30, 1980, and "Satzung der Deutsch-Türkischen Gesellschaft e.V., Berlin," Friedrichshain-Kreuzberg Museum Archive.

3 In addition to Öngören's Kollektiv Theater, another Turkish theater group, the Türkisches Arbeitertheater des Türkeizentrums Schinkestrasse, formed in 1979, also incorporated Brecht's theatrical practices. It emphasized the significance of the continuation of Turkish traditions as well as addressing their experiences as foreign workers in Germany. Comprising workers, students, and theater practitioners, it repeatedly collaborated with the Theatermanufaktur Berlin, as for example in a performance of scenes from Brecht's *The Mother* on May Day in 1980, as well as the original "Agitationsstück" *Erde und Steine sind Gold* (Earth and Stones Are Gold, 1980). The Arbeitertheater's plays, like those of Öngören, were staged in German and Turkish. The ensemble performed at the türkische Kulturwochen in 1981, the Kreuzberger Festliche Tage in 1979, and the ausländischer berliner in 1981. Moreover, they toured Germany, performing at the Landestheater Tübingen and the German Trade Union Confederation (DGB) in Stuttgart. Michael Stone, "Am Stempel hängt doch alles," *Rheinischer Merkur*, March 24, 1981.

Bibliography

A. A. "Tiyatro Basanlar Nefret Uyandırdı." *Ulus*, March 25, 1964.

Ackermann, Irmgard, and Harald Weinrich, eds. *Eine nicht nur deutsche Literatur: Zur Standortbestimmung der "Ausländerliteratur."* Munich: Piper, 1986.

Adelson, Leslie A. "Against Between: A Manifesto." In *Unpacking Europe: Towards a Critical Reading*, edited by Salah Hassan and Iftikhar Dadi, 245–46. Rotterdam: NAi, 2001.

———. "Back to the Future: Turkish Remembrances of the GDR and other Phantom Pasts." In *The Cultural After-Life of East Germany: New Transnational Perspectives*, edited by Leslie A. Adelson, 93–109. Washington, DC: American Institute for Contemporary German Cultural Studies, 2002.

———. *The Turkish Turn in Contemporary German Literature: Toward a New Critical Grammar of Migration*. New York: Palgrave Macmillan, 2005.

Agora Kitaplığı. "Genco Erkal: Politik Tiyatronun Yeniden Gündeme Geldiğini Hissediyorum." Accessed 24 September 2016. http://agorakitapligi.com/genco-erkal-politik-tiyatronun-yeniden-gundeme-geldigini-hissediyorum.

Ahmad, Feroz. *The Making of Modern Turkey*. London: Routledge, 1993.

———. *The Turkish Experiment in Democracy*. London: C. Hurst for the Royal Institute of International Affairs, 1977.

And, Metin. *50 Yılın Türk Tiyatrosu*. Istanbul: Iş Bankası Kültür Yayınları, 1973.

———. *Başlangıcından 1983'e Türk Tiyatro Tarihi*. Istanbul: Iletişim Yayınları, 2004.

———, ed. *Muhsin Ertuğrul'a Saygı*. Istanbul: Celtüt Basımevi, 1969.

———. "The Turkish Folk Theater." *Asian Folklore Studies* 38, no. 2 (1979): 155–76.

Ankara Birliği. "'Ankara Birliği' Sahnesi Kuruluş Bilgisi," *Ankara Birliği Dergisi* 1 (1970): 13.

———. "Çıkarken," *Ankara Birliği Dergisi* 1 (1970): 4.

Ankara Üniversitesi Dil ve Tarih-Coğrafya Fakültesi. "Tiyatro Bölümü." Accessed 23 September 2016. http://www.dtcf.ankara.edu.tr/tiyatro-bolumu.

Asılyazıcı, Hayati. "Bertolt Brecht Olayı." *Oyun* 9 (1964): 10–13.

Barnett, David. *Brecht in Practice*. London: Bloomsbury, 2015.

Başak, Oya. "60 Yıllık Çabanın Özeti." In *Muhsin Ertuğrul'a Saygı*, edited by Metin And, 8–28. Istanbul: Çeltüt Basımevi, 1969.

Bathrick, David. "The Dialectics of Legitimation: Brecht in the GDR," *New German Critique* 2 (1974): 90–103.

———. *The Powers of Speech: The Politics of Culture in the GDR*. Lincoln: University of Nebraska Press, 1995.

Bax, Daniel. "Deutschland, ein Wörtermärchen." *die taz*, November 20, 2004.

Berman, Nina. *German Literature on the Middle East: Discourses and Practices, 1000–1989.* Ann Arbor: University of Michigan Press, 2011.

"Bert Brecht Özel Sayısı." *Istanbul Şehir Tiyatroların Dergisi* (March 1964). Special issue on Bertolt Brecht.

Betz, Albrecht. *Hanns Eisler: Political Musician.* Cambridge: Cambridge University Press, 1982.

Bienert, Michael. *Mit Brecht durch Berlin: Ein literarischer Reiseführer.* Frankfurt am Main: Insel, 1998.

Böhm, Michael. "Verein guter Nachbarn." *Der Abend*, April 30, 1980.

Boran, Erol M. "Eine Geschichte des türkisch-deutschen Theaters und Kabaretts." PhD diss., Ohio State University, 2004.

Borman, Alexander von. "Arbeiterliteratur in der Bundesrepublik seit 1965." In Lützeler and Schwarz, *Deutsche Literatur in der Bundesrepublik seit 1965*, 99–114.

Bradley, Laura. *Brecht and Political Theatre: The Mother on Stage.* Oxford: Oxford University Press, 2006.

———. *Cooperation and Conflict: GDR Theatre Censorship, 1961–1989.* Oxford: Oxford University Press, 2010.

———. "Introduction." In Bradley and Leeder, *Edinburgh German Yearbook 5: Brecht and the GDR; Politics, Culture, Posterity*, 1–21.

———. "Recovering the Past and Capturing the Present: Özdamar's *Seltsame Sterne starren zur Erde.*" In *New German Literature: Life-Writing and Dialogues with the Arts*, edited by Julian Preece, Frank Finlay, and Ruth J. Owen, 283–95. Bern: Peter Lang, 2007.

Bradley, Laura, and Karen Leeder, eds. *Edinburgh German Yearbook 5: Brecht and the GDR; Politics, Culture, Posterity.* Rochester, NY: Camden House, 2011.

Brandt, Bettina. "Emine Sevgi Özdamar als Theatermacherin: Eine Vorstudie zu 'Karagöz in Alamania.'" In *Text und Kritik*, edited by Yasemin Dayıoğlu-Yücel, 26–36. Munich: edition text+kritik, 2016.

Brauneck, Manfred. *Ausländertheater in der Bundesrepublik Deutschland und in West-Berlin: 1. Arbeitsbericht zum Forschungbericht "Populäre Theaterkultur."* Hamburg: Hamburg University, 1983.

———. *Die Welt als Bühne: Geschichte des europäischen Theaters.* Vol. 5. Stuttgart: Metzler, 2007.

Brecht, Bertolt. "24.8.40." In *Arbeitsjournal,* edited by Werner Hecht, vol. 1, *1938–1942*, 157–58. Frankfurt am Main: Suhrkamp Verlag, 1973.

———. "26.11.48." In *Arbeitsjournal,* edited by Werner Hecht, vol. 2, *1942–1955*, 863. Frankfurt am Main: Suhrkamp, 1973.

———. "Against Georg Lukács." In *Aesthetics and Politics,* translated by Ronald Taylor, 68–85. London: Verso, 1980.

———. "Anmerkungen zur 'Mutter.'" In *Werke*, vol. 24, *Schriften 4: Texte zu Stücken*, 150–90.

———. "Anmerkungen zur Oper *Aufstieg und Fall der Stadt Mahagonny.*" In *Werke*, vol. 24, *Schriften 4: Texte zu Stücken*, 74–84.

———. "Aus dem ABC des epischen Theaters." In *Werke*, vol. 21, *Schriften 1: Schriften 1914–1933*, 210–12.

———. *Brecht on Theatre*. Edited by Marc Silberman, Steve Giles, and Tom Kuhn. Translations by Jack Davis, Romy Fursland, Steve Giles, Victoria Hill, Kristopher Imbrigotta, Marc Silberman, and John Willett. 3rd ed. London: Bloomsbury Methuen Drama, 2015.

———. "Dialektik und Verfremdung." In *Werke*, vol. 22/1, *Schriften 2: Teil 1*, 402.

———. "Epik Tiyatro" translated by Kamural Şipal, *Ataç* 17, no. 2 (1963): 18–22.

———. *Galile*, translated by Adalet Cimcoz. Istanbul: Izlem Yayınları, 1963.

———. "Kollektiv selbstständiger Künste." In *Werke*, vol. 23, *Schriften 3: Schriften 1942–1956*, 413–14.

———. "Kulturpolitik und Akademie der Künste." In *Werke*, vol. 23, *Schriften 3*, 256–60.

———. "Kurze Beschreibung einer neuen Technik der Schauspielkunst, die einen Verfremdungseffekt hervorbringt." In *Werke*, vol. 22/2, *Schriften 2: Teil 2*, 641–59.

———. "Miscellaneous Texts: B124." In *Brecht on Performance*, edited by Tom Kuhn, Steve Giles, and Marc Silberman, translations by Charlotte Ryland, Romy Fursland, Tom Kuhn, and John Willett, 98. London: Bloomsbury, 2015.

———. "Notizen über realistische Schreibweise." In *Werke*, vol. 22/1, *Schriften 2: Teil 1*, 620–40.

———. "On Experimental Theater." In Brecht, *Brecht on Theatre*, 133–46.

———. "On the Use of Music in an Epic Theater." In *Brecht on Theater: The Development of an Aesthetic*, edited and translated by John Willet, 88. London: Shenval, 1964.

———. "Round Heads and Pointed Heads." Translated by Tom Kuhn. In *Bertolt Brecht: Collected Plays*, edited by Tom Kuhn and John Willet. London: Methuen, 2001.

———. "Schluss." In *Werke*, vol. 23, *Schriften 3: Schriften 1942–1956*, 373–74.

———. "Short Description of a New Technique of Acting that Produces a Verfremdung Effect." In *Brecht on Theatre*, 184–88.

———. "Short Organon for the Theatre." In *Brecht on Theatre*, 229–55.

———. "Die Strassenszene: Grundmodell einer Szene des epischen Theaters." In *Werke*, vol. 22/1, *Schriften 2: Teil 1*, 370–81.

———. *Tiyatro İçin Küçük Araç*, translated by Teoman Aktürel. Istanbul: Can Yayınları, 1962.

———. "Über den Bühnenbau der nichtaristotelischen Dramatik." In *Werke*, vol. 22/1, *Schriften 2: Teil 1*, 227–34.

———. "Über die epische Schauspielkunst: Der Wechsel." In *Werke*, vol. 22/2, *Schriften 2: Teil 2*, 670–72.

———. "Über experimentelles Theater." In *Werke*, vol. 22/1, *Schriften 2: Teil 1*, 540–57.

———. "Vergnügungstheater oder Lehrtheater." In *Werke*, vol. 22/1, *Schriften 2: Teil 1*, 106–16.

———. *Werke: Große kommentierte Berliner und Frankfurter Ausgabe.* Edited by Werner Hecht, Jan Knopf, and Werner Mittenzwei. Vols. 21–24. Berlin: Aufbau Verlag, 1988.

———. "Zu: 'Die Mutter.'" In *Werke*, vol. 24, *Schriften 4: Texte zu Stücken*, 150–90.

———. "Zur Theorie des Lehrstücks." In *Werke*, vol. 22/1, *Schriften 2: Teil 1*, 351–52.

"Brecht Dosyası." Special issue, *Alman Dil ve Edebiyat Dergisi* 18 (2006).

"Brecht in der Dritten Welt." Special issue, *Notate* 4 (1984).

Breger, Claudia. *An Aesthetics of Narrative Performance: Transnational Theater, Literature, and Film in Contemporary Germany.* Columbus: Ohio State University Press, 2012.

Budde, Harald. "Kunst als Waffe im Klassenkampf," *Asphalt* 3 (1970): n.p.

———. "Manifest Nr. 1," *Asphalt* 3 (1970): n.p.

———. "Manifest Nr. 2," *Asphalt* 3 (1970): n.p.

———. "Manifest Nr. 3," *Asphalt* 3 (1970): n.p.

———. "Manifest Nr.4," *Asphalt* 3 (1970): n.p.

———. "Niyazi in der Naunynstrasse, oder: Das Leben in der Trümmerlandschaft." *Die Tat* 11, January 12, 1974.

———."Der Umgang mit proletarischer-revolutionären Traditionen am Beispiel der Assoziation Bildender Künstler Deutschlands (ASSO)." *Deutschland Archiv* 17 (1984): 1068–76.

———. "Von der Notwendigkeit des Schreibens," *Asphalt* 4 (1971): 1–2.

———. "Vorwort," *Asphalt* 6 (1971): 4.

Buğlalılar, Eren. *Theatre and Struggle: A Sociological Analysis of the Political Theatre in Turkey between 1960–1971.* MS Thesis, METU, Ankara, 2012.

Bullivant, Keith. "Literatur und Politik." In *Gegenwartsliteratur seit 1968*, edited by Klaus Briegleb and Sigrid Weigel, 279–301. Munich: dtv, 1992.

Çağan, Sermet, and Özdemir Nutku. *Kriegsspiel: Ein szenischer Bericht.* Translated by Max Fisch. Weinheim: Deutscher Theaterverlag, 1969.

Çapan, Cevat. "Cumhuriyet Dönemi Tiyatro Dergileri." In Insel, *Türkiye'de Dergiler*, 123–34.

Chiellino, Carmine. *Am Ufer der Fremde: Literatur und Arbeitsemigration, 1870–1991.* Stuttgart: Metzler, 1995.

Chin, Rita. *The Guest Worker Question in Postwar Germany.* Cambridge: Cambridge University Press, 2007.

———. "Imagining a German Multiculturalism." *Radical History Review* 83 (2002): 44–72.

Çoban, Murat Şevki. "Genco Ekal: Politik Tiyatronun Yeniden Gündeme Geldiğini Hissediyorum." Agora Kitaplığı. Accessed 24 September 2016. http://agorakitapligi.com/genco-erkal-politik-tiyatronun-yeniden-gundeme-geldigini-hissediyorum.

Dalmia-Lüderitz, Vasuda. "Brecht in Hindi: The Poetics of Response." In Fuegi, Voris, Weber, and Silberman, *Brecht in Asia and Africa: The Brecht Yearbook XIV*, 107–19.

Dayıoğlu-Yücel, Yasemin, and Emine Sevgi Özdamar. "'Das mutigste Mädchen, das diese steile Straße hochläuft': Gespräch mit Emine Sevgi Özdamar über ihre Begegnungen mit Schriftstellern (August 2015)." In *Text und Kritik*, edited by Yasemin Dayıoğlu-Yücel, 80–88. Munich: edition text+kritik, 2016.

Delius, F. C. "Der Erzvater, als er Anfang dreißig war." In *Ceci n'est pas une Festschrift: Aras Ören zum 75. Geburtstag*, edited by Egbert Baqué, 8. Berlin: Egbert Baqué Contemporary Art, 2014.

Denning, Michael. *Culture in the Age of Three Worlds*. London: Verso, 2000.

Deutsch-Schreiner, Evelyn. *Theaterdramaturgien von der Aufklärung bis zur Gegenwart*. Cologne: Böhlau Verlag, 2016.

"Dialog der Literatur- und Theaterwissenschaftler." In *Brecht-Dialog 1968: Politik auf dem Theater; Dokumentation 9. Bis 16. Februar 1968*, edited by Werner Hecht, 77–109. Berlin: Henschel, 1968.

Dickinson, Kristin. "Translation and the Experience of Modernity: A History of German Turkish Connectivity." PhD diss., University of California Berkeley, 2015.

"Die Geschichte des Ali aus Kesan." *Bonner Stadtanzeiger*, October 5, 1964.

Dietrich, Anne. *Deutschsein in Istanbul*. Opladen: Leske + Budrich, 1998.

Dietze, Antje. *Ambivalenzen des Übergangs: Die Volksbühne am Rosa-Luxemburg-Platz in Berlin in den neunziger Jahren*. Göttingen: Vandenhoeck & Ruprecht, 2015.

Dinamo, Hasan Izzettin. "Faşizmin Korku ve Sefaleti." *Cumhuriyet*, April 6, 1976.

Dostlar Tiyatrosu. "Tiyatro." Accessed 22 September 2016. http://dostlartiyatrosu.com/tiyatro.html.

Ebermann, Wolf, Brigitte Lange, Berliner Ensemble, International Theatre Institute: Zentrum DDR, and the Deutsche Akademie der Künste zu Berlin, eds. *Brecht-Dialog 1968: Politics in the Theatre, Lectures and Reports*. Conference report. Berlin: Centre German Democratic Republic of the International Theatre Institute, 1969.

"Ein Gespräch mit Manfred Karge." *Theater der Zeit* 46 (1991): 27–30.

Eisler, Hanns. *Materialien zu einer Dialektik der Musik*. Leipzig: Philipp Reclam jun., 1973.

———. "Schweyk und der deutsche Militarismus." In *Materialien zu einer Dialektik der Musik*, 86–87.

———. "Unsere Kampfmusik." In *Materialien zu einer Dialektik der Musik*, 86–87.

Ellis, Lorene B. *Brecht's Reception in Brazil*. New York: Peter Lang, 1995.

El-Tayeb, Fatima. *Undeutsch: Die Konstruktion des Anderen in der postmigrantischen Gesellschaft*. Bielefeld: transcript, 2016.

Emine Sevgi Özdamar, interview by Rotbuch Verlag, 6.

"Emine Sevgi Özdamar: Hermann Beil spricht den Kleist-Preis zu." *Frankfurter Allgemeine Zeitung*, July 5, 2004.

Encyclopedia Britannica Online. "Revolving Stage." Accessed March 19, 2017. http://www.britannica.com/EBchecked/topic/500684/revolving-stage.

Erkoç, Gülayşe. "1960–1970 Dönemi Tiyatro Hareketleri." *Tiyatro Araştırmaları Dergisi* 13 (2002): 6–34.

"Erlangen Tiyatro Festivalinde Türkiye'nin Kazandığı Başarı." *Milliyet*, August 11, 1965.

Frederking, Monika. *Schreiben gegen Vorurteile: Literatur türkischer Migranten in der Bundesrepublik Deutschland.* Berlin: Express, 1985.

Fuegi, John, Reinhold Grimm, and Jost Hermand, eds. *Brecht-Jahrbuch* (1974). Frankfurt am Main: Suhrkamp Verlag, 1975.

Fuegi, John, Renate Voris, Carl Weber, and Marc Silberman, eds. *Brecht in Asia and Africa: The Brecht Yearbook XIV.* Hong Kong: University of Hong Kong, 1989.

Geissler, Cornelia. "Die 40. Tür im Märchen." *Berliner Zeitung*, March 5, 2003.

"Gelecek Yüzyılların Yazarı," *Milliyet*, February 10, 1998, accessed March 18, 2017, http://www.milliyet.com.tr/1998/02/10/sanat/san2.html.

Gezen, Ela. "Aras Ören and the (West)German Literary Left." *Literature Compass* 13, no. 5 (2016): 324–31.

———. "Brecht on the Turkish Stage: Adaptation, Experimentation, and Theatre Aesthetics in Genco Erkal's *Dostlar Tiyatrosu*." *German Life and Letters* 69, no. 2 (2016): 269–84.

Gezen, Ela, and Berna Gueneli, eds. *Turkish-German Studies: Past, Present, and Future; Special Volume of Türkisch-deutsche Studien Jahrbuch 2015.* Göttingen: V&R Unipress, 2015.

Giles, Steve, and Rodney Livingstone, eds. *Bertolt Brecht: Centenary Essays.* Amsterdam: Rodopi, 1998.

Göcmener, Bettina. "Die Immigration beginnt erst jetzt." *Die Welt*, November 20, 2004.

———."In der Fremde wird die Heimat magisch." *Berliner Morgenpost*, November 27, 2002.

Göktaş, Erbil. *Vasıf Öngören'in Tiyatro Dünyası.* Istanbul: Mitos-Boyut, 2004.

Göktürk, Deniz. "Imagining Europe as a Realm of Transfiguration." *Critical Multilingualism Studies* 2, no. 11 (2014): 129–47.

———. "Interrupting Unity: The Berlin Wall's Second Life on Screen—A Transnational Perspective." In *Debating German Cultural Identity since 1989*, edited by Anne Fuchs, Kathleen James-Chakraborty, and Linda Shortt, 82–99. Rochester, NY: Camden House, 2011.

———. "Turkish Delight—German Fright: Migrant Identities in Transnational Cinema." In *Mediated Identities*, edited by Deniz Derman, Karen Ross, and Nevena Dakovic, 131–49. Istanbul: Bilgi University Press, 2001.

Gramling, David. *The Invention of Monolingualism.* New York: Bloomsbury, 2016.

———. "What Is Turkish-German Studies up Against? Occidentalism and Thigmotactics," *Colloquia Germanica* 44, no. 4 (2014): 382–95.

Grimm, Reinhold. "Falladah in Ankara, 1979: Begegnungen mit (und zwischen) Brecht und den Türken." *Monatshefte* 75, no. 1 (1983): 6–24.

Güneli, Berna. "Remixing Film Histories: Fatih Akın and the Creation of a Transnational Film History." *Colloquia Germanica* 44, no. 4 (2014): 450–66.

HA. "Şehir Tiyatrosunda Dün Gece Gençler Bir Temsile Mâni Oldular." *Hürriyet*, March 23, 1964.

Hahn, Ulla. *Literatur in der Aktion: Zur Entwicklung operativer Literaturformen in der Bundesrepublik.* Wiesbaden: Akademische Verlagsgesellschaft Athenaion, 1978.

Halle, Randall. "The Europeanization of Turkish/German Cinema: Complex Connectivity and Imaginative Communities." *Jahrbuch Türkisch-deutsche Studien* (2015): 15–38.

Halman, Talat S. "The Evolution of Turkish Drama." In *Modern Turkish Drama: An Anthology of Plays in Translation*, ed. Talat S. Halman, 13–51. Minneapolis: Bibliotheca Islamica, 1976.

———. *Modern Turkish Drama: An Anthology of Plays in Translation.* Edited by Talat S. Halman. Minneapolis: Bibliotheca Islamica, 1976.

———. "Turkish Literature in the 1960s." In *Rapture and Revolution: Essays on Turkish Literature by Talat S. Halman*, 82–95.

Häussermann, Hartmut, and Andreas Kapphahn. *Berlin: Von der geteilten zur gespaltenen Stadt? Sozialräumlicher Wandel seit 1990.* Opladen: Leske + Budrich, 2000.

Hecht, Werner, ed. *Brecht-Dialog 1968: Politik auf dem Theater; Dokumentation 9. Bis 16. Februar 1968.* Berlin: Henschel, 1968.

Hecht, Werner, Karl-Claus Hahn, and Elifius Paffrath, eds. *Brecht 78: Brecht-Dialog Kunst und Politik, 10.–15. Februar 1978; Dokumentation.* Berlin: Henschelverlag Kunst & Gesellschaft, 1979.

———. "Brecht—Werk und Wirkung." In *Brecht 80: Brecht in Afrika, Asien und Lateinamerika; Dokumentation,* edited by Werner Hecht, Karl-Claus Hahn, and Elifius Paffrath, 7–15. Berlin: Henschelverlag Kunst & Gesellschaft, 1980.

———. "Vorbemerkung." In "Brecht auf den Bühnen der Welt: Materialien zum Brecht-Dialog 1968 (1); Berichte aus den Ländern," supplement to *Theater der Zeit* 22 (1968): 3.

Heise, Wolfgang, and Heiner Müller. "Vorwärts zurück zu Shakespeare in einer auch von Brechts Theater mit veränderten Welt: Gespräch zwischen Wolfgang Heise und Heiner Müller." *Theater der Zeit* 2 (1988): 22–26.

Herrmann, Dieter. "Erlanger Impressionen, 1961." *Berliner Zeitung.* July 29, 1961.

Horrocks, David, and Eva Kolinsky, "Living and Writing in Germany: Emine Sevgi Özdamar in Conversation with David Horrocks and Eva Kolinsky." In *Turkish Culture in German Society Today*, edited by David Horrocks and Eva Kolinsky, 45–54. Providence, RI: Berghahn Books, 1996.

Hübner, Marlies. *Internationales Studententheater in Erlangen, 1946—1968.* Erlangen: Universitäts-Buchdruckerei Junge & Sohn, 1995.

———."Studententheater im Beziehungsgeflecht politischer, gesellschaftlicher und kultureller Auseinandersetzung, mit einem Ausblick auf die Theaterszene der sechziger und siebziger Jahre." PhD diss., Friedrich-Alexander-University Erlangen, 1987.

Insel Deniz, ed. *Türkiye'de Dergiler—Ansiklopediler (1849–1984)*. Istanbul: Gelişim Yayınları, 1984.

Ipşiroğlu, Zehra. *Tiyatroda Devrim*. Istanbul: Çağdaş Yayınları, 1988.

———. *Tiyatroda Yeni Arayışlar*. Istanbul: Düzlem Yayınları, 1992.

Jankowsky, Karen. "German Literature Contested: The 1991 Ingeborg-Bachmann-Prize Debate, 'Cultural Diversity,' and Emine Sevgi Özdamar." *German Quarterly* 70, no. 3 (1997): 261–76.

Joeres, Annika. "Schwarzäugig in Alemania." *die taz*, August 9, 2006.

Kaak, Heinrich. *Kreuzberg*. Berlin: Colloquium, 1988.

Karasholi, Adel. *Brecht in arabischer Sicht*. Berlin: Brecht-Zentrum der DDR, 1982.

Kaynar, Oya. *Muhsin Ertuğrul: The Leader of the Turkish Theatre*. PhD diss., University of Minnesota, 1968.

"Kısa Kısa." *Milliyet*, August 7, 1965.

Klocke, Sonja. "Orientalisierung der DDR? Spuren von DDR-Literatur und antifaschistischer Tradition in Emine Sevgi Özdamar's *Seltsame Sterne starren zur Erde*." In *NachBilder der Wende*, edited by Inge Stephan and Alexandra Tacke, 141–60. Cologne: Böhlau Verlag, 2008.

Knopf, Jan. *Brecht-Handbuch in fünf Bänden*. Vol. 1, *Stücke*. Stuttgart: Metzler, 2001.

———. *Brecht-Handbuch: Theater;Eine Ästhetik der Widersprüche*. Stuttgart: Metzler, 1980.

Koberg, Roland. *Claus Peymann: Aller Tage Abenteuer; Biografie*. Berlin: Henschel Verlag, 1999.

Kocabaşoğlu, Uygur. "Cumhuriyet Dergiciliğine Bir Bakış." In Insel, *Türkiye'de Dergiler*, 3–12.

Konuk, Kader. *East West Mimesis: Auerbach in Turkey*. Stanford, CA: Stanford University Press, 2010.

———. "Identitätssuche ist ein [sic!] private archäologische Graberei: Emine Sevgi Özdamars inszeniertes Sprechen." In *Aufbrüche: Kulturelle Produktionen von Migrantinnen, Schwarzen und jüdischen Frauen in Deutschland*, edited by Cathy S. Gelbin, Kader Konuk, and Peggy Piesche, 60–75. Königstein im Taunus: Ulrike Helmer, 1999.

———. "Taking on German and Turkish History: Emine Sevgi Özdamar's *Seltsame Sterne*." *Gegenwartsliteratur: German Studies Yearbook* 6 (2007): 232–56.

Kowalke, Kim H. "Brecht and Music: Theory and Practice." In Thomson and Sacks, *The Cambridge Companion to Brecht*, 242–58.

Krabiel, Klaus-Dieter. *Brechts Lehrstücke: Entstehung und Entwicklung eines Spieltypus*. Stuttgart: Metzler, 1993.

Kreuzberger Straßentheater. "Nachbemerkung vom Kreuzberger Straßentheater." In *Straßentheater*, edited by Agnes Hüfner, 239–41. Frankfurt am Main: Suhrkamp, 1970.

Kruger, Loren. *Post-Imperial Brecht: Politics and Performance, East and South.* Cambridge: Cambridge University Press, 2007.

Kühne, Peter. *Arbeiterklasse und Literatur: Dortmunder Gruppe 61; Werkkreis Literatur der Arbeitswelt.* Frankfurt am Main: Fischer Taschenbuch Verlag, 1972.

Landau, Jacob M. *Radical Politics in Modern Turkey.* Leiden, Netherlands: Brill, 1974.

Lang, Barbara. *Mythos Kreuzberg: Ethnographie eines Stadtteils (1961–1995).* Frankfurt am Main: Campus, 1998.

"Lehr- und Warnstück vor der Diktatur." *Erlanger Tageblatt*, February 27, 1958.

Lipovsky, Igor. *The Socialist Movement in Turkey.* Leiden, Netherlands: Brill, 1992.

Littler, Margaret. "Cultural Memory and Identity Formation in the Berlin Republic." In *Contemporary German Fiction*, edited by Stuart Taberner, 177–95. Cambridge: Cambridge University Press, 2007.

———. "Machinic Agency and the Powers of the False in Emine Sevgi Özdamar's *Die Brücke vom Goldenen Horn* (1998)." *Oxford German Studies* 45, no. 3 (2016): 290–307.

Löffler, Sigrid. "Laudatio auf Emine Sevgi Özdamar." *Jahrbuch: Bayerische Akademie der schönen Künste* 13, no. 1 (1999): 873–77.

Lucchesi, Joachim, and Ronald K. Shull. "'Die Musik wird da viel ausmachen...': Eine Einführung." In *Musik bei Brecht*, edited by Joachim Lucchesi and Ronald K. Shull, 12–87. Berlin: Henschelverlag Kunst & Gesellschaft, 1988.

Lützeler, Paul Michael. "Von der Intelligenz zur Arbeiterschaft: Zur Darstellung sozialer Wandlungsverhältnisse in den Romanen und Reportagen der Studentenbewegung." In Lützeler and Schwarz, *Deutsche Literatur in der Bundesrepublik seit 1965*, 115–34.

Lützeler, Paul Michael, and Egon Schwarz, eds. *Deutsche Literatur in der Bundesrepublik seit 1965*. Königstein: Athenäum, 1980.

"M. Ertuğrul Olayını Özel Tiyatrolar Da Protesto Etti." *Cumhuriyet*, March 19, 1966.

Mandel, Ruth. *Cosmopolitan Anxieties: Turkish Challenges to Citizenship and Belonging in Germany.* Durham, NC: Duke University Press, 2008.

———. "A Place of Their Own: Contesting Spaces and Defining Places in Berlin's Migrant Community." In *Making Muslim Space in North America and Europe,* edited by Barbara Metcalf, 147–71. Berkeley: University of California Press, 1996.

Mani, Bala Venkat. *Cosmopolitical Claims: Turkish-German Literatures from Nadolny to Pamuk.* Iowa City: University of Iowa Press, 2007.

———. "The Good Woman of Istanbul: Emine Sevgi Özdamar's *Die Brücke vom Goldenen Horn.*" *Gegenwartsliteratur: German Studies Yearbook* 2 (2003): 29–58.

———. "Phantom of the 'Gastarbeiterliteratur': Aras Ören's Berlin Savignyplatz." In *Migration und Interkulturalität in neueren literarischen Texten*, edited by Aglaia Bloumi, 112–29.Munich: Iudicium, 2002.

Markovits, Andrei S., and Philip S. Gorski. *The German Left: Red, Green and Beyond*. New York: Oxford University Press, 1993.

McBride, Patrizia. "De-moralizing Politics: Brecht's Early Aesthetics." *Deutsche Vierteljahrsschrift* 82, no. 1 (2008): 85–111.

McGowan, Moray. "'Sie kucken beide an Milchtopf': Goethe's Bürgergeneral in Double Refraction." In *Language—Text—Bildung: Essays in Honor of Beate Dreike*, edited by Andreas Stuhlmann and Patrick Suder, 79–88. Frankfurt am Main: Peter Lang, 2005.

mi. "Kritik Ankara Kriegsspiel." *Spotlight* 11, no. 8 (July 31, 1965): 3.

Minkmar, Nils. "Wir wohnen in einer weiten Hölle." *Frankfurter Allgemeine Zeitung*, November 21, 2004.

Minnaard, Liesbeth. *New Germans, New Dutch: Literary Interventions*. Amsterdam: Amsterdam University Press, 2008.

Mittenzwei, Werner, and Fritz Hofmann, eds. *Bertolt Brecht: Stücke I*. Berlin: Aufbau Verlag, 1973.

Mueller, Roswitha. "Learning for a New Society: The *Lehrstück*." In Thomson and Sacks, *The Cambridge Companion to Brecht*, 101–17.

Nekimken, Albert. *Brecht in Turkey, 1955–1977: The Impact of Bertold* [sic] *Brecht on Society and the Development of Revolutionary Theatre in Turkey*. Istanbul: Isis, 1998.

———. "The Impact of Bertolt Brecht on Society and the Development of Political Theater in Turkey." PhD diss., University of California Riverside, 1978.

Neubert-Herwig, Christa, ed. *Benno Besson: Theaterspielen in acht Ländern; Texte, Dokumente, Gespräche*. Berlin: Alexander Verlag, 1998.

Nutku, Özdemir. "Ankara'da Bir Brecht." In *Türkiye'de Brecht*, 55–59.

———. "Ayak-Bacak Fabrikası." In *Sermet Çağan Bütün Oyunları*, by Sermet Çağan, 16–20. Istanbul: Mitos-Boyut, 1993.

———. "Carrar Ananın Silahları." In *Türkiye'de Brecht*, 63–73.

———. *Darülbedayi'nin Elli Yılı*. Ankara: Ankara Üniversitesi Basımevi, 1969.

———. "Keşanlı Ali Destanı." *Türk Dili* 155 (1964): 859–64.

———. "Orta Oyununda Yabancılaştırma Kavramı." *Tiyatro Araştırmaları Dergisi* 1 (1970): 33–47.

———. *Türkiye'de Brecht*. Istanbul: Tiyatro Yayınları, 1976.

Oesmann, Astrid. *Staging History: Brecht's Social Concepts of Ideology*. New York: SUNY Press, 2005.

"Ölüm Yıldönümünde Kuramı ve Yapıtlarıyla Bertolt Brecht." Special issue, *Varlık* 911 (1983).

Onay, Yılmaz. "Im Brennpunkt des Kampfes: Zur Brecht-Rezeption in der Türkei." *Notate* 4 (1984): 3–4.

Öngören, Vasıf. "Ulusal Tiyatro Devrimci Tiyatrodur." *Ankara Birliğ Dergisi* 1 (1970): 14–16, 25.

Ören, Aras. "Arka Avlu." In *Anlatılar, 1970–1982*. Berlin: Babel, 1991.

———. *Berlin Üçlemesi: Poem*. Istanbul: Remzi Kitabevi, 1980.

———. "Dankesrede zur Preisverleihung." In *Chamissos Enkel: Literatur von Ausländern in Deutschland*, edited by Heinz Friedrich, 25–29. Munich: Deutscher Taschenbuch Verlag, 1986.

———. "Deutschland wie gut geht es dir mit den anderen?" In *Dichter predigen in Schleswig Holstein*, edited by Hans Joachim Schädich, 16–26. Stuttgart: Radius, 1991.

———. *Die Fremde ist auch ein Haus.* Translated by Gisela Kraft. Berlin: Rotbuch Verlag, 1980.

———. "Kör Oidipus." *Tiyatro* 11 (1972): 36–50.

———. *Der kurze Traum aus Kağıthane: Ein Poem.* Translated by H. Achmed Schmiede. Berlin: Rotbuch Verlag, 1974

———."Eine Metropole ist kein Völkerkundemuseum." In *Privatexil: Ein Programm? Drei Vorlesungen*, 43–60.

———. *Privatexil: Ein Programm? Drei Vorlesungen.* Translated by Cem Dalaman. Tübingen: Konkursbuchwelt, 1999.

———. "Selbstbild mit Stadt." In *Privatexil: Ein Programm? Drei Vorlesungen*, 23–41.

———. "Die Straßen von Kreuzberg." In *Mitten in der Odysse: Gedichte*, translated by Gisela Kraft, 14–16. Frankfurt am Main: Fischer, 1980.

———. "Texte." *Asphalt* 6 (1971): 5–19.

———. "Von der Würde des Künstlers gegenüber dem missionarisch-bürokratischen Egoismus." In Ackermann and Weinrich, *Eine nicht nur deutsche Literatur*, 90–93.

———. "Vorstellungskraft und Zeit." In *Privatexil: Ein Programm? Drei Vorlesungen*, 5–21.

———. "Was ist los in der Naunynstraße?" In *Deutschland, ein türkisches Märchen: Gedichte*, translated by Gisela Kraft, 95–98. Frankfurt am Main: Fischer, 1982.

———. *Was will Niyazi in der Naunynstraße: Ein Poem.* Translated by H. Achmed Schmiede and Johannes Schenk. Berlin: Rotbuch Verlag, 1973.

"Organizasyon Yönünden. . ." *Milliyet* August 19, 1964.

Özdamar, Emine Sevgi. *Die Brücke vom Goldenen Horn.* Cologne: Kiepenheuer & Witsch, 1998.

———. "Dank." *Jahrbuch: Bayerische Akademie der schönen Künste* 13, no. 1 (1999): 878–84.

———. "Dankrede." In *Der Hof im Spiegel: Erzählungen.* Cologne: Kiepenheuer & Witsch, 2001.

———. *"Kendi Kendinin Terzisi Bir Kambur": Ece Ayhan'lı Anılar, 1974 Zürih Günlüğü, Ece Ayhan'ın Mektupları.* Istanbul: Yapı Kredi Yayınevi, 2007.

———. *Das Leben ist eine Karawanserei, hat zwei Türen, aus einer kam ich rein, aus der anderen ging ich raus.* Cologne: Kiepenheuer & Witsch, 1992.

———. *Mutterzunge: Erzählungen.* Berlin: Rotbuch Verlag, 1990.

———. "Rede zur Verleihung des Kleist-Preises," November 21, 2004. Obtained from Kiepenheuer & Witsch.

———. *Seltsame Sterne starren zur Erde: Wedding-Pankow, 1976/77*. Cologne: Kiepenheuer & Witsch, 2003.

———. *Sonne auf halbem Weg: Die Istanbul-Berlin Trilogie*. Cologne: Kiepenheuer & Witsch, 2006.

———. "Spaß beiseite." *Theater der Zeit* 62 (2007): 52.

Özek, Çetin. "Mutsuz Sezuan." *Oyun* 9 (1964): 7–8.

Partridge, Damani. *Hypersexuality and Headscarves: Race, Sex, and Citizenship in the New Germany*. Bloomington: Indiana University Press, 2012.

Pazarkaya, Yüksel. "Das aufgelöste Festival." *Stuttgarter Zeitung*. August 20, 1968.

———. "Erlangen Şenliği 'Savaş Oyunu' ve Bir Kaç Nokta." *Oyun* 28 (1966): 19–24.

———. "Erlangen Tiyatro Şenliği." *Oyun* 14 (1964): 13–16.

———. "Kritik Istambul." *Spotlight* 11, no. 7 (July 30, 1965): 4–5.

———. "Literatur ist Literatur." In Ackermann and Weinrich, *Eine nicht nur deutsche Literatur*, 59–64.

———. *Rosen im Frost: Einblicke in die türkische Kultur*. Zurich: Unionsverlag, 1998.

Peitsch, Helmut. *Nachkriegsliteratur, 1945–1989*. Göttingen: V&R unipress, 2009.

"Probleme der internationalen Brecht-Rezeption." In Hecht, Hahn, and Paffrath, *Brecht-Dialog 78: Dokumentation*, 51–65. Berlin: Henschel Verlag, 1979.

Reents, Edo. "Willkommen in der Sprache." *Süddeutsche Zeitung*, 26 February 1999.

Reinhold, Ursula. *Literatur und Klassenkampf: Entwicklungsprobleme der demokratischen und sozialistischen Literatur in der BRD (1965–1974)*. Berlin: Dietz Verlag, 1976.

———. *Tendenzen und Autoren: Zur Literatur der siebziger Jahre in der BRD*. Berlin: Dietz, 1982.

Reisoğlu, Mert Bahadir. "Interlacing Archives: History and Memory in Emine Sevgi Özdamar's *Die Brücke vom Goldenen Horn*," *Colloquia Germanica* 44, no. 4 (2014): 422–37.

Remshardt, Ralf. "Conquering the South Pole and Other Places in Germany: Manfred Karge's Plays." In *Essays on Twentieth-Century German Drama and Theater: An American Reception, 1977–1999*, edited by Hellmut Hal Rennert, 312–21. New York: Peter Lang, 2004.

Richards, Sandra L. "Wasn't Brecht an African Writer? Parallels with Contemporary Nigerian Drama." In Fuegi, Voris, Weber, and Silberman, *Brecht in Asia and Africa: The Brecht Yearbook XIV*, 168–81.

Richter, Hans Werner. "Fünfzehn Jahre." In *Almanach der Gruppe 47, 1947–1962*, edited by Hans Werner Richter, 8–14. Reinbek: Rowohlt, 1962.

Rimscha, Wolfgang von. "Internationale Theaterwochen der Studentenbühnen." In *Erlanger Stadtlexikon*, edited by Christoph Friederich, 387–88. Nuremberg: Tümmels, 2002.

Rinner, Susanne. *The German Student Movement and the Literary Imagination: Transnational Memories of Protest and Dissent*. New York: Berghahn, 2013.

Rischbieter, Henning, ed. *Durch den eisernen Vorhang: Theater im geteilten Deutschland, 1945 bis 1990*. Berlin: Propyläen Verlag, 1999.

———, "Was wird bei uns gespielt? Eine Analyse der Aufführungsstatistik der letzten 6 Spielzeiten," *Theater heute* (February 1963): 22–26.

Robb, David. "The Legacy of Brecht in East German Political Song." In *Edinburgh German Yearbook 5: Brecht and the GDR; Politics, Culture, Posterity*, edited by Laura Bradley and Karen Leeder, 183–200. Rochester: Camden House, 2011.

Robert Bosch Stiftung. "Adelbert-von-Chamisso-Prize of the Robert Bosch Stiftung." Accessed 24 September, 2016. http://www.boschstiftung.de/content/language2/html/4595.asp.

Roche, Mark W. "Comic Reduction and Comic Negation in Brecht." In Giles and Livingstone, *Bertolt Brecht: Centenary Essays*, 121–32.

Rokem, Freddie. "The Meanings of the Circle in Brecht's Theatre." In Giles and Livingstone, *Bertolt Brecht: Centenary Essays*, 109–20.

Rotbuch Verlag. "Arbeitspunkte für den Rotbuch Verlag." In *Das kleine Rotbuch: Almanach 1973*, 40–43.

———. *Herbstprogramm* (1973), Academy of Arts, Aras-Ören-Archive.

———. *Das kleine Rotbuch: Almanach 1973*. Berlin: Rotbuch Verlag, 1973.

———. "Vom Wagenbach- zum Rotbuchkollektiv." In *Das kleine Rotbuch: Almanach 1973*, 52–57.

Die Rote Nelke. "Parteilichkeit ohne Parteipolitik: Die Rote Nelke—Westberlin." *Sozialistische Zeitschrift für Kunst und Gesellschaft* (1974): 61–84.

Rouse, John. *Brecht and the West German Theatre: the Practice and Politics of Interpretation*. Ann Arbor: UMI Research, 1989.

Schebera, Jürgen. *Kurt Weill: An Illustrated Life*. Translated by Caroline Murphy. New Haven, CT: Yale University Press, 1995.

Schiel, Lea Sophie. *Theater im politischen Kampf: Motivation und Konsequenz der Auflösung der internationalen Theaterwoche der Studentenbühnen in Erlangen, 1968*. Berlin: Gesellschaft für Theatergeschichte, 2016.

Schlösser, Hermann. "Literaturgeschichte und Theorie in der Literatur." In *Gegenwartsliteratur seit 1968*, edited by Klaus Briegleb and Sigrid Weigel, 385–403. Munich: dtv, 1992.

Schmidt, Sabine. "Die Türkei im Banne Brechts." *Rheinische Post*, April 22, 1998.

Schneider, Michael. "Bertolt Brecht—ein abgebrochener Riese: Zur ästhetischen Emanzipation von einem Klassiker." *Literaturmagazin* 10 (1979): 25–66.

Schülke, Claudia. "Sesshafte Nomadin." *Börsenblatt*, October 16, 2003.

Schulz, Max Walter. "Gespräch mit Haldun Taner." *Sinn und Form* 23, no. 3 (1971): 693–98.

Schütte, Wolfram. "Artisten in der Zirkuskuppel und als Bodenturner? Nach einem Besuch bei Wagenbach und im Rotbuch-Kollektiv." *Frankfurter Rundschau*, March 2, 1974.

Schwabe, Sabine, and Mithu M. Sanyal. "Ein Mund mit zwei Zungen." *Düsseldorfer Stattzeitung*, February 2, 1993.

"Şehir Tiyatrosu'nda Hadise Çıkaranlar." *Gece Postası*, March 23, 1964.

Seyhan, Azade. *Writing outside the Nation*. Princeton, NJ: Princeton University Press, 2001.

"Sezuan'ın Iyi Insanı Tepki Uyandırdı," *Ses*, March 28, 1964.

"Sezuan'in Iyi Insanı ve Istanbuldaki Tepkiler." *Ses*, April 4, 1964.

Shafi, Monika. "'Talkin' 'bout My Generation: Memories of 1968 in Recent German Novels." *German Life and Letters* 59, no. 2 (2006): 201–16.

Sieg, Katrin. *Ethnic Drag: Performing Race, Nation, and Sexuality in West Germany*. Ann Arbor: University of Michigan Press, 2009.

Silberman, Marc. "A Brief History of the International Brecht Society." Accessed March 15, 2017. http://www.brechtsociety.org/ibs_history#history.

———. "The Politics of Representation: Brecht and the Media." *Theatre Journal* 39, no. 4 (1987): 448–60.

———. "A Postmodernized Brecht?" *Theater Journal* 45, no. 1 (1993): 1–19.

Silberman, Marc, Steve Giles, and Tom Kuhn, eds. "General Introduction." In Brecht, *Brecht on Theatre*, edited by Marc Silberman, Steve Giles, and Tom Kuhn, 1–8.

Sinay, Nalan. *Yaşamı, Sanat Anlayışı ve Yapıtlarıyla Sermet Çağan*. Istanbul: Mitos-Boyut, 2012.

Slobodian, Quinn. *Foreign Front: Third World Politics in Sixties West Germany*. Durham, NC: Duke University Press, 2012.

Söğüt, Mine. *Adalet Cimcoz: Bir Yaşamöyküsü Denemesi*. Istanbul: Yapı Kredi Yayınları, 2000.

Sölcün, Sargut. *Tarih Bilinci ve Edebiyat Bilimi*. Ankara: Dayanışma Yayınları, 1982.

Soysal, Levent. "Labor to Culture: Writing Turkish Migration to Europe," *South Atlantic Quarterly* 102, no. 2–3 (2003): 491–508.

Steinweg, Reiner. *Das Lehrstück*. Stuttgart: Metzler, 1972.

Stenzaly, Georg. "Ausländertheater in der Bundesrepublik und Berlin-West am Beispiel der türkischen Theatergruppen." *Zeitschrift für Literaturwissenschaft und Linguistik* 56 (1984): 125–41.

Stewart, Lizzie. "Countermemory and the (Turkish-)German Theatrical Archive: Reading the Documentary Remains of Emine Sevgi Özdamar's *Karagöz in Alamania* (1986)." *Transit* 8, no. 2 (2013): n.p.

———. "Ümmü in Alamania? Female Voice and Song in the Premiere Production of Emine Sevgi Özdamar's *Karagöz in Alamania* (1986)." *Oxford German Studies* 45, no. 3 (2016): 252–74.

Stone, Michael. "Am Stempel hängt doch alles." *Rheinischer Merkur*, March 24, 1981.

Stuber, Petra. *Spielräume und Grenzen: Studien zum DDR-Theater*. Berlin: Links, 2000.

Sümer, Ayhan. "Haldun Taner'le." *Varlık* 620 (1964): 13.

Suvin, Darko. "Mit und ohne Skandal." *Die Weltwoche*, July 8, 1965.

Taner, Haldun. *The Ballad of Ali Keshan*. Translated by Nüvit Özdoğru. Ankara: International Theatre Institute, 1970.

———. *Keşanlı Ali Destanı*. 26th ed. Ankara: Bilgi Yayınevi, 2013.

Tatlow, Antony. "Introduction." In *Brecht and East Asian Theatre: The Proceedings of a Conference on Brecht in East Asian Theatre*, edited by Antony Tatlow and Tak-Wai Wong, 1–2. Hong Kong: Hong Kong University Press, 1982.

"Telefon-Interview von Karl-Heinz Jakobs mit Aras Ören: Deutsche Einheit ist eine Einbahnstraße." *Neues Deutschland*, 15 March 1991.

Teraoka, Arlene. "The Other Speaks Back." *Cultural Critique* 7 (1987): 77–101.

Thomson, Peter, and Glendyr Sacks, eds. *The Cambridge Companion to Brecht*. Cambridge: Cambridge University Press, 2006.

"Tiyatro Festivaline Hazırlık." *Milliyet*, November 6, 1957.

"Tiyatro Olayı Sanıklarının Duruşmasına Dün Başlandı." *Cumhuriyet*, March 27, 1964.

Torres, Maria Luisa F. "Brecht in the Philippines: Anticipating Freedom in Theatre." In Fuegi, Voris, Weber, and Silberman, *Brecht in Asia and Africa: The Brecht Yearbook XIV*, 134–51.

TÖS. *Ilk Iki Yılda Türkiye Öğretmenler Sendikası (TÖS): 1965–1967*. Ankara: Balkanoğlu, 1967.

———. *TÖS Dosyası*. Ankara: Töre-Devlet Yayınevi, 1973.

Tözer, Kemal. "Yeni Bir Tiyatro, Yeni Bir Deneme." *Cumhuriyet* November 5, 1975.

"Türkiyede Ilk Brecht «Carrar Ana'nın Silâhları»." *Oyun* 7 (1964): 5.

Ülker, Barış. "Urbanization and Modern Governmental Reason: Ernst Reuter's Exile in Turkey." *Jahrbuch Türkisch-deutsche Studien* (2015): 79–96.

Ulus, Özgür. *The Army and the Radical Left in Turkey*. London: I. B. Tauris, 2011.

"Uluslararası Kültür Şenliği Başlıyor." *Milliyet*, August 8, 1965.

Vasıf Öngören, interview by Zeynep Oral. *Milliyet Sanat Dergisi*, March 25, 1977, 3.

"Vasıf Öngören'le 'Devrimci Tiyatro' Sorunları Üzerine Bir Konuşma." *Militan* 6 (1975): 49–50.

"Vasıf Öngören'le Konuşma." *Tiyatro* 1 (1970): 28–29.

Wahba, Annabel. "Ost-Berlin roch wie Istanbul." *Der Tagesspiegel*, April 18, 2005.

Weber, Beverly. *Violence and Gender in the "New" Europe: Islam in German Culture*. New York: Palgrave Macmillan, 2013.

Weber, Carl. "Brecht Is at Home in Asia." In Fuegi, Voris, Weber, and Silberman, *Brecht in Asia and Africa: The Brecht Yearbook XIV*, 30–43.

Weinrich, Harald. "Deutschland—ein türkisches Märchen: Zu Hause in der Fremde—Gastarbeiterliteratur." In *Deutsche Literatur, 1983: Ein Jahresüberblick*, edited by Volker Hage and Adolf Fink, 230—37. Stuttgart: Reclam, 1984.

Wekwerth, Manfred. "Das Theater Brechts 1968." In *Brecht-Dialog 1968*, 65.

Werkkreis Literatur der Arbeitswelt. *Partei ergreifen: Für die Einheit der Werktätigen mit einer antikapitalistischen Literatur und Kunst*. Berlin: Verlag der Arbeitswelt, 1974.

———. *Realistisch schreiben: Der Werkkreis in der Entwicklung einer antikapitalistischen Literatur in der Bundesrepublik*. Erkenschwick: Werkkreis-Textdienst, 1972.

Willett, John, and Ralph Manheim, eds. *Bertolt Brecht: Collected Plays*. London: Methuen, 1976.

"Wörter ohne Kindheit." *Börsenblatt*, September 23, 2008.

Yalçın, Ayhan. *Türkiye Cumhuriyeti Anayasaları*. Istanbul: Geçit Kitabevi, 1982.

Yeşilada, Karin. *Poesie der Dritten Sprache*. Tübingen: Stauffenburg Verlag, 2012.

Yildiz, Yasemin. "Berlin as a Migratory Setting." In *The Cambridge Companion to the Literature of Berlin*, edited by Andrew J. Webber, 206–26. Cambridge: Cambridge University Press, 2017.

———. *Beyond the Mother Tongue: The Postmonolingual Condition*. New York: Fordham University Press, 2012.

———. "Turkish Girls, Allah's Daughters, and the Contemporary German Subject: Itinerary of a Figure." *German Life and Letters* 62, no. 3 (2009): 465–81.

"Yılın Sanatçıları Ile Söyleşi: Vasıf Öngören." *Tiyatro* 41 (1977): 36–38.

Youssef, Magdi. "The Reception of Bertholt (sic!) Brecht in Egypt." In *Proceedings of the Congress of the International Comparative Literature Association* 7 (1973): 657–61.

Yüksel, Ayşegül. *Haldun Taner Tiyatrosu*. Ankara: Bilgi Yayınevi, 1986.

"Yurttan Akisler." *Akis*, March 28, 1964.

Zuolin, Huang. "A Brief Account of Brechtian Reception in China." In Fuegi, Voris, Weber, and Silberman, *Brecht in Asia and Africa: The Brecht Yearbook XIV*, 1–3.

Archival Documents

Aras Ören, "Ahmet'le Memet-Hasan'la Hüseyin—Ustabaşı ve Makinalara Dair" (Lehrstück für türkische Arbeiter). Academy of Arts, Aras-Ören-Archive, n.p.

August 1973: Aktionsprogramm der Künstlervereinigug Die Rote Nelke Westberlin e.V., 2. Academy of Arts, Aras-Ören-Archive.

Interview with Aras Ören. Academy of Arts, Aras-Ören-Archive, call number 31.3818.

Letter from Bertolt Brecht to Hanns Eisler, Helsinki, Finland dated March 1941. Bertolt Brecht Archive, call number BBA2707.

Letter from Aras Ören to Johannes Schenk, November 23, 1970. Academy of Arts, Aras-Ören-Archive.

"Mikro a go go" Hessischer Rundfunk 3. Programm October 3, 1971. Academy of Arts, Aras-Ören-Archive, call number 31.3822.

Preface of "Kör Oidipus" (1966) booklet. Academy of Arts, Aras-Ören-Archive.

Radio Interview with Aras Ören by SWF, December 8, 1974. Academy of Arts, Aras-Ören-Archive, call number 31.3823.

Radio Interview with Aras Ören by WDR, January 9, 1972. Academy of Arts, Aras-Ören-Archive, call number 31.3823.

"Satzung der Deutsch-Türkischen Gesellschaft e.V., Berlin." Friedrichshain-Kreuzberg Museum Archive.

Index

.